HISTORY

OF THE

Episcopal Church in Connecticut.

VOL. II.

THE

HISTORY

OF THE

Episcopal Church in Connecticut,

FROM THE

DEATH OF BISHOP SEABURY TO THE PRESENT TIME.

BY

E. EDWARDS BEARDSLEY, D. D.,

RECTOR OF ST. THOMAS'S CHURCH, NEW HAVEN.

VOL. II.

NEW YORK:

PUBLISHED BY HURD AND HOUGHTON.

LONDON: SAMPSON LOW, SON, AND MARSTON.

1868.

RIVERSIDE, CAMBRIDGE:
STEREOTYPED AND PRINTED BY
H. O. HOUGHTON AND COMPANY.

TO THE

RIGHT REVEREND JOHN WILLIAMS, D. D.,

A WORTHY SUCCESSOR OF

SEABURY, JARVIS, AND BROWNELL,

THIS CONTINUATION OF THE HISTORY OF THE PROTESTANT EPISCOPAL CHURCH

IN THE DIOCESE OF CONNECTICUT,

WITH RENEWED GRATITUDE FOR HIS INTEREST IN THE WORK,

IS AFFECTIONATELY DEDICATED BY

THE AUTHOR

PREFACE TO THE SECOND VOLUME.

The publication of this volume completes the purpose which I formed when I began to write the "History of the Episcopal Church in Connecticut" I have now traced its progress, from the settlement of the Colony to the death of Bishop Brownell in 1865, — a period of more than two hundred and twenty-five years, — and given the events with as much minuteness of detail as the nature of the subject and the plan of the work would permit.

The clergy generally, in the beginning of the present century, used very little care in making and preserving a complete record of their official labors. The Missionaries of the Venerable Society for the Propagation of the Gospel in Foreign Parts, were required to send home a full report of the state of their respective missions, and in this way information was secured, which rendered it less difficult to combine and arrange the materials for a true narrative of events connected with the origin and progress of the Church in Colonial times. But for the first ten years of the Episcopate of Bishop Jarvis, there are no parochial reports to aid the historian, and no printed addresses summing up the results of Episcopal visitations. The meagre Journals of Convention, and the more meagre records of the Convocations would have been quite unsatisfactory, had I not found, among the archives of the Diocese and in manuscripts and publications of that period, statements and narratives as full of interest as they are of significance and value. When newspapers and periodicals began to appear more frequently and regularly, they were made the repository of many important facts and movements, the knowledge of which might otherwise have been lost.

It would have been an improper omission in a work of this kind, to pass by the political revolution which resulted in the overthrow of the "Standing Order," and the adoption of a new Constitution for the civil government of the people of the State. But I have not been concerned to dwell on the heats and passions of that day, — having contented myself with simply noting the ripening causes of the revolution, and the part which Episcopalians bore in bringing it on. Their influence in shaping the future government, was a natural outgrowth of the success which attended the political scheme to change the rulers of the commonwealth.

The right to characterize persons, systems, and events, according to the shades and colors which they assume, belongs to the office of a faithful historian. But the exercise of this right is a delicate business where it involves a survey of the achievements and principles of living men, or of those who have just passed from the stage of human action. In support of the statements of the text, and in justice to Bishop Brownell, I have made liberal extracts from his addresses, sermons, and charges, and allowed him to speak for himself on subjects about which some diversity of opinion may be supposed to exist outside of the Diocese. The same rule has been partially observed in reference to his successor in the Episcopate, and others who have figured conspicuously in these pages.

That I have made no mistakes, or that the work is entirely free from defects, I have not the presumption to claim. I am conscious of having been diligent in endeavoring to secure correctness, and I have been actuated by those principles of impartiality which governed me throughout in the preparation of the first volume. I have not sat beneath the arches of history to indulge in indiscriminate praise or censure. Nor have I forgotten that "Salvation is of the Lord." Much as I love and venerate the Church of my forefathers, no one will accuse me of raising it into an idol, or of exalting it above its Great Head.

My acknowledgments are again due to several friends for assisting me in my researches by kindly placing in my hands valuable manuscripts, documents, pamphlets, and rare periodicals. To those clergymen and laymen of the Diocese in particular, who have taken the pains to furnish me with brief outlines of the history of their respective parishes, I cannot be too grateful. Many of the facts and personal incidents thus obtained, which shed light on the organization and progress of the Episcopal Church in Connecticut, have been woven into the thread of the narrative, and assigned the important places which they deserve.

With this volume is issued a second edition of the first, in which a few typographical and other errors have been corrected. As I part from my work, I have a feeling of thankfulness to the Giver of all good, that I have been enabled to complete it; and I send it forth, such as it is, only asking a fair indulgence from my readers, especially from those who have not added to their pastoral duties the critical and laborious task of writing a church history.

NEW HAVEN, *October*, 1868. E. E. B.

CONTENTS.

CHAPTER I.

ELECTION OF A SUCCESSOR TO BISHOP SEABURY, AND CONSECRATION OF THE REV. ABRAHAM JARVIS TO THE EPISCOPATE OF CONNECTICUT.

A. D. 1796 – 1799.

CHAPTER II.

REMOVAL OF BISHOP JARVIS TO CHESHIRE ; ADOPTION OF AN OFFICE OF INSTITUTION; AND EFFORTS TO ENDOW THE EPISCOPATE.

A. D. 1799 – 1804.

CHAPTER III.

ECCLESIASTICAL TROUBLE; PROCEEDINGS IN THE CASE OF AMMI ROGERS; AND INTERPOSITION OF THE HOUSE OF BISHOPS INVOKED.

A. D. 1804 – 1805.

CHAPTER IV.

EPISCOPAL ACADEMY, AND RESIGNATION OF DR. SMITH; RENEWAL OF THE CASE OF AMMI ROGERS; AND ORGANIZATION OF PARISHES.

A. D. 1805 – 1809.

CHAPTER V.

ACT RELATING TO RELIGIOUS SOCIETIES; WARDENS AND VESTRYMEN A COMMITTEE; TAXING AND GRAND LEVY; PETITION TO INCORPORATE THE EPISCOPAL ACADEMY WITH COLLEGIATE POWERS; AND UNION OF PARISHES IN CURES.

A. D. 1809 – 1811.

CHAPTER VI.

STATISTICS OF THE PARISHES; SUPPORT OF THE EPISCOPATE; DEATH OF DR. HUBBARD; LIST OF ORDINATIONS; AND DEATH OF BISHOP JARVIS.

A. D. 1811 – 1813.

CHAPTER VII.

ANNUAL CONVENTION AT STRATFORD; STYLE OF PREACHING; REV. JOHN KEWLEY; AND PERVERSIONS TO ROME.

A. D. 1813 – 1814.

CHAPTER VIII.

CORNER-STONE OF TRINITY CHURCH, NEW HAVEN, LAID; DEATH OF MR. WHITLOCK; ELECTION OF A BISHOP; AND INCREASE OF THE CHURCH.

A. D. 1814 – 1815.

CHAPTER IX.

BISHOP'S FUND; CONSECRATION OF TRINITY CHURCH; SERVICES OF BISHOP HOBART; AND ANNUAL CONVENTION.

A. D. 1815 – 1816.

CHAPTER X.

SPECIAL CONVENTION, AND VISITATION OF BISHOP HOBART; DOCTRINAL CONTROVERSY; AND STANDARD EDITION OF THE BIBLE.

A. D. 1816 – 1817.

CHAPTER XI.

CONVENTION AT GUILFORD; ADDRESS OF BISHOP HOBART; VISITATION; AND AMMI ROGERS.

A. D. 1817.

CHAPTER XII.

POLITICAL REVOLUTION; CHANGE IN THE STATE GOVERNMENT; ELECTION SERMON; AND NEW CONSTITUTION.

A. D. 1817–1818.

CHAPTER XIII.

PROSPERITY OF THE DIOCESE; CORRESPONDENCE AMONG THE CLERGY; AND ELECTION OF A BISHOP.

A. D. 1818–1819.

CHAPTER XIV.

AUTOBIOGRAPHY OF THE BISHOP ELECT.

CHAPTER XV.

THE CHURCH DEFENDED; COVERT ATTACKS; "SERIOUS CALL;" AND "SOBER APPEAL."

A. D. 1819.

CHAPTER XVI.

SPECIAL CONVENTION ; CONSECRATION OF DR. BROWNELL ; GENERAL THEOLOGICAL SEMINARY ; AND REVIVAL OF THE CHURCHMAN'S MAGAZINE.

A. D. 1819 – 1821.

CHAPTER XVII.

MANNER OF PERFORMING DIVINE SERVICE; SUNDAY-SCHOOLS; CHARGE OF THE BISHOP; AND PROSPERITY OF THE DIOCESE.

A. D. 1821–1823.

CHAPTER XVIII.

CHARTER OF A COLLEGE; OPPOSITION TO ITS ESTABLISHMENT; CHANGES IN THE CLERGY; AND DEATH OF DR. BRONSON.

A. D. 1823–1826.

CHAPTER XIX.

SUPPORT OF THE EPISCOPATE; ACADEMY AT CHESHIRE; MENZIES RAYNER, AND HIS SUSPENSION FROM THE MINISTRY.

A. D. 1826 – 1828.

CHAPTER XX.

NEW PARISHES; PROPOSED CHANGES IN THE LITURGY; VISIT OF THE BISHOP TO THE SOUTHWESTERN STATES; AND LACK OF CLERGYMEN.

A. D. 1828 – 1831.

CHAPTER XXI.

RETIREMENT OF THE BISHOP FROM THE PRESIDENCY OF THE COLLEGE; CHARGE TO THE CLERGY; AND GENERAL MISSIONARY SOCIETY OF THE CHURCH.

A. D. 1831 – 1835.

CHAPTER XXII.

USE OF THE GENERAL CONFESSION; THIRD CHARGE OF THE BISHOP; ANOTHER VISIT TO NEW ORLEANS; AND MAINTENANCE OF THE CLERGY.

A. D. 1835 – 1840.

CHAPTER XXIII.

EDUCATION IN THE CHURCH; OXFORD TRACTS; FOURTH CHARGE OF BISHOP BROWNELL; AND NEW PARISHES.

A. D. 1840 – 1843.

CHAPTER XXIV.

INCREASE IN THE NUMBER OF THE CLERGY; MOVEMENT FOR AN ASSISTANT BISHOP; DEATH OF REV. ASHBEL BALDWIN; AND IMPROVED STYLE OF ECCLESIASTICAL ARCHITECTURE.

A. D. 1843 – 1848.

CHAPTER XXV.

MISSIONARY AND CHARITABLE CONTRIBUTIONS; CONVENTION AT NEW LONDON; ADDRESS OF THE BISHOP; AND TENDENCIES TO ROMANISM.

A. D. 1848 – 1851.

CHAPTER XXVI.

DEATHS AMONG THE CLERGY; ELECTION OF AN ASSISTANT BISHOP; AND THEOLOGICAL EDUCATION IN THE DIOCESE.

A. D. 1851 – 1853.

CHAPTER XXVII.

NEW PARISHES AND NEW CHURCHES; GENERAL CONVENTION; FUND FOR THE SUPPORT OF THE EPISCOPATE; AND SALARIES OF THE CLERGY.

A. D. 1853 – 1857.

CHAPTER XXVIII.

PROGRESS OF THE DIOCESE; DEATH OF DR. CROSWELL; NEW CHURCH AT STRATFORD; AND EFFORTS TO INCREASE THE RANKS OF THE MINISTRY.

A. D. 1857 – 1860.

CHAPTER XXIX.

CONVENTION AT NEW LONDON; DIOCESAN MISSIONS; EPISCOPAL DUTIES; CIVIL WAR; AND DEATHS AMONG THE CLERGY.

A. D. 1860 – 1862.

CHAPTER XXX.

MORE NEW CHURCHES AND PARISHES; PROVISION FOR THE CLERGY; DONATIONS AND BEQUESTS FOR CHURCH PURPOSES; PROLONGED RECTORSHIPS; AND DEATH OF BISHOP BROWNELL.

A. D. 1862 – 1865.

HISTORY

OF THE

EPISCOPAL CHURCH IN CONNECTICUT.

CHAPTER I.

ELECTION OF A SUCCESSOR TO BISHOP SEABURY, AND CONSECRATION OF THE REV. ABRAHAM JARVIS TO THE EPISCOPATE OF CONNECTICUT.

A. D. 1796–1799.

THE Church in Connecticut, upon the death of Bishop Seabury, was embarrassed in the selection of his successor by the want of an Episcopal fund. The petitions to the Legislature for a charter empowering a certain number of trustees to receive and hold donations for the support of the Episcopate, had not yet been granted, and the parishes had made no adequate provision for this object. Many of them, in their poverty, confined their obligations to the maintenance of their rectors, and it was natural, therefore, in choosing a bishop, to direct attention to those clergymen in Connecticut, who, with suitable qualities of head and heart, were in circumstances or occupied positions which would enable them to live and perform Episcopal duties without expecting much, if anything, from the Diocese in the way of pecuniary support.

The Constitution, adopted in 1792, required the

Presbyters, Deacons, and Lay Deputies, from the several parishes, to meet within three months from the time when a vacancy shall occur, either at New Haven or Middletown, and "select a person to fill the Episcopal chair." Accordingly, a special Convention, composed of twenty-two clergymen and twenty-six laymen, — the largest number which had yet assembled in this form, — was held in Trinity Church, New Haven, May 5th, 1796, and the Rev. Mr. Jarvis delivered on the occasion a "well-adapted sermon," having reference to the late Diocesan, a copy of which was requested for publication. Printed minutes never give the whole proceedings of a deliberative body, and in this case there appears to be unusual brevity. The two orders separated for the purpose of free consultation, and soon it was discovered that the clergy, though wishing to choose one of their own number, were divided in their preferences and unable to come to a unanimous vote. Mr. Bowden, the most scholarly among them, and the best fitted in many respects for the office, declined to be a candidate; and Mr. Jarvis, after a succession of ballotings, was declared to be elected. When the result was communicated to the lay delegates, they debated long and earnestly about the manner of proceeding, and finally agreed upon the bold and somewhat extraordinary method of giving in their yeas and nays with their names annexed. A majority of two only appeared in favor of confirming the choice of the clergy, and, unfortunately for the Bishop elect, the most influential laymen were not included in this majority.[1] The subse-

[1] MS. letter from Rev. Abraham L. Clarke to Dr. Parker of Boston, May 10th, 1796.

quent action in the whole Convention was far from being unanimous, and no cordial and liberal measures were adopted to encourage Mr. Jarvis to accept the appointment. He was ready, therefore, when waited upon for his answer, to say that he declined the office to which he had been chosen; and the Convention adjourned to meet again in the same place and for the same purpose, in the ensuing October, having first appointed a new Committee to "memorialize the General Assembly for an act of incorporation to establish a fund for the support of the Bishop of Connecticut."

In the mean time, the Annual Convention, fixed as now for the month of June, was held at Cheshire; but so little interest was manifested in its proceedings that twelve clergymen only, and half as many lay delegates were present. The principal subject of their deliberations was the reported Constitution for the Episcopal Academy, already established in that village, and no sooner had it been approved and a board of twenty-one Trustees appointed under it, than the Convention, which originally had this power, proceeded to the election of a Principal of the Institution. The ballots were all in favor of the Rev. John Bowden, who signified at once his acceptance of the office. It was an eminently responsible position, for the Academy thus founded was intended to be, not only a preparatory school of a high order, but a college and a nursery of theological learning. The old prejudices against Episcopacy which characterized the immediate descendants of the first settlers in New England, were still active, and the clergy felt most painfully the want of some literary institution where the sons of the Church might receive a thorough classical education without endangering the religious predilections of their childhood. The Trustees of Yale College, ever since the affair of Rector Cutler and his associates in 1722, had pursued the illiberal policy of preventing the admission of any one as an instructor therein who should be suspected of "inclining to Arminian or prelatic principles." Gratitude for Berkeley's benefactions and for the generosity of that churchman[1] whose honorable name the Institution bears, had not changed those severe statutes which exacted religious tests of the officers of instruction, and compelled Episcopal students to attend worship regularly in the College Chapel, except on Communion Sundays. Most of our clergy, at that period, were graduates of Yale; but the affection which they cherished for their *Alma Mater* was not so great as the love they bore to the Church. They knew that, under God, her prosperity was to be advanced by their own energy and faithfulness, and

[1] Jeremiah Dummer, agent of the Colony of Connecticut, writing to Gov. Saltonstall, from "Middle Temple [London], 14th April, 1719," says: "I heartily congratulate you upon the happy union of the Colony in fixing the Colledge at New Haven, after some differences which might have been attended with ill consequences. Mr. Yale is very much rejoyc'd at this good news, and more than a little pleas'd with his being the Patron of such a seat of the Muses. Saving that he express't at first some kind of concern, whether it was well in him, being a Churchman, to promote an Academy of Dissenters. But when we had discours't that point freely, he appear'd convinc't that the business of good men is to spread religion and learning among mankind without being too fondly attach't to particular Tenets, about which the world never was, nor never will be, agreed. Besides, if the Discipline of the Church of England be most agreeable to Scripture and primitive practice, there 's no better way to make men sensible of it than by giving them good learning." — State Library, Hartford. *Extract from Document* 110 *of vol. ii.* "*Foreign Correspondence with Colonial Agents*, 1661–1732."

much as they desired to see the number of candidates for Holy Orders increased, they would not peril the usefulness and respectability of the clerical profession by lowering the standard of literary and theological attainments.

Mr. Bowden was not without experience in the instruction and management of youth, for since his return from the Island of St. Croix, — whither he went in the autumn of 1789 to pursue the pastoral work, hoping that a residence in that climate would benefit his health, — he had been in charge of a private school for boys at Stratford, and he took the greater part of his pupils with him when he removed to Cheshire, and entered upon his new office. As the friend of Seabury, and the able defender of the Church with his pen, he had, for some time, exercised a commanding influence among his brethren; and when the adjourned Convention met on the 19th of October, attention was again turned to him as the most eligible candidate for the Episcopate. Nineteen clergymen and twenty-one lay delegates composed this Convention; but one third of the laymen were new members who had never before attended such meetings, and it is worthy of note that there is no recorded lay representation from Trinity Parish, New Haven, in whose church the body assembled, nor from the venerable parish at Stratford. That the proceedings might be confined to the object which had called them together, it was "resolved that no other business shall be done at this adjourned Convention, to be recorded, but only the business of electing a bishop." After the two orders had separated, the clergy cast their ballots unanimously for the Rev. Mr.

Bowden, and then, at his particular request, they voted to indulge him in giving a decisive answer on his election till the next annual Convention. The lay delegates readily concurred in their choice and in their resolve; and after the President and Secretary had been requested to make out the testimonials for the Bishop elect, and sign them in behalf of the Convention, an adjournment took place till the annual meeting in June.

To these gleanings from the printed Journal, something may be added from the manuscript records of the Convocation to show the hopes and designs of the clergy. They adopted measures to provide for the expenses of the Bishop elect in obtaining consecration, and requested him, in his tour to Philadelphia for this purpose, to solicit aid of pious and charitable persons or societies "for the encouragement, support, and benefit of the Episcopal Academy in Connecticut." Mr. Baldwin was desired to be his attending Presbyter, and the Standing Committee were charged with the duty of replying to a communication from the Church in Rhode Island, and of inviting a continuance under the same ecclesiastical head. "Mr. Bowden's well-known abilities and integrity," said they, "if he accepts the appointment, will, we trust, in some measure repair the loss we have sustained, and be a means of continuing and firmly establishing that diocesenal unity which has been so happily begun between us."

All these proceedings indicated a confidence on the part of the clergy, that the business which had called them together was now settled, and that the Diocese was soon to be administered by one whose learning and talents they had not failed to appreciate very highly. But to the adjourned and annual Convention held in Derby, June 7th, 1797, Dr. Bowden — for by this time Columbia College, of which he was a graduate, had honored him with the degree of Doctor of Divinity — communicated in "writing his non-acceptance of the Episcopate." The chief reason that led him to this decision was the weakness of his voice and lungs, which he had tried in vain to strengthen, and finally he was compelled to relinquish, for the most part, the public exercise of the ministry. Had he been consecrated, the mitre had rarely crowned a worthier head.

Steps were immediately taken to go into another election, and at the appointed time, the lay members withdrew to a separate apartment, and the clergy proceeded to ballot for a bishop. The Rev. Mr. Jarvis, who was not present at this Convention, was unanimously chosen by both orders, even though there were some among the laity who had strenuously opposed his election at the first special meeting held after the death of Bishop Seabury. It must have been understood that such a result would be reached, and that the candidate, when elected with entire unanimity, would accept the office. The exigencies of the Church in Connecticut at that period demanded a spiritual head. There was no neighboring bishop who could be invited to exercise Episcopal oversight or make occasional visitations. Provoost, of New York, had not much love for the primal Diocese, if the clergy of it had any love for him; and Dr. Bass, who had been consecrated just a month before for Massachusetts, was an old man, already bending under the weight of seventy years, and retaining still the charge of his parish at Newburyport.

Before the clergy dispersed for their homes, they met by themselves in Convocation, and among other resolves which they adopted, was this: "That if the Rev. Mr. Jarvis, the Bishop elect, should go to Philadelphia for consecration, the Rev. Mr. Baldwin be requested to attend him; and that it be recommended to the several churches in the State to have collections for defraying the expenses of both, by the first Sunday in August next, and that the money be sent to the Rev. Mr. Hubbard by the third of said month." There was some delay in fixing the time and place of the consecration; but when the consent of a major number of the Standing Committees in the different dioceses had been obtained, Bishop White, who was the Presiding Bishop, acquiesced in the desire of Connecticut that he and his colleagues would come to New Haven; and accordingly a special Convention was duly warned and held in Trinity Church on the 18th of October, and sixteen clergymen and twenty-seven lay delegates were present to participate in the solemn services. The sermon on the occasion was preached by the Rev. Dr. Smith, who had recently removed into the Diocese from Newport, R. I., and taken charge of St. Paul's Church, Norwalk. In England it is the common practice to select a learned presbyter to preach at the consecration of a bishop; but in this country, since the days of Dr. Smith, with a single exception,[1] no one in the second grade of the ministry has been known to perform such a high duty.

The record in the Journal reads: "The Right Rev. Dr. White acted as the officiating Bishop, and the Bishops Provoost and Bass assisted.

[1] Dr. Beasley preached at the consecration of Rev. Philander Chase.

"The act of consecration being completed, the Right Rev. Dr. Jarvis[1] was recognized by the Convention as the Bishop of Connecticut, and received their congratulations in a very affectionate address delivered by the Rev. Mr. Hubbard, to which Bishop Jarvis returned a very suitable answer. After this, he delivered an excellent charge to the clergy and laity of his Diocese." The Standing Committee, in obedience to instructions, prepared an address of thanks to the consecrating bishops, which, having been read to the Convention and approved, was presented to them with "a gratuity for defraying the expenses" which they had incurred on the occasion. "The gratuity they generously declined accepting, though Dr. Bass was at length prevailed on to accept it." The memorial to the General Assembly for an act of incorporation to establish a fund for the support of the Episcopate, was revived by a new vote, and measures were adopted to increase the endowment of the Diocesan Institution at Cheshire.

Thus terminated the interesting ceremonies and proceedings which attended the consecration of the second Bishop of Connecticut. It was a day of anxiety mingled with cheerful prospects, for the still feeble parishes had more to hope for than to enjoy in their present condition. One of the incidental fruits of this occasion was quite unexpected. Both the sermon of Dr. Smith and the charge of the Bishop were requested for the press, and the publication of the first of these brought forth a letter from Mr. Blatchford — a Congregational divine at Bridgeport — who

1 Yale College conferred upon him the Doctorate at the previous commencement.

conceived himself to be specially called upon to renew the old war against the Church, and to fight over again battles in which his predecessors had won no laurels. The Scotch blood of Dr. Smith was thoroughly roused by this fresh attempt to spread an alarm among the people, and make them look with an evil eye upon Episcopacy by stigmatizing it with the opprobrious epithet of Popery. Under the patronage, therefore, of his brethren, he published an "Answer to Mr. Blatchford's Letter," extending to about one hundred and fifty pages, and placed in the title this quaint but significant motto, copied from an old volume of the Oxford University: "Verily, these men are like Samson's foxes; they have their heads severed indeed; the one sort looking toward the Papacy, the other to the Presbytery; but they are tied together by the tails with firebrands between them, to the injury of the Church."

The "Answer" evinced great familiarity with ecclesiastical history and a thorough knowledge of the points involved in the discussion. It was written in a fearless spirit, and though it contained playful thrusts at his opponent and rambled over a wide field, it met the general assertions and sophistries of the "Letter," which Dr. Smith said he "would not call A Defence of 'the Validity of Presbyterian Ordination,' with Strictures on the Sermon delivered at Bishop Jarvis's Consecration; but The Validity of Lay Ordination Maintained, together with a Pasquinade upon Episcopacy."

At the Annual Convention of 1798, held in Norwalk, steps were taken to provide for the commencement of a fund for the Episcopal Academy at Cheshire, by ascertaining the grand levy of the Church in Connecticut; and the money formerly collected for the purpose of sending missionaries to the frontiers of the States was voted to be applied to the benefit of the same institution. It was also recommended to the several congregations in the Diocese to "collect annually for the use of the Bishop one half-penny on the pound in such way and manner as to them shall seem most expedient."

The Bishop was still in charge of the parish at Middletown, and this was a measure which looked to his separation from parochial work and exclusive devotion to Episcopal duties. His address to the Convention at this time was not printed and there are no contemporary documents to show his official acts or the extent of his visitations. He began, November 1st, with the consecration of St. John's Church, Waterbury, a new edifice which had been several years in the process of erection. But his first ordination, three weeks after the meeting of this Convention and eight months after he had been consecrated, was held in St. John's Church, Bridgeport, when Calvin White was admitted to the order of Deacons and subsequently became an assistant of Dr. Dibblee at Stamford; and on the 30th of the ensuing September, Bethel Judd and Ezra Bradley were ordained to the same grade of the ministry in St. Peter's Church, Cheshire. Several parishes in the Diocese were now vacant, and the clergy, scarcely yet beyond a score in number,[1] were charged with the oversight of neighboring or distant flocks, and to these they officiated monthly or quar-

[1] Rev. Edward Blakeslee died in 1797, and Rev. Philo Perry in 1798, the first aged thirty-one years, and the other forty-six.

terly according as their convenience would admit, or according to the more pressing demands of the parish to which their services were first due. Trinity Church, New Haven, in voting a salary to the Rector at the Easter meeting of 1797, allowed him leave of absence seven Sundays in the year, that he might officiate in West Haven, on condition, however, that the Church in that place paid to the Vestry of Trinity Parish the sum of fifty dollars for his services. This arrangement continued for quite a period, but as the vote shows, the leave of absence was not so much for the benefit of the Rector as for the relief of the parish in New Haven.

The adversaries of Episcopacy saw her feebleness, and were proud to compare their own prosperous communion and full-fed pastors with the weaker body which preferred to worship God in a Liturgy and always steadfastly believed in the Scriptural character of a threefold ministry. Bishop Jarvis was familiar with the political and ecclesiastical history of Connecticut, and understood well the nature of the high office to which he had been raised. He had all the learning, and dignity, and firmness of his predecessor, but unlike him, he was indisposed to be active; and he had not the same power to attract popular attention and to make his ministrations felt as he pursued the noiseless round of his Episcopal duties. An asthmatic difficulty which had troubled him from early life and increased upon him with advancing years, made him a poor traveller, and it is no wonder, if the Church afterwards partook in some degree of the involuntary lethargy which crept upon her new overseer.

But the clergy were too fresh yet in the recollection of the severe trials through which they had passed to be otherwise than vigilant, and therefore every care was taken, not only to maintain with firmness their distinct religious faith, but to guard against the encroachments of error and the progress of sceptical philosophy. The strong sympathy which unhappily, and on no rational grounds, prevailed in this country towards those who were leaders in the late French Revolution, as well as towards the Revolution itself, had prepared many to become the miserable dupes of their principles and declarations. "Of the immeasurable evils, under which France and her neighbors agonized, infidelity was the genuine source — the Vesuvius, from whose mouth issued those rivers of destruction which deluged and ruined all things in their way. It was seen that man, unrestrained by law and religion, is a mere beast of prey; that licentiousness, although adorned with the graceful name of liberty, is yet the spring of continual alarm, bondage, and misery; and that the restraints imposed by equitable laws, and by the religion of the Scriptures, were far less burthensome and distressing than the boasted freedom of infidels." [1]

Upon the accession of the elder Adams to the Presidency of the United States, the clergy of Connecticut sent him an address, expressive of their attachment to the government of their country and their approbation of the measures adopted by the constituted authorities thereof; and it shows how much they were alive to all flagrant assaults upon revealed truth that, at a pre-

[1] Pres. Dwight's *Discourse on Events of the Last Century*, January 7, 1801, p. 33.

vious Convocation, they directed a letter of thanks to be addressed also to Dr. Watson, the learned Bishop of Landaff, for his noble "Apology for the Bible" in answer to Thomas Paine's "Age of Reason." "Happy are we," said they in this letter, "to find that your excellent defence has in a good degree strengthened the faithful, confirmed the doubtful, roused the indifferent, and silenced the gainsayer. And we have reason to believe that it will, by the blessing of God, be a means of checking that spirit of infidelity among us which has produced such horrid scenes in a powerful nation of Europe." [1]

But the pen of the Bishop of Landaff[2] was not the only one whose influence in vindicating the truth of Christianity was felt in this country. "A Short and Easy Method with the Deists," by Charles Leslie, having been widely circulated, furnished churchmen with ready reasons for the support of their faith. "That was a great man," said Wm. Jones of Nayland writing to Dr. Bowden,[3] "and one of the great patterns from whom I learned controversial divinity in my early years. I desired a bookseller of London to lay hold of as many copies of his works as he could find; foreseeing that they would be called for. 'Ah sir,' said he, 'I could have got you a hundred copies a year ago; but the price was fallen so low, that they are now gone for waste paper.' They are among many other things disregarded by the world, which will, nevertheless, survive the fire of the last day."

1 MS. original draught.

2 Now spelled *Llandaff.*

3 MS. letter, February 28, 1799.

CHAPTER II.

REMOVAL OF BISHOP JARVIS TO CHESHIRE; ADOPTION OF AN OFFICE OF INSTITUTION; AND EFFORTS TO ENDOW THE EPISCOPATE.

A. D. 1799–1804.

In the autumn of 1799, Bishop Jarvis resigned his parish at Middletown and removed to Cheshire. He had already placed his son at the Academy under the care of Dr. Bowden, but the hopes and affections of the parents were so bound up in this child of their old age that the thought of continued separation from him was not to be endured. It formed an additional motive for his change of residence that the Institution was acquiring, in the eyes of the Church, reputation and influence as a nursery of learning, and he perceived the obvious propriety of being near to watch its infant progress and support its ecclesiastical character. Accordingly he built for himself a suitable house in Cheshire, and the village so beautiful and attractive by nature became, for a time, the general centre of diocesan interests.

The Academy prospered under the management of its scholarly Principal, and not only were contributions for its benefit obtained from New York, but the Annual Convention of 1799, held in Stratfield, declared it to be the duty of each clergyman in the Diocese, together with some respectable layman in his parish, to visit by a specified day as many of the parishioners as possible and solicit "individual donations from them for the use of the Episcopal Academy." The vacant churches were not overlooked in this attempt to raise money, for the Standing Committee was directed to communicate with them and invite their coöperation. The same Convention voted also that "one or more agents be appointed by the Trustees . . to go to Europe for the purpose of soliciting donations," as soon as there should be unappropriated funds sufficient to defray the expenses of such a mission ; and the very next year, steps were taken to ascertain, according to the grand list, the quota that each parish must pay in order to secure the sum of seven hundred dollars — that sum being designated as necessary to support the agent. The mission contemplated never was undertaken, but these votes indicate the zeal and earnestness of the churchmen of Connecticut seventy years ago, in the matter of Christian and classical education.

The clergy had not lost sight of a revision of the Articles, and in this respect they went beyond their first Bishop, who was inclined to doubt the necessity of them or "rather to believe that their object might be accomplished through the medium of the Liturgy." At a Convocation held in August, 1798, Dr. Smith and the Rev. Messrs. Shelton and Baldwin were appointed "a Committee to frame Articles of Religion," to be laid before a future meeting ; but the whole subject was taken out of their hands by the action of the General Convention in 1799, — action which was pressed upon that body at the instance of the delegates from Connecticut, and in consequence of instructions which they had received from the Diocese. The final consideration of the matter was referred to the next General Convention and resulted in the adoption of the doctrinal system of the Church as embodied in our present Articles of Religion.

Ebenezer Dibblee, whose name had stood on the list of the clergy in charge of the parish at Stamford fifty-one years, went to his rest in 1799; and the people, who loved him so well and whom he had served so faithfully, were unfortunate in the choice of a successor, and became involved in a trouble which, as will be seen hereafter, not only produced division and contention among them, but alienated them for a time from the ecclesiastical authority of the Diocese. The good instructions of the past were forgotten in the heats of passion, and the breach, small at first, was widened under the schemes and dexterous management of a bad leader.

Hitherto there had been no canons for the regulation of the clergy in Connecticut, but a special committee, previously appointed, reported to the Convention of 1799 a code, which, after due consideration and sundry amendments, was adopted and "ordered to be engrossed on the minutes." These Canons are remarkable for their comprehensive brevity, and they were first printed without any headings and distinguished merely by the numbers. Among them are directions of this sort.

"The clergy shall pay strict regard to the Rubrics of the Church and shall neither alter nor mutilate the service otherwise than they are by the Rubrics permitted.

"The clergy shall pay due attention to their dress

and shall deviate as little as possible in this respect from clerical propriety.

"All persons belonging to this State, who intend to apply to the Bishop for Holy Orders, shall make known to him their intention in writing twelve months before such application.

"Every clergyman settled in this State shall, on the next Sunday after Easter in every year, preach a sermon to his congregation on the duties which are peculiarly Episcopal; and in which he shall lay before his people the propriety and necessity of supporting the Episcopal office with becoming dignity."

Twenty years passed away before any attempt was made to amend or revise this simple code. It is true at a Convocation held in Derby on the 20th of November, 1799 — when "the new church" in that place was consecrated, — the Bishop and four of his presbyters were empowered to frame "a Canon to regulate clerical attendance upon State Conventions and Convocations; and also to address certain clergymen in the Diocese upon the subject of their neglect of those clerical meetings." But the vote resulted in no recorded action and the subsequent legislation of the Church was directed to other and more important matters.

In this year and at this Convocation an Office for inducting clergymen into vacant parishes or churches, prepared by the Rev. Dr. Smith at the request of the Annual Convention, after having been "examined, paragraph by paragraph," was approved and ordered to be printed without delay, and the Bishop was desired to transmit copies of it to the several bishops in the United States and to the standing committees of those States in which there were no bishops. The object of giving it this circulation was to open the way for its adoption and use by the Church at large, and it was first prescribed by the General Convention of 1804; and a section of the Canon then passed in reference to it declared, that no clergyman hereafter elected into any parish or church should be considered as a regularly admitted and settled parochial minister in any Diocese or State until he had been inducted according to this Office. The Diocese of Connecticut, at its Annual Convention three months before, had formally adopted it as approved by the Bishop and Clergy in Convocation. It was set forth with alterations by the General Convention in 1808, — the title changed from "Induction" [1] to "Institution," and its use made to depend upon recommendation and not upon requisition. On comparing the present Office in the Book of Common Prayer with the first printed copy, they are found to be so nearly alike as to give to Connecticut the whole credit of providing for the Church a service which, however much it may be neglected in these days, was intended to impress upon the pastor and his people their intimate, mutual, and solemn relations to each other.

The laity now began to receive accessions of prominent men from the standing order, and their delegates to the Annual Conventions regularly outnumbered the clergy. The parishes, at the commencement of the century, having recovered, in a measure, from the disastrous effects of the Revolutionary War,

1 *Induction* is that act by which a clergyman is vested with the temporalities of a living: *Institution* is the act of committing to his charge the care of souls.

had increased to sixty-three, though the number of clergymen was scarcely greater than before the Independence of the Colonies. Two persons applied to be received as candidates for Holy Orders, in 1801, and were rejected by the Convocation; and two in the Diaconate — Caleb Childs and Ezra Bradley — were degraded from the ministry. The final vote to degrade the latter was passed by the Convocation in 1804, when twenty clergymen, including the Bishop, were present. Mr. Childs, besides his doctrinal errors, was charged with being "guilty of immoralities and vices injurious to Christianity and disgraceful to the character of a clergyman," and the sentence of degradation pronounced upon him was ordered to be read in the churches of Stamford, Norwalk, and New Canaan.

The Annual Convention of that year met at Newtown, and to render the opening services more imposing, a procession formed by its members, — the clergy in their gowns, — moved from the house of the Rector, the Rev. Mr. Burhans, to the Episcopal Church, attended by a band of music. The example of that occasion was observed for many years afterwards, with the omission of the musical accompaniment. Gamaliel Thatcher was at the time advanced to the priesthood, and a lay delegate from the Episcopal congregation in Salisbury, appeared with a vote of that parish "adopting the Constitution of the Protestant Episcopal Church of this Diocese." Four of the clergy, Ashbel Baldwin, Philo Shelton, Tillotson Bronson, and Evan Rogers, and two of the laity, James Clark of Danbury and Nathaniel Perry of Woodbury, were chosen as delegates to the General Convention soon to assemble in Trenton, and a collection to defray their expenses was ordered to be made in the several parishes of the Diocese in the ensuing month, and the amounts received to be transmitted to the Rev. Mr. Baldwin. Clark attended with three of the clerical delegates, and he neutralized their affirmative in that body on a proposition to enact a Canon in the following words: "No lay deputy shall be admitted as a member of this House who shall not have been a communicant of the Protestant Episcopal Church for at least one year previous to his appointment." More than half a century elapsed before the substance of what the Church then refused to adopt was finally agreed to and ratified by the General Convention, and made an essential part of the Constitution originally accepted for the government of the Protestant Episcopal Church in the United States of America.

The Episcopalians in Hartford, whose misfortunes before the Revolution had led them to suspend the work of building for themselves a house of worship, resumed it again in 1793, but without a resident rector the enterprise progressed slowly towards completion. On the 10th of November, 1801, the Bishop and fifteen clergymen assembled in Convocation at Hartford, and the next day Christ Church was consecrated, and the Rev. Menzies Rayner, who had been recently called from Elizabethtown, New Jersey, was duly inducted into the Rectorship of the parish. It was one of the first occasions, if not the very first, on which the new Office of Institution was used in Connecticut, and joined with the services of consecration, it made the ceremonies of the day doubly impressive, and such as must have long been remembered. Ashbel Baldwin, then in the vigor of manhood and the prime of his usefulness, preached the sermon. A month later the Rev. Joseph Warren was instituted into the Rectorship of Christ Church, Middletown. Mr. Rayner preached the sermon.

One eminent presbyter, who had borne an active and influential part in the councils of the Diocese from its organization, was now about to withdraw and enter upon another field of labor. The Rev. Dr. Bowden, who for nearly six years had been at the head of the Episcopal Academy and had seen it grow into a chartered Institution,[1] with considerable funds and "generally about sixty students in a course of education," resigned his office of Principal on the 29th of March, 1802, and accepted the more comfortable position of Professor of Moral Philosophy and Belles-Lettres in Columbia College, New York. A special Convention was held in Cheshire two weeks afterwards to receive his resignation and elect a successor. The choice fell unanimously upon the Rev. Dr. William Smith, who was at that time conducting a Grammar School in New York, having relinquished St. Paul's Church, Norwalk, in the autumn of 1800, in consequence of an unhappy disagreement which arose between him and the people in regard to the permanency of a settlement. The change brought back to the Diocese an energetic, ardent, and impulsive presbyter, but it took away one whom the clergy greatly loved and revered, who was a wise and dispassionate counsellor, and whose scholarly pen could always be trusted, whether employed in defending the Church or in speaking for his brethren. Dr. Bowden, besides his classic and patristic knowledge, was

1 It was incorporated at the May session of the General Assembly, 1801.

well read in English theology and familiar with those publications of his time best calculated to encourage correct principles and sound Christian learning. He was the first to introduce into this country Daubeny's "Guide to the Church," and in a letter to the author, written at the instance of the clergy of Connecticut in the summer of 1801, and before any thought of changing his location had been entertained, he said, — "we are determined that it shall be a standard book for all our candidates for holy orders. Clergymen brought up at the feet of Leslie, Horne, Jones, and Daubeny, will not fail to be orthodox in their faith, pure in their lives, and zealous to promote the kingdom of Christ."

The proper support of the Episcopate had been a subject of consideration by the Convention and by the laity in the principal parishes from an early date in the administration of Bishop Seabury. The memorial to the Legislature for a charter heretofore several times mentioned, was granted in 1799; but so scattered were the corporators or so indifferent to their trust, that no meeting to organize was held — though donations were awaiting their action — until the last day of November, 1803. In the meantime, the Convention by special resolves had endeavored to "stir up their pure minds by way of remembrance," and three of the memorialists had applied to the General Assembly at the October session of that year for an addition to their number of two clergymen and two laymen, centrally located. The application was granted, and after an organization should be completed, five of the Board with the "president or chairman," were empowered to form a quorum. The

Treasurer, Isaac Beers, one of the new Trustees, was a resident of New Haven, and pains were taken to secure subscriptions to increase the fund, both from individuals and from the several parishes in the Diocese. By a vote of the Board, all persons who should subscribe and pay to the treasurer of the corporation the sum of thirty dollars each were entitled to have their names inserted on the records, but this inducement appears not to have been a very powerful one, for only eight names are thus entered, two of them heading the list from Stratford, — the Johnsons, father and son, — the rest were from Hartford, and the aggregate of their subscriptions was three hundred and ninety dollars. "A donation from a bishop in Scotland," of sixty pounds sterling, appears among the earliest credits.

The Annual Convention of 1804, held at Litchfield, provided for an "address" on the subject "To the members of the Episcopal Church in Connecticut," and the Trustees, meeting in October, requested the clergy to read it to their respective congregations at some convenient time previous to Easter Monday, when the parishes or individual members thereof were desired to consult together and make liberal donations. An extract from this address will show the earnestness of the Committee by whom it was prepared.

"Brethren, believing that entreaties will not be necessary to persuade you to make provision for the supreme officer in our ecclesiastical polity, we congratulate you on the opportunity now presented, of showing your zeal for the house of the Lord, and of giving to the honor of his name, 'according to the blessings wherewith he hath blessed you.' We are also putting you in mind to pay a debt, — a debt of gratitude to our common benefactor, for his merciful providence in granting to us a valid and regular succession in the ministry, with all the blessings and benefits which are connected therewith : and for such inestimable favors how disproportionate are all the returns that can be made! God hath been liberal to you in spirituals and in temporals, his goodness and his mercy accompany you — your land yields her increase and your barns are filled with plenty — but no provision is made for the fountain of Holy Orders, no maintenance made for Christ's chief minister among you! Will any of you then grudge to make God some small return ? Will any of you be backward to honor with a part of your substance that office which is the grand *vinculum* that binds and unites Christians throughout the world ? No ! brethren: rather consider the office of a bishop, as the representative of Christ, and receive those who bear it, as you would the Apostles. Remember those words of Christ to his Apostles, and in them every succeeding Bishop of his Church — 'he that receiveth you, receiveth me, and he that receiveth me, receiveth him that sent me.'

"Disposed to honor the person sent, on account of the religious reverence due to the Sender, ye need not, brethren, the force of multiplied arguments to persuade you to do in the present case what is highly for your honor, your temporal and spiritual emolument. By being liberal in your donations for this confessedly praiseworthy purpose, ye will honor the memory of your departed friends, who have 'desired to see the things which ye see,' namely, ordinations and confirmations, 'and have not seen them; and to hear the things which ye hear,' the voices of the Angels of the Churches, 'and have not heard them.' A blessing will descend upon you and your posterity; and whenever mention shall be made of the Church in Connecticut, the Bishop's Fund will be mentioned for a perpetual memorial of your zeal for the cause of God and his Church."

Notwithstanding this earnest appeal, the enlargement of the fund for several years was inconsiderable, and the support of Bishop Jarvis was regarded with a languor which neither his own private means nor any poverty of the parishes could justify.

The plans in reference to the Academy at Cheshire had not been accomplished, and steps were taken to increase its endowment in a way which was then supposed to be perfectly consistent with the dictates of Christian morality. A petition to the General Assembly for a lottery to raise the sum of fifteen thousand dollars was granted at the October session of 1802, but the net proceeds of the grant, owing to loss and perplexity and expense attending the management, were considerably less than the amount desired. The financial affairs of the institution being thus improved, its friends began to turn their attention to the original design of erecting it into a college, and, therefore, in accordance with a vote of the Annual Convention, the Board of Trustees in 1804 applied to the Legislature for a charter, empowering them to confer degrees in the arts, divinity, and law, and to enjoy all other privileges usually granted to colleges. This application failed, and no renewal of it was made until the occurrence of more propitious events. The resignation of Dr. Bowden and his removal to New York led to another change in the residence of Bishop Jarvis. He was himself a graduate of Yale College, and his son being now well prepared, he determined, in 1803, to remove to New Haven and enter him as a student at the same institution. His wife had died two years before, and this event made him more unwilling than ever to be separated from the child for whose success and welfare he was deeply solicitous. Besides, New Haven was the largest city in Connecticut, and the best located, as things then were, for a convenient administration of the Diocese.

Under the editorship of "a Committee appointed by the Convocation of the Episcopal Church in Connecticut," a periodical was commenced with the year 1804, called "The Churchman's Monthly Magazine or Treasury of Divine and Useful Knowledge." The object of it was to diffuse information concerning the Church — to furnish brief historical accounts, comments, and explanations of her feasts and fasts, her Sacraments, Liturgy, and Offices, to give a right understanding of the economy of redemption and the instituted means of salvation, and also to procure, publish, and preserve records of "the origin and progress of the individual congregations in the Diocese." The editors, in their introductory address, said: —

"That the object may be the more completely embraced, the whole will be calculated to guard against the plausible but dangerous reasonings of infidels and latitudinarians — reasonings the more dangerous, because plausible, for the laying all religions upon a level; and whose pretended liberality towards religion in every form, arises from a real coldness towards it in any, and from their wishes to bring the thing itself into contempt and insignificance.

"We have a very encouraging and noble example set us, in that country from whence we emanated, and by numbers of that Church which gave origin to ours, and under whose fostering care it was for many years nurtured. The writings of those learned and virtuous men brought over to us, exhibit the most pleasing proofs of their vigilance and ever to be admired abilities in detecting the falsehoods and repelling the subtle efforts of the enemies of their religion and peace."

It was the first and for some time the only periodical publication in this country devoted to the interests of the Protestant Episcopal Church, and though it had a precarious and troubled existence, appearing for a few years in Connecticut and then being removed to New York and New Jersey, and finally brought back and restored to life in the land of its birth, yet it must be confessed that it fulfilled a good purpose in its day, and was conducted with a spirit and ability which served to promote both the glory of God and the edification of his people. Not feeling and therefore not expressing any of that spurious liberality which would level all distinction between right and wrong, it aimed to make truth and sincerity its guide, and helped to impress those wholesome lessons which have marked the character, and lived so long in the recollections of Connecticut churchmen.

CHAPTER III.

ECCLESIASTICAL TROUBLE; PROCEEDINGS IN THE CASE OF AMMI ROGERS; AND INTERPOSITION OF THE HOUSE OF BISHOPS INVOKED.

A. D. 1804–1805.

THE peace of the Church in Connecticut was disturbed by a new and mischievous trouble which arose about this time, and extended on beyond the administration of Bishop Jarvis. It is necessary to the truth of history that the story be fully told — otherwise these pages would not be occupied with what may seem, in the view of many readers, to be unprofitable matter.

A young man named Ammi Rogers, born at Branford and a graduate of Yale College in the class of 1790, having met with opposition in his native State where his character was best known, applied for Holy Orders in the Diocese of New York, and on the strength of a certificate signed with the name of the Rev. Philo Perry, Secretary of the Convocation of the Clergy of Connecticut, — which certificate was neither written nor signed by him,[1] — he was ordained

[1] While the case was under consideration, a clerical member of the standing committee, Dr. Beach, having heard of his rejection in Connecticut, opposed his ordination. "On this, Rogers repaired to that State, with the view of procuring from the Rev. Philo Perry, the Secretary of the Convention of the Diocese, a certificate that there did not appear on the minutes any entry of the rejection of the person in question. Such a certificate

a Deacon by Bishop Provoost in June, 1792, and at a later date the same prelate advanced him to the order of the Priesthood. Of pleasing appearance and insinuating address, he made strong friends for himself; and reported as the result of his ministrations in Saratoga County, in Schenectady and other places, where he first officiated, great interest in religious things and large accessions to the Church. He continued in Northern New York some nine years and employed the influence which his zealous and apparently successful labors had gained him to promote his selfish and ambitious ends. He was a delegate from New York to the General Convention which met in Philadelphia in 1799 — having secured his election to that body over a venerable city clergyman by adroitly impressing his brethren with a conviction of his ability, earnestness, and piety. In midsummer, 1801, he returned to Branford, and assumed the charge of the parishes in that town, Wallingford and East Haven. The Bishop of Connecticut, knowing his early character and the ingenious fraud which he had practiced to obtain orders, refused to receive him, and the clergy refused to admit him a member of the Convocation, until he produced satisfactory testimonials from the Bishop and Standing Committee of the Diocese in which he was ordained and to which he properly

might have been given with great truth, because no formal application had been made. But Philo Perry being from home, Ammi Rogers fabricated a certificate in his name; not only testifying to the said fact, but going to the point of the correct life and conversation of the bearer. The last circumstance is of importance; because, although a certificate as to his not having applied for and been refused orders, was obtained from Philo Perry afterward, yet it went no further." — Bishop White's *Memoirs of Prot. Epis. Ch.* p. 188.

belonged. Had there been an explicit canon in regard to letters dimissory, such as the Church possesses now, there would have been no room for diversity of sentiment upon this subject; but the law was then to be inferred from general principles, and the friends of Rogers among the clergy, at least in the earliest stage of the proceedings, appear to have felt that he had some show of right on his side and ought to be received and recognized by virtue of his parochial cure. A month before the meeting of the Annual Convention of 1803, six Rectors in Connecticut — Dr. Mansfield, Solomon Blakeslee, John Tyler, Ambrose Todd, Joseph Warren, and Smith Miles — addressed a brief memorial to Bishop Jarvis in the following words: "That each parish has a right to choose its own Rector, and that when the Bishop's approbation is obtained he does, of course, become a member of the Convention, and that it appears from sufficient documents that the parishes under the charge of the Rev. A. Rogers have proceeded according to their right and the Canons of the Church in choosing him for their Rector, and the Bishop's actual approbation being obtained in one case, and no objections stated in the other, we therefore pray that he may take his seat in the Convention and become one of our number."

But the memorial thus supported was of no avail, nor were the letters which Mr. Rogers procured from New York satisfactory to the ecclesiastical authority of the Diocese of Connecticut. He still insisted that he was entitled to a seat in the Convention, and his claims were urged with considerable pertinacity by one or two lay-members, whom he had succeeded in convincing that he was more the victim of private persecution than an object of just censure. He was a most ubiquitous character and appeared in all parts of the Diocese, officiating wherever he could gain admittance, calumniating the Bishop, seeking to divide the clergy, to poison the minds of the laity, and thus to create an unhappy schism in the Church. In compliance with the requirements of Canon second of the General Convention of 1792, official notice was given of these irregularities to the Bishop of New York, to whom the offender was amenable, but the notice was entirely disregarded and the irregularities were repeated in an aggravated form. Failing to reach him in any other way, the clergy, at a Convocation held in Litchfield on the 6th day of June, 1804, "resolved unanimously that the Bishop be requested to suspend the Rev. Ammi Rogers from the use of the churches in this Diocese." Accordingly a circular was issued five days afterwards of which the following is a copy: —

"The Rev. Ammi Rogers, now residing in this Diocese, hath for a long time conducted himself in such a way as is contrary to the rules of the Church and disgraceful to his office, — therefore, by the advice, and at the desire of the Clergy of Connecticut, We, the Bishop, do by these presents forbid, and direct the Clergy of this Diocese to forbid the said Rogers in future to officiate in their churches and within their parishes, and in all vacant parishes the wardens are desired to do the same, and the congregations are exhorted not to give countenance to a man whose disorderly and refractory conduct is subversive of the harmony and peace of the Church."

Rogers published an immediate response to this

circular, and declared it to be without authority and of no force. His numerous adherents, in the parishes where he had been employed, also issued their solemn protest — instigated and prepared no doubt by himself — against the circular of the Bishop, but the clergy stood firmly by their chief pastor and sustained him in the act which had been performed in obedience to their request. They addressed a letter to the Standing Committee of New York, reciting generally the course of Rogers in Connecticut and enclosing a copy of his "Anti-circular" with a request that it might be laid before their Diocesan, adding, "we wish not in this communication to go into a particular detail of the many irregularities which he has been guilty of since he has been in this State. We judge his circular letter will be sufficient data for some official measures to be taken respecting him." By this time he had removed from his native place and become the accepted minister in the more ancient and wealthy parish at Stamford. Here he was quite popular, and the influence which he acquired over his supporters emboldened him to take other steps to vindicate his character and standing in the Church.

The General Convention met in the city of New York, September 1804, and confident of success, he carried his case before the House of Bishops, and invoked their interposition. That House was then composed of White, Claggett, Jarvis, Benjamin Moore, and Parker — the latter of whom was consecrated to the Apostolic office on the fourth day of the session, and the "memorial of the Rev. Ammi Rogers, accompanied with sundry documents and a letter" was introduced on the same day. A time was fixed for hearing the case, and the desire of the Bishops was communicated to the House of Clerical and Lay Deputies, that, if any members of that body "possessed information respecting the conduct of the said Ammi Rogers in the matters brought before them," they would appear at the specified time and produce the information. Bishop Jarvis, from motives of delicacy, absented himself when the question came up, but the clerical delegates from Connecticut appeared and the memorialist was called in, and documents on both sides were then read and a hearing was granted. Nothing was done afterwards in the business except in the presence of the parties concerned. "The clerical deputies from Connecticut," says Bishop White, "while they treated the man with the utmost decorum, produced ample evidence of a factious and mischievous disposition."

The final determination of the House of Bishops concerning the whole subject is entered upon their journal and quoted here without omitting a word.

"After full inquiry and fair examination of all the evidence that could be procured, it appears to this house that the said Ammi Rogers had produced to the Standing Committee of New York (upon the strength of which he obtained Holy Orders) a certificate signed with the name of the Rev. Philo Perry, which certificate was not written nor signed by him.

"That the conduct of the said Ammi Rogers, in the State of Connecticut, during his residence in that State since he left New York, has been insulting, refractory, and schismatical in the highest degree; and, were it tolerated, would prove subversive of all order and discipline in the Church; and that the statement which he made in justification of his conduct, was a mere tissue of equivocation and evasion, and, of course, served rather to defeat than to establish his purpose.

"Therefore this house do approve of the proceedings of the Church in Connecticut, in reproving the said Ammi Rogers, and prohibiting him from the performance of any ministerial duties within that Diocese; and, moreover, are of opinion that he deserves a severe ecclesiastical censure — that of degradation from the ministry.

"In regard to the question, To what authority is Mr. Rogers amenable? this house are sensible, that there not having been, previously to the present Convention, any sufficient provision for a case of a clergyman removing from one diocese to another, it might easily happen that different sentiments would arise as to this point. We are of opinion, that Mr. Rogers's residence being in Connecticut, it is to the authority of that diocese he is exclusively amenable. But as the imposition practiced with a view to the Ministry was in New York, we recommend to the Bishop and Standing Committee of that State, to send to the Bishop in Connecticut such documents, duly attested, of the measure referred to, as will be a ground of procedure in that particular.

"We further direct the Secretary to deliver a copy of the above to the clerical deputies from Connecticut, and another copy to the Rev. Ammi Rogers. And we further direct that either of the aforesaid parties be permitted to have any document respectively delivered in by them, a copy of it being first taken; except the petition and affidavit of the Rev. Ammi Rogers, of which he may have a copy if desired — as may either of the parties have of any document delivered by the other party."

This decision, embracing the opinion of the bishops on all the points contained in the memorial, was not entirely free from canonical difficulties. It sent the petitioner back to Connecticut under a sentence of condemnation by the very body from which he had sought redress; and hence the impression was produced that Ammi Rogers had been tried by the House of Bishops and that nothing remained but to declare him degraded. The whole proceeding was somewhat loose and irregular. Bishop White thought that in giving an opinion, the House should have stopped with an incidental notice of "the iniquity which had come within their knowledge," during the investigation. "But unfortunately," he continued, "one of the bishops having proposed that there should be included a recommendation to degrade the man from the Ministry, the others, under the sensibility excited by the evidence of his great unworthiness and his flagitious conduct, consented to the proposal. This was ill-judged." It seemed to close the case to further scrutiny, and furnished the Bishop and clergy of Connecticut with a reason for their subsequent action.

The mode of trying a clergyman in this Diocese at that time was prescribed by a Canon, which required the accusers of an offending minister to make written application in the first instance to the Standing Committee, and if it appeared to them that there was ground for the charges, they should report thereupon to the bishop, who was then to call a convention of his clergy — not less than seven — and after a full and fair trial and examination he, with the advice of those present, should pronounce sentence against the guilty party. Rogers complained that in his case the provisions of the Canon were not regarded; and, technically speaking, there was room for complaint, unless the hearing, which he had himself invited, is to be understood in the light of a trial before a higher court. It was so understood by Bishop Claggett, whose ill-health compelled him to leave the city and return home before the business was finished or rather before any judgment had been delivered. Others could not refrain from taking the same view; especially as witnesses were called, testimony heard, and an authoritative decision rendered.

"The ground on which the Bishops consented to give their sentiments on the question, as to the jurisdiction to which Ammi Rogers belonged, was," says White "in the urgent solicitations of both the parties; which were thought to justify the expression of opinion." His amenability to the Diocese of Connecticut having been affirmed, a Convocation was held in Cheshire on the 3d day of October, — two weeks after the adjournment of the General Convention, — when the Bishop and ten presbyters were present. No allusion to the episcopal decision appears upon the records of that meeting, but simply this entry: "Bishop Jarvis presented a sentence of degradation against the Rev. Ammi Rogers, which was unanimously approved and the same ordered to be published in the usual form," an order which was, of course, immediately obeyed. A terrible storm now arose and threatened to be followed by serious consequences to the Church in Connecticut. The friends of the degraded minister rallied around him with increased earnestness and the congregation of St. John's Church in Stamford, for which he had been hired on the previous Easter Monday to officiate six months, held a meeting, and by a major vote called and settled him as their Rector, and stipulated to pay him annually a definite sum during his natural life, "any order, determination, or decree of the Bishop and clergy of this or any other State to the contrary notwithstanding." The minority, who endeavored in vain to get the Bishop's circular and documents from the General Convention read, remonstrated against this proceeding, and claimed that those who instituted it had forfeited their right to be the representatives of the parish and the guardians of its interests. Internal troubles followed, and suits at law were commenced against Rogers to eject him from the incumbency on the ground that he was a trespasser, and in the trial of these suits came up the question of his displacement from the ministry in due and canonical form. The courts decided virtually in his favor, and held that the papers issued and published by Bishop Jarvis concerning him were not, in themselves, sufficient to deprive him of his standing in the Church, and consequently of his living amongst those who had accepted him as their lawful and settled minister. The points of law turned upon the nature of the Episcopal office, and the interpretation of the Canons which prescribed the mode of trying a clergyman in Connecticut. Disorderly and schismatical conduct, unbecoming a priest of God, and subversive of the peace and harmony of the Church, was not the issue before the civil court, but it was whether the man, with this particular sentence of degradation pronounced upon him, had the same clerical rights as before.

The Bishop with his clergy met in Convocation at Stamford on the 14th day of October, 1805, when besides himself thirteen were present, including two visiting brethren from New York. The object of the meeting was to confer, in a friendly and unofficial way, with the principal adherents of Rogers; and as soon as they had organized for business a committee was appointed to wait upon Mr. Cary Leeds, one of their number and their authorized "agent to negotiate a settlement of all the unhappy differences and disputes," and inform him that the Convocation was now ready to enter into a conference with him respecting those ecclesiastical proceedings of the Diocese which were so unsatisfactory to him and his friends. The answer brought back by the committee was—"That Mr. Leeds informed them that he could have no personal conference with the Convocation." The Bishop had previously made a gentle requisition upon him for the keys of St. John's Church, that it might be used for the meetings of the clergy while in town; and had told him that "his compliance in this particular would be in strict conformity to ecclesiastical duty." But the keys had been given up to the exclusive control of Rogers, and to him therefore a more peremptory requisition was sent, but without avail. Several letters or notes passed between the parties, and finally the "Rev. Philo Shelton, Rev. Daniel Burhans and Rev. Tillotson Bronson were appointed a committee to draft an answer to the last communication from Cary Leeds to this Convocation;" and they submitted the following statement, which was approved unanimously and ordered to be engrossed upon the minutes.

"To Cary Leeds, Alexander Bishop and others who are dissatisfied with the ecclesiastical proceedings of the Bishop and clergy of the Diocese of Connecticut in regard to Mr. Ammi Rogers: —

"The Bishop and clergy of the Diocese of Connecticut, sincerely desirous to promote the peace and preserve the authority of the Church, have met at Stamford in the hope that, by friendly conference with you, it would be in their power to satisfy you of the propriety and duty of submitting to the sentence pronounced upon Mr. Ammi Rogers. They regret that your refusal to engage in a personal conference has prevented that full and fair discussion of the subject which in every point of view was so desirable. By persons who profess themselves churchmen in principles and in practice, they still cherish the hope that the following statement of facts from the authority of the Church will be duly regarded."

They then proceed to give a minute history of the hearing before the House of Bishops and to call attention to every step taken in that body with reference to this matter. Their answer next goes on to say: —

"By recurring to the Journal, you will find that the above is an impartial statement of facts, and that the following particulars undeniably result from it. Mr. Ammi Rogers brought this business himself before the House of Bishops, and, in the words of his memorial, declared that 'he has never shunned investigation, but on the contrary has always requested it, and *now* prays that a candid and impartial inquiry may be made as to his conduct and character.' It appears that Mr. Rogers presented to the House his documents; and that a full hearing of the case was at different times made in the presence of both parties; that Mr. Rogers confirmed the wish that he expressed for an inquiry by always attending for the purpose, and it was not until the close of the inquiry, and until he had reason to fear the unfavorable result to himself that he expressed to the Bishops that he did not wish them to come to any decision. Now as persons deeply interested for the peace of the Church and your spiritual welfare, we entreat your conscientious attention to the following considerations. Can you suppose, that, if Mr. Rogers did not wish for an inquiry into his conduct by the House of Bishops, he would have permitted them to engage in it, without entering his solemn protest against it? Can you suppose that the Right Rev. Bishop White, whose impartiality and mildness are so universally acknowledged, — that Bishop Moore, who had been represented by Mr. Rogers as friendly to him, — that Bishop Parker, who had just made his solemn vows at the altar, would have forced Mr. Rogers to an inquiry if he had not solicited it; — would declare that they had made a full inquiry and fair examination of the subject, if such inquiry and examination had not been made? Can you suppose that these venerable Bishops of the Church would have violated every obligation of truth and justice as well as the most solemn vows of office by condemning an innocent man? Could Mr. Rogers have had a trial before a more impartial tribunal? Or can you suppose that, after the

House of Bishops had made a full inquiry and pronounced their opinion, anything else was left to the Bishop of Connecticut than to carry their decision into effect? Mr. Rogers made an appeal to the House of Bishops. They thought proper to investigate his conduct and pronounce a decision. The Canons of the Church of Connecticut in regard to the trial of clergymen could here have no operation. The Bishop of Connecticut was the agent to carry the decision of the House of Bishops into effect. Mr. Rogers has been solemnly degraded from the ministry after a full investigation of his conduct, and a discussion in regard to him by the highest authority in the Church. We entreat you by your character as churchmen, by the memory of your forefathers who cherished the Church with inviolable fidelity; — we entreat you by the prospect of that awful tribunal at which all mankind must be judged, to regard the Divine injunction, 'Hear the Church.' In the language of the Apostle, we exhort you, brethren, 'Put from you that unworthy person.' Remember the injunction of our Lord: 'If any man refuse to hear the Church, let him be unto you as a heathen man and a publican.' In the spirit of meekness and affection, we entreat you. Rend not that Divine body, the Church which your Redeemer purchased with his blood. For ourselves we most solemnly declare, that mindful of the commission given to us by our Divine Master and relying on his promise, that He will be with His Church alway, even to the end of the world, we shall esteem it our sacred duty to preserve inviolate the authority committed to us: and we trust that what is thus done by the lawful governors of the Church on earth, will be ratified in heaven."[1]

A copy of the foregoing document, signed by Mr. Bronson as chairman of the Committee, was delivered to Mr. Leeds and a resolution of the Convocation next morning shows the manner of its reception, and the extent to which the misguided adherents of Rogers had allowed their passions to run. The resolution was, — "That Mr. Cary Leeds be informed that the Convocation have received his communication of October 16th, accompanied with a certain vote of a meeting held at St. John's Church in Stamford on the 27th day of May, 1805, attested by Isaac Holly, Jr., by which they have declared that they are not under the direction, nor amenable to the authority, of any bishop. This Convocation have therefore no further communication to make to Mr. Leeds on this subject."

Here was a step in the direction of actual schism. It was breaking away from the counsels which ought to have been heeded, and rashly setting aside the order and polity of the Church. No parish pursuing such a course could expect to be represented in the Diocesan Convention, and it was not surprising, therefore, that a vote was afterwards passed in that body, excluding a lay representation from those "who should employ any person to officiate among them, who had been suspended or degraded from his clerical office." This action might have been regarded, for a time, with indifference by the friends of Rogers; but in the end, even supposing the sentence of the ecclesiastical authority against him premature, it

[1] MS. Records of Convocation.

would operate to their disadvantage and put them in the wrong for rejecting wholly the discipline of a kingdom which is not of this world. "Religion" says Dr. Chandler, "being a matter of free choice, for which we are ordinarily accountable to Him only who will hereafter judge us for our moral behavior; and the Church, considered with relation to civil power, being, in the very nature of it, a voluntary society; it is left to men's consciences to determine whether they will become members of it or not. But after they have become members, the laws of the Church are in force against them, and they are subject, in ecclesiastical matters, to the authority of those who govern it." Principles cannot be made false by mistakes or oversights, nor does the mere use of the Book of Common Prayer constitute a man an Episcopalian. He must love and honor the teachings of his communion and recognize the authority of a bishop — of a bishop, too, who has a canonical claim to his allegiance.

CHAPTER IV.

EPISCOPAL ACADEMY, AND RESIGNATION OF DR. SMITH; RENEWAL OF THE CASE OF AMMI ROGERS; AND ORGANIZATION OF PARISHES.

A. D. 1805–1809.

GENERAL inquiries into the state of the Institution at Cheshire were authorized from time to time, and from the report of a special committee to the Annual Convention of 1805, which is entered in full upon the journal for that year, it appears, that instead of flourishing, "the number of students was gradually diminishing, the building going to decay, and the institution itself sinking in reputation." It was not determined whether these unfavorable appearances arose from any deficiency in its organization, neglect or mismanagement of those entrusted with its interests, or from the place of its establishment. The belief, however, was expressed that they resulted "in some measure from its location in the vicinity of a flourishing university, and in a town where it received very little patronage or encouragement;" and further inquiry into its affairs, and into the causes of its present condition was recommended and approved.

The next Annual Convention, composed of fifteen clergymen and twenty-two laymen, was held in Cheshire, and though no report appears upon the journal of that year in regard to the further inquiries which had been previously recommended, yet there is an important entry made towards the close of the session, which covers the whole ground and lets us into the secret history of the declining reputation of the institution. It is the resignation of the Rev. Dr. Smith, couched in peculiar phraseology and addressed: "To the Convention of the Protestant Episcopal Church of Connecticut, in session this fifth day of June, A. D. 1806.

"Whereas missives have passed between the Board of Trustees and me, whereby certain articles have been interchangeably acceded to by both parties, I hereby request this Convention to accept of my resignation of the office of Principal of the Episcopal Academy of Connecticut, and upon their acceptance of the same, I shall consider myself as detached from all connection with the said Academy, either as to its internal or external regimen or the emoluments thereof, from and after the first day of October next."

The resignation was accepted, and the Convention, without appointing a successor, adjourned to meet in Newtown on the eighth day of the ensuing October. The "missives" that passed between Dr. Smith and the Trustees were not, as may be inferred from the tenor of his letter, altogether of a pleasant nature. Charges amounting to an impeachment were brought against him, and the records of the Board show that the final adjustment of the matter was far from being mutually satisfactory. Perhaps the measures resorted to by one party to effect their object, were not taken with sufficient reference to the peculiar temperament of the other. The dignity of self-respect, like any other moral quality, is more easily lost than regained;

and corporate bodies, dividing up the responsibility of their actions, seldom allow enough for private and individual character.

The Convention, which adjourned to meet in Newtown, elected the Rev. Tillotson Bronson to supply the vacancy thus created, and he accepted the office and entered at once upon its duties. For about eight years he had been the Rector of the parish in Waterbury, but towards the close of 1805 "the high price demanded on all the necessaries of life and the increasing expenses of his family obliged him to ask for a proportionable increase in his salary." This, though advocated by many of the more substantial friends of the Church, was refused, and consequently he took his leave of the people in a farewell discourse, and removed to New Haven, to conduct the "Churchman's Magazine." He was the editor of that useful periodical, when appointed to the charge of the Academy, and except during the interval of its publication out of the Diocese, he continued to add to his other labors the responsibility of arranging the matter and superintending the press.

At this adjourned Convention in Newtown, an effort was again made to reopen the case of Ammi Rogers, and John Nichols, a lay delegate from Waterbury, introduced a resolution requesting the Bishop to revoke his sentence of degradation and leave the offender "to be proceeded against agreeably to the Constitution and Canons of the Episcopal Church in Connecticut." The Convention decided that it was not competent to judge respecting the sentence, and after its final adjournment the Bishop and clergy met in Convocation and declared "that in their opinion the only proper board for redress of grievances complained of by said Rogers in consequence of his suspension and degradation" was the House of Bishops, to whose decision they expressed themselves ever ready to submit. Through a committee they also prepared a letter, which they directed to be signed by the Secretary and transmitted to the several bishops who were present at the last General Convention. The letter is given here in full, for it shows their desire to bring this troublesome business to an end in any way that would preserve "the honor of God's Church," and further "the prosperity of true religion."

"RIGHT REV. SIR: The Bishop of Connecticut, with the advice of his presbyters in Convocation assembled at Cheshire in the month of October of the year 1804, passed sentence of degradation against Mr. Ammi Rogers. In taking this step, the Bishop conceived himself warranted by the proceedings had with regard to the said Mr. Rogers before the House of Bishops at New York. This opinion was formed on the consideration of the full and solemn hearings that were given to Mr. Rogers and the delegation from Connecticut, and on the conceived impropriety of again calling in question facts which the highest ecclesiastical authority in our Church had said were proved. Having nothing in view, as is hoped and believed, but the honor of God's Church and the prosperity of true religion, it is found with regret that a different opinion has been expressed by two of the members of the House of Bishops, in their affidavits given to Mr. Rogers; which has exposed the Church in Connecticut to much inconvenience and trouble, and the dangers of an unhappy schism are greatly increased by the efforts now carried on by the said Rogers and his adherents.

"If these evils are to be ascribed to the governors of the Church in Connecticut in consequence of their erroneous conclusions from what was done at New York, they flatter themselves that it was the error of the head and not of the heart. But however this may be, they stand ready to be corrected by the competent authority. And being disposed to do everything in their power for the peace of the Church, they do hereby request that you will, in conjunction with the other bishops concerned, transmit a statement of your view of the whole subject, together with your advice to Connecticut how it would be prudent in the present state of things to proceed; and particularly whether it would be advisable to give Mr. Rogers a new trial on the ground of nullity in the act of degradation.

"Your advice on this, or any other point that may tend to remove the unhappy embarrassments under which the Church is laboring, will be thankfully received and seriously weighed and considered."

Answers to this letter from the three bishops to whom it was severally addressed were read to the Convocation which met at Watertown on the second day of June, 1807. Bishop White, in his "Memoirs of the Protestant Episcopal Church,"[2] has a note in reference to the Clergy of Connecticut desiring advice on the question of again taking up the case of Ammi Rogers and granting him a new trial. Both he and Bishop Moore were in favor of the measure; "but," he adds rather sharply, "it did not take place. It would

[1] MS. Records of Convocation.

[2] P. 190

have been more discreet in them to have withheld their advice, until they should have known that it would have effect." Bishop Claggett, who went very extensively into the merits of the sentence of degradation and recited the history of the action which led to it, differed in opinion from those two prelates, and thought that nothing but reordination could "restore Mr. Rogers to his former standing in the Christian ministry." His letter,[1] which is too long to be inserted in this place, undoubtedly had its influence in preventing the Bishop and clergy of Connecticut from pronouncing their own degradation a nullity.

The excitement produced by his imaginary wrongs was meat and drink to Rogers, and he poured his complaints into the ears not only of those who sympathized with him, but of all who were disposed to listen. For many years, hardly a convention or convocation in the Diocese was held that he did not flood with his papers or visit with his importunities. He had his friends to bolster up his cause, and afford him a medium through which to operate, and hence Bishop Jarvis, in his address to the Annual Convention of 1807, — which was the first address ever printed in the Journal, — called attention to the office of the Episcopate and earnestly rebuked any disregard of its rights and powers.

"The firm belief," said he, "that ecclesiastical authority, in its fullest extent, was essential not only to the well ordering, but even to the very being of the Church in this country, caused our predecessors to plead so strongly as they did for the obtaining of it. From their public communications, we learn what evils

1 Appendix A.

they expected would be remedied, and what benefits would be enjoyed, by having resident bishops in the American Church. One particular advantage, preëminently conducive, in their opinion, to its welfare and reputation, would be the complete information which the bishop could obtain, or the personal knowledge he would have of those who should be presented to him for ordination; and thereby the greater security would be established that no disqualified or unworthy persons would get admission into the ministry. But in case such instances should happen and the Church should suffer scandal, the bishop would be at hand, to correct, to suspend, and, if necessary, to silence, to depose from their office, and even to excommunicate from the society of Christians, the vicious and incorrigible.

"I ask, then, gentlemen, whether the Episcopate in possession be considered as holding primitive powers; and whether it be now viewed in the same light in which they viewed it, who contended so long and so earnestly to procure its establishment among us? Is it found to be a remedy for the evils complained of, and does it experimentally yield to the Church that good which was expected? During the time in which our Church was destitute of resident bishops, there were among the clergy men of acknowledged abilities, and of characters approved for their activity, learning, and piety. How watchful were the endeavors of these clergymen may be easily imagined; and yet by them we have it asserted, as one of the evils for which they solicited the Episcopate as a redress, that vicious men from this country, by means of testimonials, either forged or obtained, God knows how, procured ordination in England; and after having been invested with the sacred office, had been sent back to take charge of the souls of others — in the prosecution of which work they acted as if they had not or imagined that they had not any souls of their own.

"Are we not compelled to own that the same fact has taken place since bishops have been present among us? After a solemn investigation, full proof of fact, and actual deposition from office, have not numbers arisen to support the degraded person, even while he continues to minister, in defiance of the authority which has stripped him of all right so to do? By this contumelious and ruinous procedure, a schism commenced, the future extent and continuation of which is indeed uncertain; but most certain has been the contempt shown to ecclesiastical authority. The false tongue of the transgressor has found listening ears, and minds disposed to credit his tales, and to associate with him in the work of mischief. By them the bishop's character has been loaded with obloquy and reproach, and Korah (though thus to use the name is degrading even to Korah), in the eye of his company, has become the saint and the bishop the sinner.

"Repeated efforts to bring this subject before the Convention, though every attempt to do it was, in my apprehension, a fresh outrage upon the order and authority of the Church, is the cause of my speaking in this manner. Had circumstances been such as would have directed me to call your attention to the ordinary concerns only of the Church, according to her well known rules, and sound doctrines, it would have been far, far more congenial with my wishes."

Failing in all his attempts to be recognized and restored, and furnishing, as an eminent lawyer of that time said, an example of the triumph of justice over law, Rogers again ventured to carry his case before the House of Bishops in the shape of an appeal from the sentence of degradation under which he lay. Two bishops only — White and Claggett — were present at the General Convention which met in the city of Baltimore, May, 1808, and on the fourth day of the session, the "documents signed Ammi Rogers," accompanied by a letter from his counsel, were under consideration; and in the final decision[1] which was rendered, the House both confirmed its previous action and refused to interfere with the proceedings of the Bishop and clergy of Connecticut. Not satisfied with this decision, he sent in, on a subsequent day, "certain petitions addressed to the General Convention," but as the resolution had been taken by the Bishops to dismiss the subject of his case finally from consideration, they passed them, without opening, to the House of Clerical and Lay Delegates, where the action upon them was equally summary and decisive.

Soon after this, Rogers left Connecticut and removed to New York, locating himself in the neighborhood of his earliest ministrations. While there he brought a suit against Bishop Jarvis for slander before the Circuit Court of the United States, to be holden at New Haven, April, 1811, claiming damages in the sum of twenty thousand dollars. The Convention of the Diocese appointed a committee of laymen to employ legal counsel to defend in the suit thus instituted, and great pains were taken to collect testimony

[1] Appendix B.

to rebut his witnesses and establish the righteousness of his degradation from the ministry. Declining to appear when the case was called, he was non-suited, and "the Court considered that Bishop Jarvis should recover against him $316.24 — cost and charges laid out by him for his defence" — and accordingly he had execution for that amount.[1]

But the anger of this degraded priest was not yet burnt out, and Bishop Jarvis going afterwards to the City of New York to assist in the consecration of Griswold and Hobart, was sued by him before the Supreme Court of that State and damages once more laid at twenty thousand dollars for issuing papers against him without authority, breaking up his settlements, and causing distress and trouble to himself and family. The suit was pending when death came to the Bishop and terminated all further proceedings. He had been, in a measure, unable to silence the discontents which sprang up in certain quarters from the operation of what he conscientiously believed to be the exercise of his Episcopal duty. The disturbance of the Diocese was to him, with his infirmities, a personal trouble, and this wretched business for years gave him no peace. Perpetually recurring in different forms, and sometimes instigated or encouraged by those who undoubtedly had the welfare of the Church at heart, it was the one great trial of his Episcopate and shaded with oppressive sorrow his latest days.

The General Convention which met at Baltimore in 1808 was composed of two bishops, fourteen clergymen, and thirteen lay delegates. Seven States were

[1] Records of Circuit Court, New Haven, 1811.

represented; among them, Connecticut and Rhode Island. Bishop Jarvis was prevented by the state of his health from attempting the journey, but two clerical and two lay delegates were present from this Diocese, and bore a conspicuous part in the deliberations of that body. Though thinly attended it was an important meeting. For then all the Canons were revised, thirty new hymns adopted, certain resolutions in regard to duels and divorces passed, and a committee appointed to make a solemn and affectionate address to all the dioceses and urge upon them "the propriety, necessity and duty of sending regularly a deputation to the General Convention." A pastoral letter from the House of Bishops, prepared in compliance with a Canon enacted in 1804, was now for the first time issued, and efforts were put forth to secure in future fuller statistics and a more accurate and general view of the state of the Church throughout the country. The pastoral letter touched upon doctrine, worship, discipline, and the end of all, a holy life and conversation. The part relating to discipline opened with this paragraph: "And here we wish our clerical and our lay brethren to be aware, as, on one hand, of the responsibility under which we lie; so, on the other, of the caution which justice and impartiality require. The Church has made provision for the degradation of unworthy clergymen. It is for us to suppose that there are none of that description, until the contrary is made known to us in our respective places, in the manner which the Canons have prescribed: and if the contrary to what we wish is, in any instance, to be found, it lies on you, our clerical and lay brethren, to present such faulty conduct; although with due regard to proof; and, above all, in a temper which shows the impelling motive to be the glory of God, and the sanctity of the reputation of his Church."

The first published statistics of the Diocese of Connecticut appeared in the Journal of the Annual Convention for 1809, under the head of *Notitiæ Parochiales.* Eight clergymen, holding pastoral relations to nineteen parishes, reported the number of their respective families, communicants, baptisms, marriages, and funerals. This was in obedience to the recently enacted Canon of the General Convention "providing for an accurate view of the state of the Church from time to time," but the requirements of the Canon appear to have been little heeded and the view of the Church was fragmentary, for returns were made by only one clergyman in New Haven County, Rev. Chauncey Prindle, and by none of the rectors of parishes in the towns lying along and east of the Connecticut River. The whole number of clergy in the Diocese at that date, including the Principal of the Academy at Cheshire, was twenty-six, and to them was committed the care of souls scattered through seventy-three parishes and mission stations. Though they had full enough to do to occupy and till the old ground without striking out into new and promising fields of labor, yet they watched the opportunities of extending the Church, and sowed good seed wherever they had reason to believe it would germinate and grow.

In the period embraced by this and the two preceding chapters, parochial organizations were effected, or houses of worship begun and partially completed in Meriden, Woodbridge (now Bethany), in Salem (now Naugatuck), in New Stratford (now Monroe), in

Bridgeport, Bethlehem, Kent, Litchfield, Milton (a part of Litchfield), Salisbury, Sharon, Warehouse Point, and Glastenbury. Sometimes, after the organization of a parish, the private dwelling of a zealous and influential churchman served as a sanctuary, until better provision could be secured. A few months before the consecration of Bishop Jarvis, movements were made to build a church at Chewstown, now Seymour, which were ultimately successful; and in other places where the clergy performed occasional services an interest in the Liturgy was shown, and a love for the Episcopal form of worship ripened into substantial efforts to provide for its maintenance. Dissensions in the Congregational societies growing out of the old doctrines of Calvinism frequently sent many of their members adrift, and more would have found their way into the Church, had the clergy been numerous enough to supply the demand for ministrations, and the Bishop been ready to give personal attention to exigencies as they arose. Revivals of religion in the standing order, from the beginning of the century and for some time before, had been very general not only in Connecticut, but throughout New England, and our own Communion quietly reaped its share of the abiding fruits.

The parish at New Preston (now Marbledale in Washington), originally numbering among its members churchmen from several adjoining towns, and which had a house of worship before the Revolution, was one of the first to reorganize after the acknowledgement of American Independence and to quote its own record "as the late law of the State doth direct." The old dilapidated building, which had been nearly destroyed during the war, was finally disposed of, and in 1796 the parish purchased the "Friends' Meeting-house," an edifice situated within the limits of New Milford, a little more than a mile west of the present church in Marbledale. It was built for the noted enthusiast, Jemima Wilkinson, and there for a time she published her religious extravagances and obtained followers. The better purpose to which it was afterwards put for thirty years shows that her teaching, like that of all fanatics, left behind no permanent impression.

The Congregational minister at Bethany, Isaac Jones, — a graduate of Yale College and a descendant of William Jones, Deputy Governor of the New Haven Colony, — changed his ecclesiastical relations in 1808, and a large portion of the people whom he had been serving followed him into the Episcopal Church. It was a secession which marked an important passage in the history of the Diocese, and traces of its influence remain to this day in the town where it occurred. The parish there — which took immediate steps to erect a new and larger house of worship — passed a vote, Nov. 6, 1809, recommending Isaac Jones "as a person worthy and well qualified for a Gospel minister in the Episcopal Church," and early in the autumn of the next year he was ordained a Deacon in New York by Bishop Benjamin Moore, and subsequently a priest by Bishop Hobart. The new church at Bethany was consecrated by Bishop Jarvis, September, 1810 — the parish at that time being under the pastoral oversight of the Rev. Reuben Ives of Cheshire, who was a judicious and zealous moulder of the crude material that had been suddenly thrown into his hands. This was the eleventh and last church in the Diocese consecrated by the second Bishop of Connecticut. The same number had been consecrated by his predecessor.[1]

Under the auspices of Mr. Rayner, Rector of Christ Church, Hartford, congregations were gathered about this time in Warehouse Point and Glastenbury, and in both places edifices of wood were soon constructed. He himself, in his parochial report at the Annual Convention of 1812, which was the year after his removal from Hartford to Huntington, says: "In 1802, 1803, and 1804, collected and organized a parish at Warehouse Point, consisting of about one hundred families, who have erected an elegant church, and a clergyman in deacon's orders is now settled with them."

1 "Churches consecrated in Connecticut by Bishop Seabury: St. Paul's Church, Norwalk; St. James' Church, New London, Sept. 20, 1787; Christ Church, Norwich Landing; St. John's Church, Stratfield; Trinity Church, Newtown, Sept. 19, 1793; St. John's Church, New Milford, Sept. 25, 1793; Christ's Church, Westbury, Nov. 18, 1794; ——— Church, Tashaway, June 8, 1795; St. Stephen's Church, East Haddam, Oct. 18, 1795; St. Matthew's Church, Plymouth, Oct. 21, 1795; St. Mark's Church, Harrington [Harwinton], Oct. 22, 1795.

"This record is made from an entry on a loose piece of paper, written, attested, and signed in the following words:—

"'The above is a list of churches which have been consecrated in Connecticut by SAMUEL,

'*Bishop of Connecticut and Rhode Island.*'

"Churches consecrated by Bishop Jarvis: St. John's Church, Waterbury, Nov. 1, 1797; St. Peter's Church, Plymouth, Nov. 2, 1797; Trinity Church, Fairfield, Oct. 18, 1798; St. James' Church, Derby, Nov. 20, 1799; Christ Church, Hartford, Nov. 11, 1801; St. James' Church, Danbury, Oct. 6, 1802; St. John's Church, Bridgeport, Sept. 16, 1807; St. Peter's Church, New Stratford, Sept. 18, 1809; St. Andrew's Church, Symsbury, Oct. 11, 1808; Christ Church, East Haven, July 25, 1810; Christ Church, Bethany, in the town of Woodbridge, Sept. 19, 1810." — MS. of Bishop Jarvis in possession of his grandson, Rev. S. Fermor Jarvis.

About the time of Mr. Rayner's removal to Ripton, the church in that place was rebuilt on the foundations of the second edifice, erected some twenty years before; and which had been burnt to the ground through the carelessness of a young man in shooting at a dove upon the roof. He left Hartford in the autumn of 1811—some warm friends desiring his stay, and the majority of the parish as desirous of a change that they might "continue together in the true Church, without schism or separation."[1] He was succeeded by the Rev. Philander Chase, who, for the sake of educating his son, had returned from New Orleans to the North, and was then residing at Cheshire to avail himself of the advantages of the Episcopal Academy.

Thus the Church in Connecticut slowly advanced, and gaining a little strength, the clergy became more active and the laity more and more interested. Occasionally a pamphlet appeared, written by some metaphysical controversialist, who in defending his own tenets would severely assail the principles and faith of those who could neither accept the system of religious revivals and awakenings nor the cheerless and uncomfortable doctrine of predestination in the Calvinistic sense. But there was always a pen ready to answer such attacks and out of them grew "A full length portrait of Calvinism," in all its comely features and beautiful proportions! by Dr. Bowden, not from the painting of his own imagination, but from the writings of Calvin himself and from those who were his ablest defenders.

[1] MS. Letter of John Morgan to Bishop Jarvis, Oct. 5, 1811.

CHAPTER V.

ACT RELATING TO RELIGIOUS SOCIETIES; WARDENS AND VESTRYMEN A COMMITTEE; TAXING AND GRAND LEVY; PETITION TO INCORPORATE THE EPISCOPAL ACADEMY WITH COLLEGIATE POWERS; AND UNION OF PARISHES IN CURES.

A. D. 1809–1811.

The law of the State of Connecticut under which the parishes after the Revolution were organized, contained no reference to the Episcopal Church as such. All societies and congregations, instituted for public religious worship, were placed on precisely the same footing and allowed to manage their affairs in their own way, subject of course to the limitations of the statute. They had "power to provide for the support of public worship by the rent or sale of the pews or slips in the meeting-house, by the establishment of funds, or in any other way they might judge expedient." At their annual meetings they each appointed what was called a "society's committee" to whom was entrusted, for the ensuing year, the proper business of the society and the adjustment and settlement of all legal claims. The language of the law was Congregational and not in accordance with the rules and usages of the Church. The word *Parish* gave way to *Society*, and a *Committee* was substituted for *Wardens* and *Vestrymen* — those ancient ecclesiastical officers who had always sustained a relation to the rector, and been understood to be the legitimate guardians of the interests of the parish. This led to some confusion or irregularity in the practice of the new Episcopal organizations. To preserve the language of the Church and yet to act, as they supposed, strictly according to law, many of them not only chose wardens and vestrymen, but a separate committee also, and Bishop Jarvis called attention to this irregularity in his address to the Annual Convention of 1807. He claimed that it was a needless surrender of our rights to adopt the phraseology of the law; that as wardens and vestrymen were "the ancient ecclesiastical officers of a parish, to substitute a committee in their stead was to needlessly change the principles of the Church, and to adopt those which were independent and Congregational." The object of his animadversion was to bring all the parishes of the Diocese to one uniform practice and to make them see that they were not infringing the statute in its true intent by conforming to the cherished rules and customs of their own body. He proceeded briefly to define terms and explain principles.

"In the sense," said he, "in which it is used by the Church, 'society' means the whole body of Christians, or the Church universal, comprehending under one term both the priesthood and the laity. To apply this appellation to small companies or parcels of people in particular districts, is as improper, according to the sense and usage of the Church, as it would be to call a finger, or any other member of a man, his body. The idea of the sectaries is entirely different; according to their notion of it, any number of people agreeing among themselves, and united for the support of assembled worship, is a society or church, in the full meaning of the word, and consequently independent of all others. This, in our understanding, is to make Christ have churches by thousands; whereas, consistent with the unity of his body, he has and can have but *one.* The Church Catholic in its parts, takes distinct denominations from the different countries, and different civil governments under which it is placed. Hence its notation is national, and those general branches are again subdivided into provinces, dioceses, and parishes. In all these divisions and subdivisions, the clergy, in their different grades and several departments, preside over it, for the administration of the sacred ordinances, for instruction and for government, as overseers of the flock. We deduce it from Scriptural doctrine, illustrated by primitive practice, that in things spiritual the Church is to be ordered and governed by those to whom Christ hath given it in commission to take the oversight.

"Agreeably to the Canons, the parish ministers are to be aided by wardens, chosen by the parishioners. Hence, wardens are the committee of the parish to perform certain duties and functions connected with those of the minister and needful for the better fulfillment of his office, and for the welfare of the parish. Laying aside, therefore, the supposition of any speciality which may render it necessary for the officers of the Church to appear in the character specified by the law of the State, in order that they may enjoy the benefit of it, we should in our ecclesiastical business, direct our practice solely by the rules and injunctions of the Church; in which the words *Parish* and *Warden* bear a very different construction from the legal forms, *Society* and *Committee*."

The counsels thus given were not followed, and the practice of the different parishes at their annual meetings continued with little variation as before. For half a century, the general law was untouched or unexplained [1] by the authority that enacted it, though several attempts in the mean time were made by the Convention to secure from the Legislature an act or form of incorporation for parishes, more in accordance with the spirit and usages of the Episcopal Church. The Saybrook Platform, as a legal establishment in Connecticut, was no longer in force, but the voluntary system of supporting religion had not yet been adopted. If all were left free to worship, and connect themselves with whatever denomination they preferred, all were still compelled to pay a tax for the support of some church. They could not escape this liability by setting up the claim that they were "Jews, Turks, Infidels, and Heretics" and had no interest in the maintenance and propagation of Christianity.

The Episcopal parishes taxed their members to

[1] A supplemental act was passed by the Legislature of 1842 in these words: —

"Whereas doubts have arisen in the minds of some, whether the Episcopal Societies in this State have been legally organized:

"*Be it enacted by the Senate and House of Representatives in General Assembly convened*, that the acts which have been done by ecclesiastical societies of this State, organized under the Episcopal order, according to the rules and customs of said societies, shall be good and effectual in law. And that the wardens and vestrymen of said societies shall hereafter be a society's committee, and shall have all the powers in managing the affairs of said societies, as are granted to the committees of all religious societies in this State by the statutes in such case made and provided."

build churches, and to sustain religious services; and the Diocesan Convention assessed the parishes to provide both for the endowment of the Institution at Cheshire and the increase of the Bishop's Fund. Each parish was required to make an annual return of what was called the "Grand Levy,"—that is, its taxable list, according to the last enrollment,—and upon this return rested the right of a lay delegate to his seat in the Convention. The resolution which fixed this rule was adopted in 1803, and the first published Grand Levy appeared in the Journal of 1806, and from that time onward for fifteen years the roll of the lay delegates was accompanied by the taxable list of the several parishes which they represented. If the list of any parish exceeded the sum of ten thousand dollars, such parish was entitled to send to the Convention two delegates.

It is interesting to note the changes since that period in the relative wealth of the Church in Connecticut. In those early days, as reported, Litchfield was stronger than Waterbury or Hartford. Woodbridge was stronger than Meriden, Huntington than Derby, Redding than Bridgeport, and Newtown than New Haven. The agricultural towns and rural districts have been drained to supply the great centres of population, and the prosperity of the manufacturing interests has given importance to localities which were once poor and thinly inhabited. The change in the modes of inland travel and transportation, the substituting of the speedy rail-car for the slow stage-coach, the opening of thoroughfares through hitherto untrodden swamps and forests, the making rocky hills smooth their faces and smile under the hand of public industry, the multiplicity of new inventions, creating new kinds of traffic and a demand for the skill and labor of numberless overseers and operatives, the increase in the facilities for making and spending money, the love of luxury and self-indulgence, the pursuit of learning, the culture of the arts, the progress of science, all these things have helped to form new centres of influence and to transfer the muscle of energy and successful wealth from the country to the town, and from the eastern to the western States. Occasionally, the merchants who have become princes, and the manufacturers whose prosperity has flowed in upon them in a full and steady stream, have returned to the scenes of their nativity, and still holding by inheritance or repossessing themselves of the lands of their fathers, have enriched them with fertilizing agencies and beautified them with the taste and improvements of modern cultivation. Such men in their retirement have not forgotten their duty to the village church; but where all enterprise has disappeared from among the people and decay has written itself upon their dingy dwellings and barns, and there is no leading mind to quicken and direct, it is not surprising to find spiritual coldness and indifference with irregular ministrations.

The Convention, at the annual meeting in 1810, renewed its efforts to obtain an enlargement of the charter for the Diocesan Institution at Cheshire. As the preamble expressed it, doubts had arisen whether the Trustees were "invested with the power of conferring upon the students the degrees and testimonials of literary proficiency, usually granted in colleges," and as the great objects contemplated by the

Convention could not be accomplished without such power, it was resolved to request the Trustees "to prefer a petition to the next General Assembly of the State of Connecticut, praying that said Academy may be constituted a college, by the name and style of the Episcopal College of Connecticut." The memorialists on the part of the Board were Jonathan Ingersoll, John Bowden, Daniel Burhans, Nathan Smith, and Burrage Beach; and in their petition they mentioned that the permanent and productive fund amounted to nearly fourteen thousand dollars, and that the number of students who had resorted to the Academy from different parts of the United States and from the West Indies had generally been from fifty to seventy. Among other reasons why their application should be granted they said: "That Institution, which has been most justly the pride and boast of this State, was established for the open and avowed purpose of propagating the religious sentiments of its founders. This is the very language of its constitution, which has often received the sanction of the General Assembly. The General Assembly early adopted, protected, patronized, and richly endowed it, in a manner highly honorable to itself, and vastly beneficial to the State. Notwithstanding this, Yale College has shared largely in the munificence of Episcopalians, both in this country and in Europe. The donations which have, from time to time, been made by the General Assembly, have been drawn equally from Episcopalians, in proportion to their numbers and property, as from other denominations. This, however, furnishes no ground of complaint to Episcopalians, nor to the liberal and ingenuous of other denominations. None can justly complain that too much has been done for Yale College. For it never can, for a moment, be presumed that the General Assembly of Connecticut will grant privileges to one denomination which, upon suitable application, it will deny to others.

"Episcopalians, as a body of Christians, are in point of numbers respectable, as supporters of legitimate government and friends to good order they yield to none. About thirty colleges have been established in different parts of the United States by Presbyterians, Baptists, Lutherans, Methodists, and Roman Catholics, all of which have received the sanction of the Legislatures of the States in which they have been founded. But not a single college *now* exists in any part of the Union, which is under the government and instruction of Episcopalians." [1]

The application, thus urged at the October session of the General Assembly was granted in the Lower House, but denied in the Council or Senate. It was encouraging to be heard with favor in the popular branch of the Legislature, and again the efforts were repeated to obtain a charter. The General Convention met in New Haven the next year, and understanding that the establishment of a second college in Connecticut under the auspices of churchmen was contemplated, each House adopted a resolution expressing entire approbation of the measure and earnest wishes for its success. The Church throughout our country at that time had reached its lowest depression and passed the depths. Not unfrequently the legislative body which does nothing, does wisely,

[1] Original MS. of petitioners.

and this was somewhat true of the General Convention which met at New Haven in 1811. Two bishops only — White and Jarvis — were present. Bishop Claggett, who engaged to preach the opening sermon, left his place of residence on his way to the city, but was obliged by indisposition to return. The consecration of Griswold and Hobart [1] therefore, whose testimonials had been duly signed, was postponed until the week after the adjournment, when the two Bishops proceeded to New York and summoned the disabled Provoost from his retirement to assist them in the solemn act. [2]

1 The Rev. Alexander V. Griswold was elected Bishop of the Eastern Diocese, composed of Massachusetts, Rhode Island, New Hampshire and Vermont, May 31, 1810, and the Rev. John H. Hobart, D. D. was elected Assistant Bishop of New York, May 15, 1811, — Bishop Moore having been stricken by partial paralysis and rendered incapable of active duty. Though last elected and younger than Mr. Griswold, Dr. Hobart was first consecrated. Bishop White, the presiding bishop, undoubtedly observed in this case the rule referred to in the following extract from a letter written by him to correct "a mistake" which had appeared in the *Churchman's Magazine*, "as to the consecration of Bishop Claggett."

"On the subject of precedency, no discourse ever took place between Bishop Provoost and me. From what I know of myself, and from what I believe of him, I venture to pronounce it impossible that any dissatisfaction should have arisen on that ground. As he is my senior in years, I accounted for the priority of my name in the instrument of consecration, and in a communication of the Archbishop which concerned us alike from the circumstance of my being the senior Doctor in Divinity, as our papers must have shown, and as I know to be according to a rule which governs in England, and governed among our clergy in America before the Revolution." — *MS. Letter to Rev. John C. Rudd, July* 18, 1815.

2 "The author left home under the hope of inducing Bishop Provoost to go on to New Haven, although he had never performed any ecclesiastical duty since the consecration of Bishop Moore in 1801. But besides Bishop Provoost's being under the effects of a slight stroke of the paralytic [paralysis], sustained two years before, he was, at this time, only beginning to recover from the jaundice. He found himself utterly incompetent to the taking of a journey; but promised, if possible, to assist in a consecration, if it

By this time, the number of the clergy in Connecticut had increased to thirty, and from a report then made, it appeared that between four and five hundred families had been added to the Church since the last General Convention. The congregations of the Diocese were in a flourishing condition, several new churches had been built, and with the zeal and exertions of the clergy, the expectation was cherished that the power as well as the form of godliness would greatly advance. The moral support which the effort to secure a charter had gained by the action of the General Convention, encouraged the clergy to persevere, and at a Convocation held in February, 1812, it was resolved that a petition be preferred to the next Legislature by the Bishop and clergy of the Diocese of Connecticut, with the consent and approbation of the Board of Trustees of the Episcopal Academy — praying that said Academy may be erected into a college. Five prominent clergymen were appointed to draft the petition and advocate the same before the General Assembly, but their movements are not recorded, and other events afterwards came in to stay entreaty and absorb the ecclesiastical and legislative sympathies.

The second pastoral letter from the House of Bishops, issued in 1811, was brief, and after glancing

should be held in the city of New York. With the expectation of this, Bishop Jarvis, after the rising of the Convention, came with the author to the said city; as did the two bishops elect. To the last hour, there was danger of disappointment. On our arrival, a day also having been publicly notified for the consecration, we found that Bishop Provoost had suffered a relapse during our absence. But finally, he found himself strong enough to give his attendance, and thus the business was happily accomplished." — Bishop White's *Memoirs*, etc., p. 209.

at topics and doctrines formerly considered, it called the special attention of the clergy to their duty in reporting the state of their respective cures; and in preparing and presenting young persons and others for the holy rite of Confirmation.

As the Church at large increased, it was quite important to know where it was the strongest and where it was growing most steadily and rapidly. The objects of the XLVth Canon contemplated that careful parish registers be kept, transcripts of which were to form the parochial reports at every annual convention; but independently of the canonical requirement, "the keeping of these records" said the bishops, "is occasionally of so much consequence to the fortunes, and in some instances to the reputation of individuals, that we do not know how any clergyman, negligent in this particular, can answer it to God and to society."

The extent of their dioceses, their parochial engagements, and the necessity of travelling in stage-coaches and private conveyances, rendered it impossible for the early American prelates to make frequent visitations and administer the apostolic rite of Confirmation. The first Bishop of Massachusetts (Bass), though he exercised his office for a period of six years, never penetrated to the distant parishes of his charge in the valley of the Housatonic, and the whole body of communicants in that region was therefore left to welcome the feet of his saintly successor, and to receive from him the hand of blessing and hear the prayer to God for their future growth in grace. The original Canon, providing for an accurate view of the state of the Church, did not require the minister to include in his parochial report the number of confirmations, but the connecting link between Baptism and the Lord's Supper was not on this account to be forgotten. "It has not been unobserved by us," is the language of the Pastoral, "how zealous and how successful some of the clergy have been in aiding our efforts in this branch of the Episcopacy; and even in soliciting our visits to their respective churches, with a view to it. And if the same cannot be affirmed of all our reverend brethren, we are aware that, in some instances, it may have been less owing to indifference and neglect, than to the difficulty of introducing a practice which, until within these few years, was unknown in this country, however in itself coeval with our holy religion."

In 1808, Bishop Jarvis stated that he had visited six parishes of his Diocese, confirming three hundred and eighty-six persons, and in 1809–10 he visited eight parishes and confirmed four hundred and thirty-seven. In 1811, he confirmed, in three parishes, two hundred and eighty-four persons; and the next year, which embraced the last of his reported visitations, he administered the rite in five parishes to one hundred and eighty. The whole number on record as confirmed by him during his Episcopate is three thousand and sixty-eight, an average of about two hundred a year from the date of his consecration. It shows that the clergy of Connecticut were not unmindful of their responsibilities in this respect, and only needed a more active head to quicken their zeal and stir the hearts of the laity.

The Annual Convention which met at New Haven in 1808, composed of fifteen clergymen and seventeen laymen, undertook to ascertain the bounds of the several cures in the Diocese, partly with a view of providing ministrations of some kind for all the places where parishes had been organized, and partly to give more permanence and regularity to the support of the rectors. According to the arrangement then adopted, not one of these rectors had a single charge, and many of them were required to look after the scattered families of the Church in towns remote from their residences. There were seventy-three parishes or localities in the Diocese which called for Episcopal services, and only twenty-six clergymen to supply them; so that several of the feebler churches were almost constantly vacant. Much was done to keep them alive by lay-reading and by the circulation of instructive books and pamphlets; and a voluntary Society, called a "Society for the Promotion of Christian Knowledge," of which more will be said hereafter, was formed in New Haven on the last day of October, 1808, to publish and circulate, at reduced prices, such useful religious works as would best conduce to the advancement of piety and Christian knowledge. From the lack of properly authorized ministers to officiate in the vacant churches, sprung a class of "preaching candidates," whom Bishop Jarvis thus reproved in his address to the Annual Convention of 1807:—

"An intention to enter into the priesthood is a self-offering, and it is required that a declaration of this intention be made one year previous to ordination. The rule supposes that the name of the person is put on record, and that he is afterwards considered as a candidate. Hence a preposterous idea seems to have been adopted, that the candidate is authorized to officiate in reading the prayers of the Church and in preaching. In consequence of this idea, the people, either through ignorance of the principles of their own Church, or from a desire of bearing a nearer affinity to the dissenters, have grafted into our clerical character a new grade, — I mean that of licensed preachers, — and this has been done without their pretending even to the shadow of a license, unless it be the before-mentioned record. If the vacant congregations would be contented to have a lay-reader, until they could be supplied with a priest, and if, provided no one among them should be proper or willing to perform the office, they would procure a candidate to lead them in the prayers and read a sermon to them, no particular objections would arise. But on the sole ground of being a candidate, a circumstance which has no connection with preaching or with any clerical services in the devotions of the Church, for him to undertake to preach, and for the people to do anything to promote it, is in both a palpable contradiction to the principles of the Church. On the part of the parishioners, it is entirely absurd; on that of the candidate, it is a direct bar against his admission into the priesthood."

The union of parishes in cures was not unalterably fixed by the Convention. The whole scheme was but recommendatory, and nothing was done which might not be changed by a simple vote of the same body. Disputes between churches respecting their parish lines, or difficulties between a rector and a portion of his cure, were sometimes best settled by separating the parts which had been previously united for the sake of convenience and strength. Some of the cures were long vacant, and these furnished temptations to the clergy to absent themselves occasionally from their own flocks, with results which, in general, were not salutary. "It may be a subject deserving your attention," said the Bishop,[1] "whether a real injury is not done to the Church by clergymen leaving the churches particularly assigned to their charge, and officiating too frequently in those vacant churches which might, and if so, ought, to have a clergyman settled among them: whether such practice be not disorderly, and does not merit such aid as the Convention may give to the Bishop, to correct the disorder, as having a tendency to hurt their own churches, and to cherish a spirit of indifference and lukewarmness among those vacant churches towards the Liturgy and Offices, and the general interest and prosperity of the Church." As the ranks of the ministry were increased and younger men appeared to enter with fresh zeal upon self-denying labors, a few of the weak parishes rose up with resolute purpose to provide for more frequent clerical services; but the evil here complained of still continued, and the history of the Church in Connecticut for several years presented a picture with the same dark and sombre shades.

[1] Address to Convention, 1812.

CHAPTER VI.

STATISTICS OF THE PARISHES; SUPPORT OF THE EPISCOPATE; DEATH OF DR. HUBBARD; LIST OF ORDINATIONS; AND DEATH OF BISHOP JARVIS.

A. D. 1811–1813.

Ten presbyters and thirteen laymen attended the Annual Convention which met at Middletown in 1811. The Bishop was absent, as he had been also from the Special Convention held at Cheshire on the 3d day of the preceding October; and out of all the rectors in the diocese, four only — Ashbel and David Baldwin, Elijah G. Plumb, and Philo Shelton — reported the state of the nine parishes with which they were severally connected. From such partial and imperfect statistics, no fair representation of the Church could be gathered, and the chief advantage of publishing them must have been to draw attention to the matter and show that there was a Canon of the General Convention which almost the whole body of the clergy habitually neglected. It is to be lamented that more care in this respect was not observed at that early day. Many, who were no doubt zealous and self-sacrificing in their work, appear to have kept their records for personal convenience and to have felt themselves to be under no obligation to obey the Canon, and make annual parochial reports. Loose sheets of paper and the blank leaves of a Prayer-book were sometimes used for entries of official acts, instead of a parish register, which could be easily preserved and conveniently consulted. Whether the admonition of the pastoral letter from the House of Bishops, referred to in the previous chapter, had any effect or not, the *Notitiæ Parochiales* for the next year increased from nine to nineteen, and ever since that time there has been in Connecticut a general compliance with the requirements of the Canon. The returns have not, by any means, been complete, but they have been full enough to convey some definite idea of the condition and growth of the Church in successive periods of her history.

The infirmities of Bishop Jarvis were now very great, and his constitution, originally strong, was shaken by the inroads of the disease from which he had so long suffered. To himself as well as to others the close of his stewardship appeared not far distant.

On the 19th day of February, 1812, he met his clergy in Convocation at New Haven, when a dozen were present, and delivered an "affectionate address," in which he took occasion to refer to the unhappy difficulties then existing in the Diocese of New York. These difficulties grew out of the election and consecration of Dr. Hobart to the Episcopate. One of his associates in the rectorship of Trinity Church, — the Rev. Cave Jones, a native of New York City, — while the election was yet pending, had published an ill-judged pamphlet reflecting upon his fitness for that high office, and with an imagination perturbed by jealousy, had cited, from his intercourse with him, examples of hasty temper and petty contention which a better mind would have buried in oblivion. A long personal controversy followed and opened "the scene of Bishop Hobart's apostolic labors with a picture foreign to their holy and peaceful spirit." It was a sad controversy, for while these dissensions among the shepherds of the flock were raised, the wolf of the world was looking with malignant joy over the pales of the fold and preparing to make a fatal entry. Connecticut was incidentally mentioned in this clerical quarrel. A few of her leading presbyters, a short time before, had interchanged thoughts upon the plan of choosing an assistant bishop, and had gone so far as to communicate their views to an old and fast friend of the Diocese (Dr. Bowden), and ask him if, under certain conditions, he would consent to accept the office. An unwarrantable use was made of this informal movement in the pamphlet of Mr. Jones, and the peace of the Church in Connecticut was touched by the disturbance of the neighboring Diocese. Very properly, therefore, did Bishop Jarvis bring the matter before his clergy, from whom a committee was appointed to advise with their brethren of New York and take such "prudential measures" to remove the existing difficulties as, by the blessing of God, might be in their power. It was not officious meddling in them to wish that the parties involved might correct their misunderstandings, sacrifice their worldly resentments, if they had any, at the foot of their Master's cross, and henceforth proceed, hand in hand, as champions of the faith, to build up the kingdom whose sublime watchword was "Glory to God in the highest, and on earth peace, good will towards men."

The last occasion on which Bishop Jarvis presided

in the Convention of the Diocese was in 1812, and he opened his annual address then with touching allusions to his lengthened age as compared with that of his more vigorous and healthy predecessor. His experience in the Episcopate and the situation of the Church made him anxious for the future, and his thoughts were turned to the continuance of the important office which he filled and to the means and style of its support. He would not have it dependent upon a parish; and no parish in the Diocese could afford an adequate living for a bishop and provide, at the same time, for a supply of services while he was absent on his Episcopal visitations. "But," said he, "if we had a church sufficiently able to do it, would it be desirable? Would it be for the best to have the office so attached to any one church as to give that church a control over the choice of a bishop. When our first Bishop, who, after much expense and trouble, obtained and introduced the office into the country, took his residence amongst us, the sentiment generally pervaded the body of the Church in the State, that it was necessary and their duty to make some provision for his living among us. The churches accordingly, by their delegates, repeatedly met on that business. A contribution according to a certain *ratio*, in form of a tax, was agreed upon, and recommended to all their respective churches. The measure thus attempted, being left upon so general a footing, probably from that very circumstance, proved inefficient; and all that my worthy predecessor received from the Diocese I believe did not amount to the interest of the money he expended of his own property to accomplish for us the object of our wishes.

This was succeeded by an effort to procure from the Legislature an act incorporating a board of trustees for the establishment of a fund. After some time and much exertion the act was obtained. And, as if nothing more was intended by the zeal that was shown to procure it, there it rested. The attention that has since been given to it, and what has been done to carry into effect the purpose expressed in the act, you all know. As I mean only to remind you of what has passed, with the feeling hope of exciting more attention for the future to a matter of such weighty concern, I will barely request you to advert to several successive resolves passed in different conventions."

He then proceeds to recite these resolves and delicately to intimate that they contemplated other and intermediate provision for the Bishop, until that provision should be acquired by the operation of the proposed fund. Too modest to set up any claim for himself, he could not plead for better care of his successors without stating the facts and recalling the measures of the past. He added, moreover: —

"Now, gentlemen, if you will examine what stands upon the journals, successively from the year 1798, and compare the several proceedings, with the receipts of moneys from the churches of the Diocese, subject to your inspection, if desired, you will see with what languor the support of the Bishop has hitherto been regarded. You will see with how much reason they who feel an unfeigned interest in the welfare of the Church are concerned for the unpleasant prospect that the Episcopate in this Diocese must fail, unless some more energetic measures are pursued to prevent it.

"My mind would have been more highly gratified to have had this subject brought forward to your particular notice at this time, by some member of the house; and however sentiments of delicacy under a different situation might have laid me under some restraint from doing it myself, yet I perceived that restraint lessened by the consideration that I can, at my advanced period of life, indulge no rational prospect of any great length of days to come; and therefore must be less personally affected by the future events which may await the Church than probably will be the case with most, perhaps all of you, my brethren, who are now present. Little, indeed, have been the aids afforded by the Church towards the support of the office, since we have had the privilege of enjoying it. From this, if duly considered as from a visible cause, we may infer the want of that salutary influence essential to its respectability and to the powers of doing good, annexed to the office in its original institution.

"When we were subjected to the many difficulties attendant on a hazardous and expensive voyage to England, to obtain our priesthood, it was then viewed in that state of deprivation, as a matter which would have been of incalculable privilege, to have a resident bishop among us. And, while laboring under the disadvantages, an honorable provision for his maintenance would have been considered as a real gain in the article of expense."

The Convention referred the address to a committee, and some earnest steps were immediately taken to provide in future such a salary as seemed indispensably requisite to support the Episcopal dignity in the Diocese. The general poverty of the Church was a great bar to any schemes for creating a respectable endowment, and the infrequency of the Bishop's visitations had hitherto prevented him from exciting much interest among the laity in the matter of his personal support. The parishes, especially those most remote from his residence, complained of his neglects; but he may have justly pleaded in excuse ill-health and the lack of sufficient provision to defray the expenses of journeying. In mercy and consideration to him, the clergy acquiesced in the limited exercise of his public duty, and were generally content, in the latest years of his life, with such offices as could not be omitted without detriment to the essential interests of the Church. With a tremulous voice and a very deliberate enunciation, — the effect perhaps of his painful asthma, — he became somewhat wearisome as a preacher; and for a considerable time before his death, he seldom made his appearance in the pulpit.

National events at this period were beginning to assume a threatening aspect and to absorb the popular attention. The old sores between the United States and Great Britain were not all healed, and the right of searching American vessels, claimed by the government of the mother country, and of impressing from them British seamen, opened these sores afresh and brought on the fever of resistance to foreign aggression. In June, 1812, the United States declared war against Great Britain, and it was prosecuted with various success for nearly three years, during which the Americans attempted in vain the conquest of Canada, and the British squadrons were repulsed in several attacks upon the principal maritime cities.

The people of the New England States were, for the most part, opposed to the measures of the administration, and being destitute of the national protection and liable to the ravages of the enemy, they were in great alarm and dread. Their fears were not a little increased by the course of their friends in Congress. Thirty-four members of the House of Representatives, including the whole Connecticut delegation, addressed their constituents in the outset on the subject of the war with Great Britain, and, among other things, said, "It would be some relief to our anxiety, if amends were likely to be made for the weakness and wildness of the project, by the prudence of the preparation. But in no aspect of this anomalous affair can we trace the great and distinctive properties of wisdom. There is seen a headlong rushing into difficulties, with little calculation about the means, and little concern about the consequences. With a navy comparatively nominal, we are about to enter into the lists against the greatest marine on the globe. With a commerce unprotected and spread over every ocean, we propose to make profit by privateering, and for this, endanger the wealth of which we are the honest proprietors." But when the war, blazing over the length and breadth of the land, had reached Connecticut, she was ready to rise in her own defence, and the heroic spirit with which the inhabitants of Stonington repelled, at a moment's warning, the invasion of her eastern borders, has been at once the admiration of the historian and of the whole country.

Religion never thrives amid the clashing of hostile swords, and the tread of opposing armies. Though the

Episcopal Church stood in no such odious or suspicious relations to the war of 1812 as to the Revolutionary conflict, yet, in common with other communions, she suffered from its operation and effects. In Connecticut, she not only felt the weight of the burdens which war always brings, but the consequences of the great commercial embarrassments which followed the conclusion of a treaty of peace. Nevertheless, as will be shown hereafter, some noble enterprises for her advancement were undertaken at this season, and prosecuted to a successful issue.

For fourteen years but two of the clergy of the Diocese had died — one, the venerable Dr. Leaming, early in the autumn of 1804, and the other, the Rev. Mr. Todd of Huntington, in midsummer, 1809. The infirmities of age had been creeping upon Dr. Hubbard; and the people of his parish, who began previous to Easter, 1811, to confer together on the subject of building a new church, took an equally important step that same year in procuring and settling a permanent assistant. The Rev. Henry Whitlock, a graduate of Williams College, who had been seven years in charge of the parish at Norwalk, was chosen; and accepted the position with an annual salary of eight hundred dollars. He was in the prime of life and had already won the reputation of an earnest, eloquent, and faithful clergyman. The neatness and care with which he noted his official acts in the parish register cast quite into the shade the slovenly record of his senior associate, kept, as a tradesman keeps his journal, with all the different entries running together and following each other in the order of their dates.

Events showed that provision for an assistant to the

Rector of Trinity Church, New Haven, was not premature. In fifteen months from the time of the Institution of Mr. Whitlock into his office, the declining health and strength of Dr. Hubbard terminated in death — and he was buried on the 9th of December, 1812, with the lamentations of a people among whom, for forty-five years, he had gone in and out to administer comfort and impart instruction. His assistant, now, by the terms of his settlement, succeeding to the rectorship, delivered a discourse at the funeral which was printed by request of the vestry, and extensively distributed in the parish and among the friends of the author. It may be regarded as a fair specimen of his beautiful style of sermonizing; and the allusions to himself and his flock in it are as delicate as the portraiture of the departed servant of the Lord is faithful.

"I will not believe," said he, "that the services and example of your venerable Rector have been ineffectual, or will soon cease to have influence. Though dead he yet speaketh and will be regarded. Long may his doctrine, his character, his courtesy, his devotion, his zeal for the Church and her holy services, abide in you, and be exhibited in your lives. For you he prayed, for you he labored, for you he exhausted his life. Through the whole course of his late sickness, the prosperity of this church was his favorite subject of conversation. And it was a source of peculiar satisfaction to him, that in proportion to the decline of his health and usefulness, the affection of his people was increased and was manifested in the most substantial manner, not only by continuing his customary maintenance but by procuring an assistant; and that, instead of being cast off as a burthen, he has received from you every token of respect, every tender assiduity, which could alleviate his infirmities, soothe his pains, and cheer the evening of his life. With this truly honorable and Christian treatment, his heart was full — it overflowed. My dear friends, in this season of affliction and of mourning for one of the best of ministers, may suitable impressions sink deep into your hearts, sanctify your sorrows, confirm your faith, and invigorate your virtue.

"As for me, I need not tell you my grief; I will spread it before Him, who hath taken away my head, my father, and my friend.

"When Elijah ascended into heaven, and his mantle fell from him, it was taken up by Elisha, who had witnessed his ascent: from which time it was said, 'the spirit of Elijah doth rest on Elisha.' So far as our departed father had the temper of a Christian minister, may his spirit be found to rest on his successor! Most eagerly would I take up his mantle, put on his virtues, wear his character, and like him, enjoy your affection. Brethren, I beseech you, pray for me, that, stirring up the gift that is in me, I may attain to the maturity of the pastoral character, discharge with fidelity the arduous duties of my holy office, and be an instrument of bringing many sons to glory."[1]

Two weeks after the death of Dr. Hubbard, ere the days of mourning were ended, Bishop Jarvis held an ordination in Trinity Church and admitted to the priesthood Daniel McDonald and Frederick Holcomb. These were the last names which he affixed to his list of ordinations, numbering in all sixty-one — thirty-three deacons and twenty-eight priests. Bishop

[1] *Sermon*, pp. 18 – 19.

Seabury, who exercised his Episcopate for a period of little more than eleven years, ordained ninety-three, — forty-nine deacons, and forty-four priests — but candidates from other sections of the country came to him before White and Provoost were consecrated to the apostolic office. Bishop Jarvis, though he had entered the sixteenth year of his consecration, had seldom performed any services for the Church beyond the limits of his own Episcopal charge. As Frederick Holcomb was the last to receive from him the priestly office, so he is the last surviving [1] link in the chain of ordinations that unites the clergy of the Diocese with the second Bishop of Connecticut.

It was not many months before the funeral solemnities of the Bishop followed those of his old friend and valued companion, Dr. Hubbard. Together they went forth on the voyage to England for Holy Orders; together they had walked in the house of God as brothers, and in death they were scarcely divided. On the 3d of May, 1813, after a short and severe illness, Bishop Jarvis died at his residence in New Haven, just at the completion of his seventy-fourth year. He was buried in the public cemetery then recently opened; but upon the erection of the present Trinity Church in that city, his remains were disinterred and deposited beneath the chancel of this edifice, which he had hoped to see erected.[2] His son and only surviving child, — the Rev. Samuel F. Jarvis, — whom he advanced to the priesthood about two years before his death, was permitted to honor his memory

[1] March, 1868.

[2] ——— "Hujusce templi, quod, ut exstructum adspiceret
Eheu non oculis mortalibus, magnopere sperabat." — *Inscription.*

by placing over his dust a mural monument of chaste design and exquisite workmanship, with a Latin inscription, reciting his ecclesiastical dignity and position, and his own filial and affectionate sorrow.

Bishop Jarvis was an admirer of the old school of divines, and his manners were formed after the type of an English gentleman of the last century. Those who knew him in the latter years of his life speak of him as preserving great dignity of deportment, gravity of speech, and professional decorum. A profusion of white locks covered his head, which resembled somewhat an old-fashioned wig, and added much to the venerableness of his appearance. He had a capacious mind, a correct taste, and great sensibility of heart. He watched with a good degree of jealous care the dignity and prerogatives of the Episcopal office, and at times was rather arbitrary and unyielding in the pursuit of what he conceived to be the true line of his duty. Thoroughly versed in the history of the Church, her constitution and government, her doctrines and Liturgy, he was so far forth fitted to be a wise counsellor and guide; and his few published writings bear marks not only of his opposition to needless innovations, but of his undeviating advocacy of apostolic order and primitive usage. He rigidly adhered to rubrics, and had no patience with those who would shorten the Liturgy for the sake of the sermon.[1]

[1] The gentlest rebukes are frequently the most effective. During his residence in New Haven, a young clergyman from the South spent a Sunday with him, and was engaged to officiate in the morning. On their way to the church, he whispered in the ear of the Bishop that he had rather a long sermon, and with his permission, he would like to omit the ante-Communion service. The Bishop waited for a moment and then laying his hand upon his young friend, said, — "My dear Sir, if you have anything better

It has been seen that he had some serious troubles to contend with in the matter of discipline, particularly in the case of Ammi Rogers, and it added sharpness to his trial that all the clergy of the Diocese did not approve of his policy in that unhappy affair. He was slow to form conclusions and not very quick to act, but inflexible when he had taken his ground. He magnified points of minor importance, and sometimes allowed them to stand in his way, when, to the view of others, he seemed to be forgetting the real welfare of the Church. He would postpone the ordination of candidates for slight reasons, and he was so nice about their dress that occasionally when they appeared before him in unsuitable apparel, he would supply from his own wardrobe what, in his judgment, was necessary to present them "decently habited." He had a tenacious memory and a large fund of information, and towards the close of his life he repeated anecdotes and sketches of personal history with such minuteness of detail as to be tedious to his listeners. The art of brevity in narration was not among his attainments.

The family of his predecessor had been left "in all temporal things unprovided for," but Bishop Jarvis never suffered from "the chill hand of want and pecuniary distress." Though the Diocese had done too little for his support, Providence had blessed him with a competency; and his son had inherited a handsome property through his mother, who was a niece of the wife of Rev. Dr. Leaming. Not one of

than the Ten Commandments and the Epistle and Gospel for the day, by all means omit the service, but if not, hold fast the form of sound words." It is needless to add that there was no omission of the service.

his clergy could lay any claim to so large a private fortune. In view of his cup and of the portion of his inheritance, the Bishop might have said with the Psalmist: "Surely goodness and mercy shall follow me all the days of my life; and I will dwell in the house of the Lord forever."[1]

[1] Psalm xxiii. 6.

CHAPTER VII.

ANNUAL CONVENTION AT STRATFORD; STYLE OF PREACHING; REV. JOHN KEWLEY; AND PERVERSIONS TO ROME.

A. D. 1813–1814.

A MONTH only intervened between the death of Bishop Jarvis and the meeting of the Annual Convention at Stratford. The clergy and laity on that occasion were equally divided, — twenty-nine of each order being present, — and the Rev. Tillotson Bronson delivered a sermon in which he set forth "the divine institution and perpetuity of the Christian priesthood," and made appropriate allusions to the bereavement of the Church in Connecticut and the character of her late Diocesan. The sermon was asked for publication and printed. It opened thus: "In the course of Divine Providence, that portion of the Church here assembled in Convention, has lately been deprived of its visible head. Our late venerable Diocesan has received that summons which all must obey, and is gone from this to the world of spirits. His sacred office is vacant. He will no more preside in this body. His seat is left to be filled by another. Under the immediate view of such an event, it becomes all seriously to reflect on the ways of God in his government of the Church, during its continuance in this transitory state.

"Especially should we, my brethren of the clergy,

be deeply reminded of the solemn vows we made at our ordination; and resolve, before God, to feed the flock committed to our care, with the sincere milk of his word, and neglect not to stir up the gift that is in us by the laying on of hands. This gift many of you received through the instrumentality of those hands, which have been lately consigned to the tomb, and are mouldering into dust. Though they have ceased any more to perform the sacred rite, yet should they be active through you in the spiritual work, to which you are called in repairing the waste places of Zion."

The thoughts and deliberations of the Convention, though not summoned for that specific object, were naturally turned to the election of a successor in the Episcopate. The Rev. Tillotson Bronson and eleven laymen, two of them (Nathan Smith of New Haven and Samuel Tudor of Hartford) not members of the Convention, but "present with many others from a feeling of interest in the result" were appointed a committee to devise ways and means for increasing the Bishop's Fund, and in their report, which was made on the second day of the session, they directed that the Secretary should transmit to the several parishes throughout the Diocese a circular, earnestly recommending the necessity of raising a sum which would afford an adequate and reasonable support of the Episcopate; that the Standing Committee, by themselves or by agents of their appointment, should solicit donations and subscriptions in all the parishes, and that on or before the 20th day of July, 1813, every rector in the State be requested to preach a sermon to his people, "strongly enforcing the importance of accomplishing this most desirable object."

No time was lost in acting upon the letter and spirit of this resolution. The establishment of an ample Episcopal fund had been a subject of serious consideration for many years, and the last annual address of Bishop Jarvis, noticed in the previous chapter, invoked a renewal of the efforts, which had hitherto been attended with very little success. The laity evinced a more hearty interest in the matter, and felt that a system of neglect so discreditable to the Diocese should not be permitted to continue. At the Special Convention, therefore, on the 3d day of the ensuing August, warned by the Standing Committee to assemble for the purpose of electing a bishop, steps were taken to ascertain the proportion of each parish in the Diocese, according to its taxable list, towards the endowment of the Episcopate. The election of a bishop was postponed until the last Wednesday in November, and having secured for publication a copy of the sermon delivered at the opening services by the Rev. Philander Chase, then Rector of Christ Church, Hartford, the Convention adjourned and awaited the result of the movements which had been thus initiated.

The assessments on the parishes or the proportion of each, as estimated by a committee appointed at this Convention, contemplated an amount in money for the principal of the fund which, at simple interest, would yield an income of not less than one thousand dollars a year, this being the limit of the charter, and as much as the Episcopalians deemed it prudent to ask of the General Assembly, when the act of incorporation was solicited. The amount of assessments in 1813 upon seventy-two parishes or congregations, was sixteen thousand five hundred and seventy dollars, but experience shows that taxes are more easily levied than collected, and not quite one half the sum here named was afterwards received.

When the adjourned Convention met in November at New Haven, the election of a bishop was again postponed, and Charles Sigourney, the treasurer of the trustees for receiving donations, appointed upon the death of his predecessor three months before, was requested to visit the various parishes in the Diocese and obtain from them the amounts which they had severally raised towards the proposed fund. The winter was approaching and the treasurer at first did no more than address them in a printed circular, laying before the members their duty in respect to the Episcopate and urging them to its immediate performance. The returns came in slowly, and a few months later he travelled through many towns in the western part of the State, where the Church was the strongest, and held personal interviews with leading Episcopalians on the business of his mission. The result was not particularly encouraging, and at the next Annual Convention, which was also an adjourned one, held in Woodbury, June 1, 1814, no perceptible progress in the movements of the Diocese towards filling the vacant Bishopric was made. After the Convention had divided to vote in the usual manner by orders, the "clerical delegates" resolved to sit with closed doors. What transpired in that secret meeting, the warm discussion, the sharp conflicts of opinion, the delicate scrutiny of personal character, the earnest advocacy of favorite candidates by different clergymen, the representation of the absolute need of Episcopal oversight and of the drift towards the Church by members of the standing order which every day was becoming more apparent, all these things are unknown to us, for when the veil of secresy had been removed, the only record of the proceedings was: "Whereas, the fund contemplated for the support of a bishop is not yet adequate to that purpose, therefore resolved that it is inexpedient to proceed to the election of a bishop at this time."

The question upon this resolution was taken by yeas and nays, and eighteen out of twenty-one voted in the affirmative. It was communicated to the House of Lay Delegates, who returned it with their unanimous concurrence; and once more the Convention adjourned to meet in New Haven on the 26th day of October, it being understood that the object of the adjournment was to give opportunity for carrying into effect the plan of raising an Episcopal fund. But when October came and nineteen clergymen and thirty-three laymen assembled to renew their deliberations, the point of highest importance was still in the distance, and again an adjournment took place till the annual meeting in June, the Convention having first directed the Standing Committee, "upon application from any church or churches in the Diocese, to request any bishop in the United States to attend an Episcopal visitation among them." Thus the clergy and laity met in convention three times in 1813, and twice in 1814, to arrange and perfect measures for advancing the general interests of the Church in Connecticut.

The Episcopate, however, and the duty of providing for its support, were not the only subjects of solicitude with the delegates. At the Annual Convention of 1814 a Diocesan Missionary Society was projected, which looked both to the supply of vacant parishes and the aid of young men in their education for the Christian ministry. Though it yielded no immediate fruit and was afterwards combined with another agency, yet the formation of this society is some proof of the zeal of the churchmen of that day and of their desire, as was stated in the preamble of the Constitution, to "extend a knowledge of our holy religion." The Rev. Bethel Judd, at that time Rector of St. Paul's Church, Norwalk, and one of the most active of the thirty-four clergymen in the Diocese, was the head of the movement, and took especial pains to further its design. There was need enough then for an increase of the ministry. The Church in other States was but poorly supplied, and the whole number of Episcopal clergymen throughout our country was scarcely above two hundred, and one sixth of these resided in Connecticut. The adoption of the missionary principle, therefore, in connection with the proffer of assistance to young men seeking an education with a view to Holy Orders, was a step forward, and all the more to be commended because it was taken at a period when the tone of general feeling was not in sympathy with a broad and large-hearted charity.

The generation which knew Bishop Seabury and fell under his instructions had not yet passed away. He was remembered in the older parishes with gratitude and affection, and the new ones, which had been recently engaged in erecting houses of worship, were guided in their type of churchmanship by the principles of which he was an admirable exponent and defender. His disinterested and primitive zeal in the cause of the Apostolic Church was often recalled, and men spoke of him with a reverence which had respect as well to his personal character as to his office. It was about this time that his discourses on several subjects, in two volumes, were published by subscription for the benefit of his family, from manuscripts prepared by the author himself, and with a dedication, "To the Episcopal Clergy of Connecticut and Rhode Island, . . . in token of the regard and esteem of their affectionate Diocesan." Lay-readers used them freely in the vacant parishes, and probably no sermons were more familiar to the churchmen of Connecticut half a century ago than these. They helped to teach them sound Christian doctrine and to preserve in their minds the image of a godly and sainted prelate. An original portrait of the first Bishop of Connecticut, painted by Thomas S. Duché, and presented to the Diocese through Bishop White by a sister of the painter,[1] now hangs in the library of Trinity College, and no one acquainted with his history can look at it, without a feeling of gratitude to God for the noble work which He enabled Seabury to accomplish.

[1] "In the room where I am writing at this time, I have before my eyes a very good picture of Bishop Seabury, the painter of which was my particular friend. He painted another fine picture for the front of my church organ, where it is now to be seen, and is much admired ; but it so happened (*longa est historia*) that that picture was the occasion of his death." — *MS. Letter, Wm. Jones of Nayland to Dr. Bowden*, 1799.

Thomas Spence Duché, the son of Rev. Jacob Duché of Philadelphia, died in England, in 1790, in his twenty-seventh year, and was buried in Lambeth church-yard.

The great business of the Christian ministry is to preach the Gospel, and all themes in their treatment should converge to its one centre, "Jesus Christ and Him crucified." Men are influenced by the tone of religious sentiment around them and by the age in which they live. At the beginning of the nineteenth century, the staple of the pulpit in New England was largely made up of scholastic essays and dry metaphysical disquisitions; and among the people there was an extensive prejudice against the sterner features of Calvinism. While in the neighboring commonwealth of Massachusetts, some voice from time to time was heard, uttering what many feared or hesitated to believe, while single ministers called out to admonish all of the rapid current, which, without a breath of air, was wafting them away into Socinianism — in Connecticut the rigid, dogmatic theology of the Puritans was still received and accepted as a whole by the Congregationalists; or where intelligent minds among the laity renounced it, they renounced it, not to deny the Lord that bought them, but to join a communion in whose venerable Liturgy the doctrine of the Trinity is most thoroughly recognized and taught. Hence if it be true that the intelligent religious sentiment of Massachusetts, restless under the severe teachings of the prevailing denomination there and separating from it, became Unitarian, it is also true that the same sentiment under like conditions in Connecticut fled for satisfaction and repose to the bosom of the Episcopal Church.

This may account in part for the general style of preaching among our older clergy at that period. Controversy had sharpened their logical powers and made them feel that it was necessary to draw attention to the Christian doctrines embodied in the Book of Common Prayer, and to the essential and practical duties of life. With some of them, perhaps, there was too much zeal for forms: the scaffolding prepared for use in erecting the building was watched at the expense of the building itself. They sprung to the opposite extreme from Calvinism and were apparently more diligent in explaining the government and external order of the Church than in enforcing the great and vital truths of the Gospel. Their sermons were chiefly plain, didactic essays, correct but cold, and calculated to instruct the judgment rather than to warm the heart. Hubbard at New Haven, and Tyler at Norwich, both good men and faithful ministers for life in their respective parishes, were types of a school in theology which laid much stress upon the inculcation of moral duties. Rayner at Huntington, and Barber at Waterbury, both afterwards recreant to the Church, were as remarkable for earnestness and ability in the defence of their favorite tenets as for sowing the seeds of mischief and discontent along their paths. Mansfield, now for more than half a century the grave and sensible pastor at Derby, Ashbel Baldwin, Bronson, Burhans, Ives, and Shelton were all examples of those embassadors for Christ who will not believe that it is any violation of charity to maintain stoutly, as this Church understands it, "the faith once delivered to the saints."

With these was intermingled a class of minds differently tempered — not less tenacious of the externals of religion, but more zealous in the proclamation of its saving truths. In the spring of 1809, the

Rev. John Kewley, M. D., of Maryland, formerly a Romish priest, became Rector of the parish at Middletown, and for nearly four years he was one of the most active and influential presbyters in the Diocese. He was an eloquent and evangelical preacher, who gained a wide popularity and impressed his hearers in all places with a conviction of his entire earnestness. In the summer of 1811, he delivered a discourse at the institution of the Rev. Henry Whitlock as Assistant Minister of Trinity Church, New Haven, and another in October of the same year, at the anniversary of the Episcopal Academy of Connecticut. Both these discourses were subsequently printed, and in a preface to the latter, this reason is given for its publication: "The devotional exercises of the day had not long been finished, before the author was credibly informed that some of the brethren present had expressed the opinion that it was a Calvinistic discourse, and consequently, in their opinion at least, not in conformity with the established doctrines of the Protestant Episcopal Church. In justice, therefore, to himself, and to prevent misconstruction and misrepresentation, and to enable his respected clerical brethren to form a just judgment of it, he commits it to the press, with these remarks: That if the doctrines he herein advocates are peculiarly Calvinistic, he must confess he is unable to decide to what other system the Articles and Liturgy of the Church give countenance; and if it appears that the sentiments contained in this discourse are in agreement with the established standards of Church doctrine, as he believes they are, and the clergy teach them not, he cannot but express a desire that a reformation may soon take place in this particular."

Dr. Kewley closed his useful and acceptable ministry of the church in Middletown on the 10th of March, 1813, when he delivered a valedictory discourse to his people which, at their request, was published. A brief extract from it will show the tone of his piety and the style of his preaching. "Unless we feel ourselves undone by the holy, pure, and perfect law of God, we shall never duly prize the Gospel of the Lord Jesus Christ; we shall discover nothing in it to command a hearty joy and gratitude to God for its promulgation. Unless we are convinced of the plague of our nature, and of our spiritual diseases and infirmities, we shall never apply to that heavenly Physician who alone is in possession of those remedies which can relieve us and make us whole. But if we are truly and thoroughly convinced of our sinful and depraved nature; if we behold with horror its evil effects as manifested in our lives and dispositions; if we have a lively sense of the dreadful consequences which must ensue, and groan under the burden of our guilt and condemnation; if our conscience is thoroughly awakened, and we are laboring in all the auguish of a wounded spirit; then the Gospel will be truly to us glad tidings; the grace of the Lord Jesus Christ, the love of God, and the communion of the Holy Ghost will be esteemed the most valuable blessings; we shall seek after them as after a pearl of great price; we shall joyfully embrace them; Christ will then appear to us precious, altogether lovely, and the chief among ten thousand."[1]

During his residence in Connecticut, Dr. Kewley had been honored with the confidence of his breth-

[1] Pages 7 and 8.

ren, had been chosen a member of the Standing Committee, and a delegate to the General Convention; and when he removed from the Diocese, it was to assume the rectorship of St. George's Church in the city of New York. Here he manifested the same zealous interest in the salvation of souls, and for three years filled the position which he had reached with distinguished ability and success. But one morning, his arrangements for leave of absence having been previously made, Bishop Hobart was startled by a note from him, written on board the vessel that was to bear him to the shores of Europe, in which he stated that he was returning to his mother, the Church of Rome, to whose service he should henceforth devote himself and all his energies. Many have believed that, while acting in our communion, he was but a Jesuit in the disguise of Protestantism. It is certain that while in Connecticut, he tampered with one or two of the theological students at the Episcopal Academy, and advocated the duty of celibacy in the clergy with all the zeal of a cloistered bachelor in the middle ages. The only notice which Bishop Hobart takes of his relapse in his annual address for 1816, is, "the Rev. John Kewley, M. D., formerly Rector of St. George's Church, has removed to Europe."

Coeval with this event was the perversion of the Rev. Virgil H. Barber, ordained a Deacon by Bishop Jarvis in 1805 and for several years Rector of St. John's Church, Waterbury. In connection with his ministerial duties he engaged in teaching a school of a higher order, required his household to converse in Latin, and when he relinquished his parish in the spring of 1814, and removed from Connecticut to

Fairfield in the State of New York, he still united the same occupations. He had already signalized himself in the defence of one peculiar tenet. He and the Rev. Benjamin Benham of Brookfield memorialized the General Convention of 1811 to procure from that body a declaration of the invalidity of lay-baptism. The subject of the memorial was debated, but it was resolved to be inexpedient to take any order thereon. Mr. Barber professed to be conscientiously scrupulous about admitting as members of his congregation persons who had received no other baptism, and the very next year after the rejection of his memorial, in giving the statistics of his parish, he reported as the number baptized fifty-nine infants and eleven adults, "seven of whom had previously received lay-baptism." Such teachings and such a course were calculated to disturb the minds of Christian people, and their unhappy effects lingered in Waterbury and its vicinity long after his departure. But in 1817 he had sundered all domestic ties, left his family (whom his own treatment had learned to undergo a severe discipline), and joined the Church of Rome — a church in which it is so far from being heretical to accept lay-baptism, that it is not uncommon for midwives to baptize. "It is a well known property of extremes," says Bishop White, "that they are often seen making the connecting points of a circle."

Mr. Barber was a son of the Rev. Daniel Barber of Vermont, whom Bishop Seabury ordained a Deacon in 1786; and the steps of the father were not far behind those of the son in entering the Romish Communion. The elder, after leaving his Protestant friends, spent his life in Georgetown, D. C., but the son repaired to the seat of the papacy, and there, in a College of the Jesuits, under the name of Signori Barberini, a travelling clergyman of our Church found him in Passion Week, 1818, and the brief interview must have revived for both the recollection of better days. [1]

These defections from the Church, being events of singular occurrence, excited at the time much attention. They were soon followed by another, that of the Rev. Calvin White of Derby, — "a humble country clergyman, whose quaintness, learning, and goodheartedness cast a sunbeam upon poverty itself;" and who, in writing to Bishop Hobart, then in charge of the Diocese of Connecticut, touching his views of Roman Catholic authority, said: "If holding these opinions is inconsistent with my holding a peaceable stand upon *Protestant ground*, I can retire in peace, unwilling to give my Bishop or brethren a moment's discomposure, — my importance in the Church is not worth it, — only asking the blessedness of sitting under mine own vine and mine own fig-tree, disturb-

[1] "On being conducted to this person's room, I found him whom I had sought, transformed in appearance as well as name. He received me with great cordiality and joy, but without any wonder or surprise. I spent a short time with him very pleasantly. He spoke with freedom of the rites and ceremonies of his adopted religion, but with perfect delicacy, and the most studied regard to my feelings. There was even a liberality in censuring what he thought blame-worthy, which was somewhat surprising in a new convert.

"A hard bed, laid on bare planks, a table, a desk, two or three chairs, a small crucifix, and the pictures of some Romish saints, were all the articles with which his solitary chamber was furnished. He was dressed in the coarse black cassock, which is the habit of his order; the crown of his head was shaved, and both in his countenance and in all the objects around him there was an air of austerity and mortification." — Rev. Wm. Berrian's *Travels in France and Italy*, pp. 122, 123.

ing no man, and by none disturbed. I repose my concern upon your paternal bosom, waiting for a reply."[1]

At a later date he was displaced from the ministry by the Bishop of Connecticut, according to the provisions of the Canon, and lived henceforth the life of a quiet layman in sight of the sanctuary where he had so long officiated. Not one of his children then followed him in his doctrinal errors, and he himself at times evinced such an affection for the Episcopal Church as to lead some of his charitable friends to think that his early faith was still in his heart. He did not, however, renounce his connection with the Church of Rome, and died in her communion.

1 *Professional Years of Bishop Hobart*, p. 332.

CHAPTER VIII.

CORNER-STONE OF TRINITY CHURCH, NEW HAVEN, LAID; DEATH OF MR. WHITLOCK; ELECTION OF A BISHOP; AND INCREASE OF THE CHURCH.

A. D. 1814–1815.

THE original proprietors of the township of New Haven reserved for public uses a handsome central square. From the beginning, it was occupied with a house of worship and the graves of the dead; and then with a second meeting-house, and such other buildings as were needed for the convenience and protection of a well-ordered community.

Besides the Chapel of Yale College and a small wooden structure for the Methodists, the only houses of public worship in New Haven in 1812 were the "Middle Brick Meeting-house," belonging to the First Ecclesiastical Society; just north of this a wooden building, the church of the "United Society;"[1] both Congregational—and Trinity Church, east of the Gregson Glebe. The First Ecclesiastical Society, rich and prosperous, and led on by a few of its wealthiest members, prepared at the close of that year to re-

1 The house built for the "White Haven Society," known as the Blue Meeting-house, was also standing on the corner of Elm and Church Streets, but the congregation had joined the "Fair Haven Society" on the Green, and the two were incorporated under the name of "The United Societies of White Haven and Fair Haven." They worshipped alternate months in each building. The Legislature in 1815 reduced their corporate title to "The United Society."

move the "Middle Brick," which had become too small for the congregation, and to erect on its site a larger and more imposing edifice after designs and specifications furnished by a skillful architect. The contractors had scarcely demolished the old building and commenced their new work before the "United Society" — not willing to be outdone by their neighbors — engaged in a similar enterprise, and proceeded to build a "costly and splendid meeting-house." Taxation, the usual method adopted in such cases to raise the necessary funds, was not resorted to here, since a number of leading men in each society stipulated, on certain conditions, to complete the buildings and to reimburse themselves for their expenditures by the sale of pews.

The plan to erect a new church had, for some time, been simmering in the minds of the vestry of Trinity Parish, and these movements on the part of the Congregationalists served to quicken those of the Episcopalians. They could not but feel that it would greatly promote their prosperity to substitute for the old wooden edifice on Church Street, a stately Gothic structure built of stone in a commanding position on the public square. Drawings were, therefore, obtained from the same architect who had been employed by the First Ecclesiastical Society, and a novel and unique scheme was immediately set on foot to secure their execution. At a legal meeting of the parish, held October 18, 1813, the plan or agreement submitted by the vestry for raising funds to build a church, was accepted on the terms and conditions therein named. The preamble of this plan stated that the members were "desirous of erecting a new church on the Green, south of the Court house, for the better accommodation of the congregation, and at the same time to provide that the parish, by the rents of the pews, shall be enabled not only to defray the charge of building such church, but also eventually to discharge thereby the annual expenses of the Society." The amount of expense of the new church was divided into shares of fifty dollars each, payable in installments as the money should be wanted, and the wardens and vestrymen for the time being, under whose direction it was to be built, were authorized to proceed with the work when four hundred shares were subscribed for, but no subscriber was to be liable for more than fifty dollars upon each share of stock. When the building was finished, certificates were to be issued to the stockholders, the stock being transferable, and the annual rent of the pews was to be considered as pledged for the payment of the interest at the rate of six per cent. per annum, and any surplus was to be applied from time to time towards the reduction of the principal, but in no event was the "Society of Trinity Church to be held responsible for the payment of such principal or interest, or any part thereof." The Society might redeem at its pleasure "the amount of the capital stock or any part" of it, and upon its redemption in full the new church was to become the absolute property of Trinity Parish. There was another stipulation in these words. "If at any time after the expiration of four years from the completion of the new church, it shall appear that the rents of the pews and slips shall be insufficient to pay the interest upon the stock, then the wardens and vestry may sell said pews and slips, or any part thereof at their discretion, and apply the avails of such sales to the payment of the principal and interest of said stock, provided, however, that no such sale shall be made without the consent first obtained of stockholders to the amount of three hundred shares; and provided, also, that the consent to such sale shall be given by the Bishop of the Diocese; and in case the Episcopal office be vacant, then no such sale shall be made without the consent of the Standing Committee."

The subscription to all the articles of agreement was upon the further condition that when the new church was built, it was to be used by the Episcopalians of the city, and the old edifice on Church Street was to be no longer occupied as a place of public worship. Upwards of five hundred shares had been subscribed for when the parish voted its approval of the plan and authorized the vestry to proceed.[1] Thus three costly houses of public worship were going up

[1] "In all the official proceedings with regard to the new church, the site is uniformly designated as on the Green, south of the Court-house. As the old Court-house has long since passed away, the meaning of this may not be well understood without a word of explanation. The Court-house was an old and ill-looking structure, located near the southeast corner of the centre green, and projecting into what is known as Temple Street. It stood nearly on a parallel line with the old meeting-house of the First Ecclesiastical Society. That meeting-house was at the time to be demolished, and a portion of its place occupied by the graceful and symmetrical building, called the Centre Church. On the opposite or northeast corner of the Green, a new meeting-house was also in progress of erection for the 'United Society' so called in law, but generally known as the North Church. The right of building Trinity Church on the corner south of the Court-house was obtained with great difficulty, on account of the jealousies existing on the part of the Congregational societies. After it was obtained, therefore, no legal measure or usage was omitted that might be necessary to secure and hold its possession."—Rev. Dr. H. Croswell's *Annals of Trinity Parish*, MS.

on the Green, side by side and nearly equidistant from each other, at the same time during the war of 1812, — a war which so far had not diminished the gains of the merchants and traders of New Haven. The 16th day of May, 1814, was fixed upon for the ceremony of laying the corner-stone of Trinity Church, and the Rector, the Rev. Henry Whitlock, being absent on a journey for his health, the Rev. Samuel F. Jarvis of New York, "son of Abraham, late Bishop of Connecticut," was requested to perform divine service on the occasion and make the address. The religious ceremonies were postponed until the 17th on account of a storm, and on that day the congregation assembled in the old church for Morning Prayer, and then a procession was formed to the foundations of the new edifice, where the remaining services were held in the presence of a large concourse of people. The address of the Rev. Mr. Jarvis was a finished production, in which he spoke of "the elegances of life and the refinements of taste," being the gifts of God as much as any other blessings that we enjoy, and added: — "In this view, it is a source of great pleasure, that you, my brethren, will set a laudable example to your fellow-Christians by erecting your church according to a mode of architecture of which, as yet, there is not a perfect and pure specimen through the whole of the American republic." Before such an assemblage and at such a time, some allusion to Dr. Hubbard and his own father, both recently deceased, was natural, and the address concluded thus: —

"If blessed spirits, after they have left this busy stage of being, take any interest in its affairs (and I know not that either reason or religion will forbid the thought), with what delight must your late venerable Rector, and the friend of his early years, his companion in life, and his speedy follower in death, behold this present scene! You will remember with what interest they thought and spoke of this event. For more than five years did they cherish the hope of seeing this church erected; nor was it till after repeated disappointments, that at length they discarded with reluctance, what seemed at that time to be a fruitless expectation. The feelings of our nature compel us to regret that their evening hours were not gilded by the same prospect which now cheers our view. But it would not become us to repine at the dispensations of Heaven. All events are in the hands of an omniscient God, and it was his pleasure to remove them, we trust to a happier state of being, without having the warm wishes of their hearts gratified. Instead of lamenting their absence, let us rather be thankful that we are permitted to be present on this joyful occasion; and let us learn from this signal instance not to despond, if engaged in a laudable cause, even when our exertions seem to be most ineffectual. The providence of God often brings about events when they are least expected. Eighteen months have scarcely elapsed since all hope and all expectation that this stone would be laid, seemed as unsubstantial as a morning dream."

While the walls of the new church were slowly rising, the hopes of the parishioners in regard to the recovery of their Rector were gradually diminishing. The health of Mr. Whitlock slowly declined. The progress of the disease which had fastened itself upon him was not abated by the suspension of his labors, and he began to feel that he should never be able to resume his parochial duties. In the summer of 1814, when his pulpit was supplied from Cheshire, the Rev. H. Croswell of Hudson, N. Y., then in deacon's orders, spent a Sunday in New Haven, and it so happened that both of the clergymen who had been officiating temporarily were absent on that day, and a theological student had been sent to take their place as lay-reader. The services of the visiting minister, therefore, were solicited, and he filled the vacancy with great acceptance to the congregation. "On the following morning," said he, "I called to pay my respects to Mr. Whitlock. It was my first and only acquaintance with him. I was struck with his saint-like appearance. A spectacle of more lovely Christian faith and humility I never witnessed. He was pale, emaciated, feeble, and could scarcely speak above a whisper. He seemed under a little restraint, while his family were present; but the moment he found himself alone with me, he expressed his views of his condition with entire freedom."[1]

In the hope of prolonging his days and possibly of being in a measure restored, Mr. Whitlock resolved to seek a southern climate, and early in the autumn of this year he made his arrangements, and leaving his family behind took his departure from New Haven. Soon after the commencement of his journey, he communicated his proposal to retire from the rectorship, in consequence of ill health, and "requested the parish to join with him in asking of the ecclesiastical authority of the Diocese, a dissolution of their pastoral connection." His request was acceded to and

[1] Annals of Trinity Parish, MS.

the parish voted to pay him, annually, two hundred and fifty dollars for a period of four years, from October 21, 1814, the date of his letter of resignation. At the same meeting (October 31st) measures were adopted to fill the vacancy thus created, and the Rev. Harry Croswell was invited to settle as the minister of the parish at a salary of one thousand dollars per annum, which had been the salary allowed to Mr. Whitlock. He ultimately accepted the invitation, and preached his introductory sermons on the first day of the ensuing January, which was Sunday, and made an affecting allusion in one of them to the former rector of the church "even now," to quote his words, "in a distant land, withering as the grass and fading as the flower under the hand of disease." It heightened the melancholy interest of the occasion that, on the same day, an infant daughter of Mr. Whitlock, born during his absence, was presented for baptism by the mother in conformity with the wishes of her husband. Intelligence at that period travelled slowly, and though he was arrested in his progress further South, and had died at Fayetteville, N. C., on Christmas-day, yet the news of his decease did not reach New Haven until the lapse of nearly a fortnight.

Of the fourteen years of Mr. Whitlock's ministry, the last ten were passed in Connecticut, where he was honored and greatly beloved by his brethren. He was but thirty-six when he died, and few clergymen were ever more truly enthroned in the affections of their people, or had richer prospects of usefulness than he, when he became prostrated by the disease which finally terminated his life. His three published discourses, one delivered before the Convention of the Diocese in 1806, another at the institution into the rectorship of Christ Church, Hartford, of the Rev. Philander Chase, — whom he calls "my dear brother and friend of my youth," — and the third delivered at the interment of Dr. Hubbard, all bear marks of Christian scholarship, and of a mind sanctified in the love of his Divine Master, and devoted to the edification of "the Church of the living God, the pillar and ground of the truth."

At the Annual Convention, which met in Middletown on the 7th of June, 1815, twenty-nine clergymen and thirty-eight lay-delegates were present. There were some new names in both orders; and in the clerical, two or three that afterwards filled a prominent place in the history of the Diocese. Reuben Sherwood had been added to the list of deacons; and Harry Croswell, who in the earlier portion of his life had been familiar with the schemes of wary politicians, took his seat for the first time in that Convention. "I entered this ecclesiastical body" said he, "with some shades of distrust. But I feel bound and glad to confess, that I was most favorably impressed with the general appearance of this council of the Church. And although it was easy to perceive that it was not wholly exempt from the strivings of ambition, and the workings of jealousy and prejudice, these feelings were more than overbalanced by the general air of reverence and devotion which pervaded the whole assembly."

Bishop Griswold of the Eastern Diocese, composed of all the New England States, except Connecticut, was present at this Convention, having been invited just a month before by the Standing Committee, under the resolution referred to in the previous chapter, to officiate in certain parishes where Episcopal visitations were desired; and to hold a special ordination. He was not present, however, to preside, and his name is entered upon the Journal as a visiting brother. The Convention paid him the compliment not only of waiting upon him, by a committee, with a request that he would take a seat in the House, but also of asking, for publication, a copy of the discourse which he had delivered at the ordination held by him in the church at Middletown. He seems to have regarded the Diocese as placed under his canonical charge, but no trace of any record to this effect can be found, and therefore, in the judgment of charity, either the purport of the invitation was misunderstood, or the Standing Committee overreached their authority, and failed to comprehend the spirit of the Canon.[1] Bishop Hobart, upon a similar invitation, visited the parishes at Stratford and Trumbull, in the summer of 1815, and confirmed one hundred and sixty persons.

A proposition was introduced at this same Convention, to request Bishop Griswold to add Connecticut to his Episcopal jurisdiction. There was some diver-

1 "Since the last meeting of this Convention, being invited, according to the directions of the XXth Canon, I have visited some of the churches in Connecticut, and confirmed, in Middletown, Hartford, and Warehouse Point, one hundred and thirty-one persons. I admitted Ezekiel [G.] Gear and Reuben Sherwood to the order of Deacons; and the Rev. Birdsey G. Noble, Alpheus Gear, Harry Croswell, and Aaron Humphrey, Deacons, were ordained Presbyters. I have heard, though not by any official notice that the churches in Connecticut have since placed themselves under the care of Bishop Hobart. The invitation previously given is therefore, no doubt, revoked." — *Address to Convention of the Eastern Diocese, September* 25, 1816.

sity of opinion and feeling, in regard to the election of a successor to Bishop Jarvis, and those opposed to going out of the Diocese for a candidate were ready to adopt any measure which would keep alive their hopes, and delay decisive action upon the important question. Among the elder of the Connecticut clergy, several might be found who were not deficient in many of the best qualifications for the Episcopal office, but no one combined in his character all the requisites, or stood sufficiently prominent to secure a respectable majority of the votes of his brethren. The leading laity were inclined to prevent further divisions and jealousies by selecting for the office some presbyter of commanding talents and good reputation, who had proved his Christian armor well in another Diocese. The proposal to invite Bishop Griswold to take Connecticut under his charge was overruled, not with any unkind or uncourteous feelings towards him, but from a belief that the duties of his already extensive Diocese would not permit him to give to the Church in Connecticut the services and supervision which her condition demanded.

In these circumstances there appeared to be no other alternative, and on the second day of the session, it was resolved to proceed to the election of a bishop. The Convention divided, and the lay-deputies withdrew, and then, according to the entry in the Journal, the votes were taken in the clerical order, and being counted "were as follows: Rev. John Croes, 10; scattering, 17; Rev. John Croes, 14; scattering, 13. The Rev. John Croes of New Brunswick, in the State of New Jersey, was declared to be duly and canonically elected."

From this it might be inferred that two ballots only were taken, but the record does not tell the whole story. There were several ballotings and several candidates from the clergy of the Diocese; among them Chase of Hartford had his little circle of supporters. No one from the first, however, received a higher number of votes than Mr. Croes, and the greatest disappointment at the final result was betrayed by those for whom the fewest were cast.[1] The lay-delegates reported their concurrence in the choice and resumed their seats in the clerical body, and a committee, consisting of Rev. Messrs. Shelton, A. Baldwin, Hon. S. W. Johnson, and Burrage Beach, was appointed to "make a communication from this Convention to the Rev. John Croes, D. D."

But Providence wisely ordered that these proceedings should not be consummated; for while the committee were in correspondence with the bishop-elect, in regard to his support, consecration, and removal, the Convention of New Jersey, which met about two months after that of Connecticut, elected him with great unanimity to the Episcopate of that Diocese. New Jersey was his home, — the place of his birth, and of his long residence — and the Church there was the object of his fond affection, for whose welfare he had labored, and for whose respect and confidence

1 "The compiler," meaning the Secretary of the Convention, "probably out of delicacy, deemed it expedient to suppress the names of the other candidates, and sum them up under the term 'scattering.' How far any of these clergymen were willing to be considered as candidates, I know not. It was easy to observe, however, that two at least of the number, and those the candidates who had received the smallest number of votes recorded as 'scattering,' betrayed much disappointment at the result. — *Annals of Trinity Parish, MS.*

he was grateful. Hence it was natural, with two mitres before him, to take the one which would allow him to remain among his old friends, and to decline the other, which would oblige him, at the age of fifty-three, to seek new acquaintances and a new home. He was therefore consecrated Bishop of New Jersey, on the 19th day of November, 1815; and the vacancy in the Episcopate of this Diocese still continued.

The war of 1812 was ended, and with peace came unexpected political issues which were beginning to shape the destiny of the Standing Order in Connecticut. The current towards the Episcopal Church was swelling, and the accession of members to her communion was not the result of increased emigration to the Diocese; but rather of better acquaintance with the forms of the Liturgy, and of dissatisfaction with the management and illiberality of the Congregationalists. It was no sudden rush from the established ecclesiastical system into new relations; but all over the State there were signs of a kinder feeling on the part of individuals towards the Church, so that from the hills of Litchfield to the towns by the sea-side, she gathered her intelligent families and rejoiced in the prospect of higher advancement. In some places the old houses of worship were improved, or completed, and in others new ones were projected to meet the wishes of churchmen, and fulfill their most sanguine expectations. More perfect statistics, according to the Canon, were called for, and the Convention of 1815, in a formal manner, declared it to be the duty of the President to admonish all such clergymen as neglected, without assigning satisfactory reasons, to report the number of their baptisms, communicants, marriages, and funerals, and generally any matters that might throw light upon the state of their parishes. The life indicated in these ways was quickened by subsequent events, and Episcopalians became a power in the State, whose influence was very perceptible in overthrowing the ancient dynasty, and securing the adoption of a new Constitution for the government of the people.

CHAPTER IX.

BISHOP'S FUND; CONSECRATION OF TRINITY CHURCH; SERVICES OF BISHOP HOBART; AND ANNUAL CONVENTION.

A. D. 1815–1816.

THE fund to support a bishop had been gradually accumulating, and several parishes had paid in full or in part the Conventional assessments for this object. In the spring of 1814 an association of gentlemen petitioned the General Assembly of Connecticut to incorporate a new banking institution at Hartford, to be called the Phœnix Bank, and offered, "in conformity to the precedents in other States," to pay for the privilege of the charter a certain per cent. upon the capital stock, to be appropriated, if the Legislature should deem it expedient, partly to the Corporation of Yale College for its Academical and Medical departments, and partly to the Corporation of the Trustees of the Bishop's Fund; "or to be otherwise disposed of for the use of the State." It is unnecessary to recite the measures and management which preceded the charter. The bank was incorporated with a capital of one million, and five per cent. of this amount, fifty thousand dollars, went into the Treasury of the State to be applied in pursuance of the conditions suggested by the petitioners and modified by the Legislature. At the same session an act was passed authorizing twenty thousand dollars of the bonus to be paid out of the first moneys received, to three persons living in New Haven, who, as trustees, were to expend and appropriate the sum "for the use and benefit of the Medical Institution of Yale College." The Upper House or Senate originated a bill, distributing the remainder, and granting ten thousand dollars to the Trustees of the Bishop's Fund, but although this bill twice obtained the almost entire approval of that branch of the Legislature, yet it was repeatedly rejected in the Lower House, and among other reasons for the rejection, Episcopalians were told that the country was then at war, that the Treasury of the State was in want of money, and that however just the claim might be, it was inexpedient to allow it at such a time.[1]

At the October session of the General Assembly, nearly a year after the treaty of peace, the trustees again sent in their memorial and spread their case before the consciences of the law-makers, but unaccountable as it may appear, the members of the Upper House now, with a solitary exception (Hon. S. W. Johnson), completely changed their ground, and joined the popular branch in voting down the very claim which they had hitherto nursed and defended. The grant to the Medical Institution had virtually established the principle on which the distribution of the bonus was to be made, and the course pursued by the Legislature was felt by Episcopalians to be a violation of good faith and a blow aimed at their order. It was in vain to say that the public funds of the State ought not to be turned to the exclusive advantage of any "religious sect," for churchmen claimed that on no

[1] *Bishop's Fund and Phœnix Bonus*, p. 18.

such ground was the appropriation sought, but rather because it was a donation from a set of individuals, who, for the privilege of a charter, were willing to send their bounty in this direction. If the allowance to the Medical Institution had been withholden, there would have been no room for complaint.

The subject at the time was the source of much irritation and a sharp controversy began and was carried on in the "Connecticut Herald," a New Haven paper, by parties who dipped their pens into the history of matters remotely connected with the merits of the question. The illiberal policy of Yale College, the test oaths demanded from her officers of instruction, the repeated refusal of the Legislature to charter another collegiate institution, "the Divine right of Presbyterianism and the Divine right of Episcopacy," were among the subjects discussed by these anonymous laymen with peculiar zeal and ability. The pieces were afterwards compiled and published with notes and additions in a pamphlet form by their respective authors; but as neither party was willing to trust the other in editing the matter, two separate editions appeared, one omitting personal invectives and irrelevant statements; the other professing to "contain the whole controversy just as it was given warm from the press." The compiler of the latter edition was opposed to the grant of ten thousand dollars to the Bishop's Fund, and the motto from Shakespeare, set in the title-page of his pamphlet, was intended to be significant: —

> "Liberty plucks justice by the nose,
> The baby beats the nurse, and quite athwart
> Goes all decorum."

These things occurred on the eve of a memorable crisis in the civil history of the State. The Episcopalians had already been drawn in sympathy to that political party which favored toleration and desired to break down the existing rule of authority, and the final rejection of their memorial by the Legislature was one of the spurs to their diligence in securing at the next "Freemen's Meeting," the election of Jonathan Ingersoll, a warden of Trinity Church, New Haven, to the position of Lieutenant Governor. It was the first interruption in the chain of Puritan succession to that high and honorable office, and was important mainly as being a forerunner of the more complete victory to be achieved by the same political party at the next annual election. A notice of the new issues and changes in the legislation of the State will fall very properly under the head of a subsequent chapter.

But the Bishop's Fund was increased in a way wholly unexpected when the assessment upon the parishes was made, or the Phœnix Bank charter solicited. The State had received from the General Government, to reimburse it for expenses incurred in the late war with Great Britain, sixty-one thousand five hundred dollars, and the Legislature, a majority of whose members still favored the party which had been in power since the Revolution, passed an act in 1816, appropriating the money to the different religious denominations, then commonly classed under three heads, — the Congregationalists or Standing Order, the Episcopalians, and the minor sects. The measure was an unpopular one, and the Methodists and Baptists spurned the share which fell to them in the division. But Nathan Smith, of New Haven, an eminent lawyer and a sagacious manager, saw at once that this was a good opportunity to increase the Episcopal Fund, of which he was a trustee, and he immediately put in operation a plan to accomplish his object. One seventh part of the whole amount thus went into the treasury of the "Trustees for receiving donations for the support of a Bishop," and was invested in bank stocks. And here it may be mentioned, though a little in anticipation of the order of events, that the claim upon the Phœnix Bonus was not on this account relinquished. The trustees renewed their petition to the General Assembly at its May session in 1820, for "a sum of money," to quote their own words, "heretofore paid to the Treasurer of the State by the President and Directors of the Phœnix Bank for the use of the petitioners." They accepted, in answer to the prayer of their memorial and in commutation of the claim, the grant of a lottery, and the trustees met on the 5th day of the ensuing June, and assigned the grant to other parties, from whom they ultimately obtained for the corporation $7,064.88. In their corporate capacity, they had no hesitation to accept such kind of *liberality* from the State, because the propriety of lotteries was not then questioned, and the character of the Phœnix Bank Bonus, closely analyzed, might not rise much above the same class of public moralities.

The close of the year 1815 saw the spacious Gothic church for Trinity Parish, New Haven, completed and opened for services. The neighboring edifices of the two Congregational Societies had both been dedicated and occupied, and public attention was now turned to the consecration of this and to the imposing ceremonies to be witnessed on that occasion. Many persons, while the building was in progress, had indicated their purpose to attach themselves in due form to the Episcopal Society, and at the leasing of the pews which took place twelve days before the festival of the Nativity, there was a large accession of families, and such was the demand for seats that "the rents amounted to an annual interest of six per cent on about sixty thousand dollars, being nearly double the whole cost of the church, including organ, bell, and other furniture."[1] The leasing was for a period of five years from the first of January, 1816, and in this arrangement deference was paid to the old system of individual proprietorship, while the way was prepared for the policy of annual renting which now prevails in all the parishes of the Diocese.

The day fixed upon for the consecration was Wednesday, the 21st of February, 1816, and the eloquent and energetic Hobart, then Bishop of New York, was present by special invitation to officiate in the services, and preach the sermon. Churchmen from the adjoining towns and nearly all the clergy of the Diocese were drawn to New Haven on this occasion, and not only were the sittings in the vast building compactly occupied, but the aisles and galleries were literally crowded with standing auditors, so that the whole number was estimated to be not less than three thousand. At the conclusion of the grand and impressive services, the venerable Dr. Mansfield, the senior among the clergy, and in the ninety-third year of his age, exclaimed in amazement to the Rector of Trinity, as he cast his eyes upon the slowly retiring

1 Annals of Trinity Parish, MS.

multitude: "I can remember when there were but two or three Church families of reputation in all New Haven, the rest were of no great account."

The church, built of stone obtained from West Rock in the vicinity, was, at that date, the largest structure of the kind in New England, and for simple elegance and architectural design was perhaps unsurpassed by any in the whole country. The original drawings provided for an apsidal chancel, with a convenient vestry-room, but such an addition was in advance of the times and offensive to Puritan prejudice, and the building committee unwisely consented to its omission — an omission which impaired the symmetry of the edifice, and no subsequent attempt to supply it has been successful. The sermon of Bishop Hobart at the consecration was published by the request of the vestry, and the following paragraph deserves to be quoted: "The style of architecture in the edifice which has been raised by your zealous exertions, carries back the contemplative observer to that remote period, when, according to a theory which seems to have some foundation in nature, the sacred groves in their stillness and gloom cherishing the devout affections, their lofty trees shooting up into slender summits, and their branches interlacing in irregular and pointed arches, suggested, for the purposes of worship, the Gothic temple. The design was worthy of your taste; its execution is honorable to your munificence. May this temple prove to you, to your children, and to your children's children, the house of God, and the gate of Heaven. Accept, on an occasion that consecrates to the God of your fathers an edifice not unworthy of those exalted services which you are to offer in it, my liveliest congratulations." [1]

On the day after the consecration, another service was held in the church, not so attractive to the multitude, but quite as interesting and important to the parties immediately concerned. The Bishop officiated at the institution of the Rev. Mr. Croswell into the Rectorship of the parish; but the sermon on this occasion was preached by the Rev. Philander Chase of Hartford.

Still the spiritual feast continued, and on the third day, an immense concourse of people assembled to participate in the services and to witness the reception of the rite of Confirmation by one hundred and seven candidates. That large class was chiefly composed of persons of mature age, some of whom had been waiting during the vacancy in the Episcopate, for an opportunity to ratify their baptismal engagements, and others had but recently come out of Congregationalism and conformed to the Church. It was a most affecting spectacle, and Bishop Hobart seemed to catch a new inspiration from it, and to address the

[1] The architect was Mr. Ithiel Town, and in a description of the building by himself, appended to the sermon, he thus speaks of a portion of the interior: "The pulpit and canopy are constructed like those in the Cathedral at York, in England, and are richly ornamented. The ornaments of the ceiling are also similar to those in that Cathedral. The chancel floor is elevated three steps, and enclosed by a mahogany railing, with suitable ornament work under it. The altar is composed of the imitation of eight large books, relating to the government and worship of the Church, two of which, in front, are open; the idea is a very interesting one, and the execution of their painting is masterly. The front of the galleries, the reading desk, architraves of the doors and windows, etc., are finished in a corresponding style with the other parts. The slips are capped with mahogany, and painted dead white, as are also the front of the gallery, columns, pulpit and other inside work." (page 29.)

candidates and the people with more than his usual unction, eloquence, and impressiveness.

When all was over and he was about to take his departure from New Haven, two gentlemen, deputed by the vestry, waited upon him and presented him with a purse of gold as a suitable remuneration for his expenses and services. He accepted the handsome gratuity only with the understanding that he might appropriate it to the benefit of an eccentric, yet venerable and retired clergyman,[1] long resident in the Diocese, whose fortune it had been, like that of many others, to gather more learning than money, and to be in straits, when he ought to have had abundance. After reaching New York, he wrote again to one of these gentlemen, and referring to the fact that he had lodged the gift of the vestry "in the hands of Mr. Shelton, at Bridgeport, for Dr. Smith's use," he added, "My visit to Connecticut was a delightful one, spiritually and socially delightful, and in the gratification which I received I am more than repaid for any services which I have rendered." [2]

Large as was the class of candidates at New Haven, the Bishop confirmed, in the same week, a larger number at Cheshire, and fifty-four in St. John's Church, Bridgeport. He was himself surprised at the interest which his visit awakened, and more than ever impressed with the life and power of the Church in Connecticut. On all occasions when the audiences were filled in with Congregationalists and members of "the minor sects," he loved to present our services in their best and most pleasing attire, and nothing on his part was omitted which might serve to produce a

[1] Rev. Wm. Smith, D.D. [2] Annals of Trinity Parish, MS.

favorable impression of the dignity and importance of his office. He was taken from New Haven to Cheshire in the private carriage of a legal gentleman, at that time prominent in the councils of the Diocesan and General conventions ; and not much of the journey had been travelled before the Bishop suddenly discovered that the valise which contained his Episcopal robes was left behind. He suggested whether it would not be worth while to return for it, but the gentleman said he did not think it important, inasmuch as there would be only a few candidates for Confirmation and probably a small attendance. In this way his regret of the oversight was soothed, and they rode on and reached the village; and at the appointed hour of service, the Bishop proceeded to the church. The Rector was there to welcome him, and throngs of people, such as the old sanctuary had seldom received before, were pressing to its portals. When the prayers and sermon were ended, the candidates were called for, and one hundred and thirty, more than one fourth of the whole congregation, rose and advanced towards the chancel. The sensibilities of the Bishop were excited, but he went through the remaining services with his wonted animation, and at their close cordially congratulated the Rector on the prosperity of his parish. Coming outside of the church he fell in with his legal friend, and said to him very energetically and somewhat reprovingly: "Do you call this a small number of candidates? How mortified I am, that I should appear before such a congregation and in such a service without my official robes?"

The accessions to the Church at this period were

stimulated both by religious revivals and the feverish state of public opinion. Some driftwood of course came in, which was afterwards found to be worthless, but the Episcopal clergy watched all the changes that were going on, and with a few exceptions, stood at their posts like men who remembered that they must give an account. It was yet a fashion common to the people of Connecticut to frequent the house of public worship. The custom of their forefathers and the reverence for a Christian life required this; and the clergy, who were pastors as well as preachers, helped to keep it up by personal appeals and by familiar intercourse with their parishioners. The towns were not so populous, the habits of social life were not so constrained and artificial, and the movements of men were not so rapid, as to make it difficult to find them in their homes and know their views of Christian truth and duty.[1]

On the 5th day of June, 1816, the Annual Convention of the Diocese was held in Trinity Church, New Haven, when thirty-two clergymen and thirty-nine lay-delegates, representing thirty-six parishes, attended. The Rev. Jonathan Judd, at that time Rec-

1 "In the year 1816, New Haven contained about seven thousand inhabitants. The distances from the centre of the city to any point of its circumference were short, and it was easy for a clergyman to ascertain the ecclesiastical relations of the people, and to discover families as well as individuals who did not consider themselves attached to any religious society or church. Both public opinion and statute law moreover, may be said then almost to have forced every one into some sort of connection with a professedly Christian congregation."—Rev. Dr. Harwood's *Semi-Centennial Sermon*, 1866, p. 9.

The law was still in force which empowered the "Standing Order" to collect for its support a tax from every citizen not duly enrolled in another denomination.

tor of St. John's Church, Stamford, preached the sermon, and the Rev. Philo Shelton, the senior presbyter present, presided agreeably to the Constitution, as he had done at all the conventions since the death of Bishop Jarvis. An effort was again made to obtain a charter for an "Episcopal College to be erected in this Diocese," and the Rev. Messrs. Chase and Burhans, Charles Sigourney, Asa Chapman and Nathan Smith, were appointed a committee to prefer a petition in the name and behalf of the Convention, to the General Assembly at the next October session, "provided they should think it expedient." The powers of the committee were continued for two succeeding years, and then the memorial was withholden for a time, while other objects of more immediate interest engrossed the attention of the Church.

It was impossible for the clergy and laity to come together in council at that season, without discussing the question of the Episcopate. So long had it been under consideration that some really wished it finally disposed of; but the influence of the larger parishes prevailed, and it was resolved to be inexpedient to proceed to the election of a bishop. In this vote regard was had to a temporary provision. The late visit of Bishop Hobart to Connecticut was before the minds of the clergy like an enchanting picture, and the proposition to call in his assistance had only to be mentioned to meet with general favor. It was "resolved unanimously, that an invitation be given to the Right Rev. John Henry Hobart, Bishop of the Diocese of the State of New York, to visit and perform the Episcopal offices in this Diocese, according to the XXth Canon of this Church;" and two clergymen and two laymen were authorized to tender him the invitation, and, on his accepting the trust, to stipulate to pay him a suitable compensation for his services. This was altogether unlike in character the resolution which authorized the Standing Committee to solicit, as occasion required, the services of "any Bishop in the United States." It put the whole Church in Connecticut under the charge of a provisional Diocesan.

CHAPTER X.

SPECIAL CONVENTION, AND VISITATION OF BISHOP HOBART; DOCTRINAL CONTROVERSY; AND STANDARD EDITION OF THE BIBLE.

A. D. 1816–1817.

Bishop Hobart consented to take the Diocese under his Episcopal oversight, and a Special Convention was held in Trinity Church, New Haven, on the 16th day of October, for the purpose of completing the arrangement. Twenty-four clergymen, entitled to seats, and thirty-two lay-delegates were present. The Bishop preached the sermon and admitted to the Priesthood the Rev. William Cranston from Savannah, Georgia.

In his communication to the Convention, he quoted the resolution adopted at the annual meeting in June, and then said; "I have considered it of so much importance that the respectable and important Diocese of Connecticut, which has supplied the Church in other States, and particularly the State of New York, with many most useful clergymen and lay members, should be furnished in its present exigencies with the regular exercise of Episcopal functions, that I have deemed it my duty to accept the invitation contained in the above resolution of your body, sanctioned as this resolution is by a Canon of the Church. In conformity, therefore, with the XXth

Canon of the General Convention, I do hereby consent to exercise the Episcopal offices in the Diocese of Connecticut, agreeably to the Constitution and Canons of the Church."

The Convention, in a formal manner, accepted the terms, resolved unanimously to acknowledge him as the "Bishop of this Diocese" and through a committee, communicated a copy of the resolution which had been adopted. Not to be misunderstood, he wrote in reply: "I deem it proper to observe, that, agreeably to the invitation to me, contained in your resolution, at your session in June last, and to the sentiments expressed in my former communication to you, I can consider myself as Bishop of the Diocese of Connecticut, only according to the tenor of the XXth Canon of the Church. And on this view of the subject, I conclude your resolution of yesterday was founded. Permit me further to remark that, while it will be my duty, in conformity with that Canon, to bestow as much attention on the Diocese of Connecticut as shall be compatible with the paramount charge of the Diocese of New York, I shall be exceedingly gratified when, a bishop being elected and consecrated for your Church, my Episcopal charge of it, according to the Canons, will be no longer necessary."

He commenced a visitation immediately after the close of the Convention, and passed from New Haven to Meriden where, on the 18th, he consecrated St. Andrew's Church, and confirmed thirty-eight persons. The next day, he crossed over to Southington and confirmed twenty-seven, and continued his journey to Waterbury, where he spent the Sunday. At that period, there were no railroads; and the passage from one place to another was necessarily accomplished in stage-coaches and private conveyances. Peculiar interest and attraction marked the services in Waterbury. Not since Seabury made his first visitation to the same parish thirty years before, and confirmed two hundred and fifty-six candidates, had so large a class been presented in this Diocese, or perhaps in this country, for the Apostolic rite. It numbered two hundred and twenty-six, and exceeded any single class which afterwards came before Bishop Hobart. The candidates were parishioners from the whole cure of the Rector, which then embraced the congregation in Salem, now Naugatuck. On Monday, the Bishop proceeded to Oxford, consecrated St. Peter's Church, and confirmed seventy-four persons. Woodbury, Watertown, Plymouth, and Litchfield were successively visited, and some congregations within the limits of his own State also. On his return to the city of New York, he descended the valley of the Housatonic and took on his way New Milford, Brookfield, Ripton, New Stratford and Newtown. At St. Paul's Church, Norwalk, he held another Confirmation on the 4th of November, and admitted at the same time the Rector, Rev. Reuben Sherwood, to the order of the Priesthood.

The total number of persons confirmed in Connecticut, during this visitation, which occupied less than three weeks, was eleven hundred and fifty-eight. The interest attending the progress of the Bishop was surprising. He won the admiration of all by the charms of his eloquence, and churchmen, not content with a single service, followed him to the adjacent towns, and seemed never satisfied with listening to the tones of his voice. In his address to the Annual Convention the next year, he noticed these official acts, and said, "I feel it my duty to express the high gratification which I received in my visitation of the Diocese, not only from the efforts of both the clergy and the laity to make my stay among them personally agreeable, but principally from the evidence which I received of the flourishing state of the churches which I visited. The services, though generally on week-days, were attended by numerous congregations. The order and the solemnity with which divine worship was celebrated, have not been exceeded by any congregations in which I ever officiated; and may, I trust, be considered as an evidence that the affections of the people were engaged in the sacred exercises in which, with so much impressive reverence and decorum, they united. The numbers confirmed in the respective churches were unusually great on these occasions. The highly gratifying spectacle was exhibited of a collection of young people, principally between the ages of fifteen and twenty, solemnly assuming their Christian obligations, and presenting themselves before God for his favor and blessing.

"I was happy to find also that this was not the impulse of the moment. The persons who were confirmed had previously been visited by their respective pastors, excited to take upon them their baptismal engagements, instructed in the nature of the obligations which they were to assume, and prepared for receiving with an enlightened, fervent, yet sober faith and devotion, the Apostolic laying on of hands. I could not resist the conviction which I have since repeatedly expressed, excited by this circumstance, and justified by all the information I have obtained, of the laborious and faithful zeal of the clergy, in their pastoral and parochial duties."

While candidates were thus publicly and privately instructed by their pastors, it is evident that they were not all expected to become immediate partakers of the Lord's Supper. In that day more than in this, Confirmation was regarded as a rite which, in one sense, was to release parents and sponsors from the solemn engagements into which they had entered at the time of the baptism of their children. It was indeed the commencement of a new and better life with the individual,—his voluntary assumption of religious obligations, —the first public confession before the world that he had chosen the Lord, to serve Him, but it was not understood to be presently followed by strengthening and refreshing the soul with Eucharistical food. The approach to the Communion was a holier step that often lay quite in the future, and for this another preparation was generally to be made. For instance, the very next year after the large Confirmation in St. John's Church, Waterbury, the Rector, in his parochial report, stated the total number of his communicants to be one hundred and fifty-nine, —new communicants thirty-one; and in St. Paul's Church, Norwalk, where one hundred and three persons were confirmed on the same visitation, the corresponding statistics gave a total of one hundred and twenty-two communicants, and fourteen additions. Undoubtedly many of the candidates had been previously enrolled under the rubric which allows the admission to the Holy Communion of those who are "ready and desirous to be confirmed." Very few of the parishes had been favored with an Episcopal visitation for a long time, and as, before the Revolution, they had learned to do without that rite which, in the order of the Church, forms a connecting link between Baptism and the Lord's Supper; so now the law of necessity had governed the clergy, and compelled them to enroll persons as communicants without knowing when they would have an opportunity of welcoming the presence of a bishop.

The Christian education of children, however, at that period was by no means neglected. They were nurtured in the love of obedience to the divine commandments, and of lowly and reverent respect towards "all their betters." The day of Sunday-schools in this country was just beginning to dawn, and parents had not yet learned to turn over to the operation of this agency any portion of their own responsibilities and duties. Under the influence of domestic training and faithful catechetical instruction, children were prepared, as they reached the years of discretion, to enter on the Christian life, and to become, through the exercise of faith and the renovation of the soul, "heirs of the kingdom which God hath promised to them that love Him." By some of the parochial clergy great diligence was used in teaching the young the government of the Church, and the meaning of her services. In self-defence, they explained her doctrines, and sought to promote a spirit of religious inquiry, and of rational and pious devotion. They threw around their teachings fresh and happy illustrations, and if they were not aided in their work by a prolific press, they were not hindered by its continual sensations and rapid reproduction of an unchristian literature.

In 1816, a revival prevailed in some parts of Connecticut, which was attended with the usual excitements and extraordinary awakenings. It was conducted by ministers of the "Standing Order," and novel and alarming representations were made to excite the fears and arrest the attention of the young. In several places, schools and academies were visited and the students addressed in a pathetic manner, and not unfrequently in language which neither the word of God nor the judgment of charity would sanction. The nature of conversion and of regeneration was taught in a way which reflected upon the Episcopal Church and set inquirers to examining her doctrines and standards and comparing them with Scripture. The result was an increased attendance upon her worship, and many who before had believed that she was a teacher of bare morality and encouraged her members to expect salvation by their works only, were led to change their opinions, to relinquish their old associations, and eventually to connect themselves with her communion.

The Episcopal clergy wisely confined themselves to their parochial duties and seldom took any notice of the revival, except in cases where it was necessary to instruct their parishioners and guide the minds of honest inquirers. But the Rev. Menzies Rayner, of Huntington, who held the pen of a ready writer, and was rather fond of controversy, published "A Dissertation upon Extraordinary Awakenings or Religious Stirs," in which he enlarged upon conversion, regeneration, conference meetings, and topics of a kindred nature, growing out of the religious excitement of the times. The publication was issued on his own individual responsibility and without any encouragement on the part of his clerical brethren. He described quite graphically the theory of revivals, and reviewed concisely the doctrines of the Church, in whose defence he had not yet learned to falter. "With respect to extraordinary awakenings or religious stirs," said he, "in the ideas which appear to be generally entertained of them, and in the manner in which they are usually carried on, the Episcopal Church knows but little about them. She has her ancient landmarks and rules, from which neither her clergy nor people are allowed to deviate. No pretences to immediate inspiration, — no extraordinary zeal or religious fervor, are supposed to supersede their utility, or cancel the obligation to adhere to them. Order is her first law; with which, from Scripture, as well as from long experience, she is convinced her Redeemer is well pleased. Neither the convulsions of nations, the revolutions of governments, nor the ravings of fanaticism, have prevailed on her to depart from her well regulated forms and offices of devotion, the pride of her children and the admiration of strangers. With an even tenor, she pursues her course through this inconstant and changing world, marking the footsteps of her Saviour, and tracing his bright example, from the manger which first received his infant body, to the right hand of the Eternal Father, where he ever lives, her glorious Advocate and Intercessor."[1]

All this was very true, and much more that might

[1] *Dissertation*, pp. 20-21.

be quoted; but the Episcopal clergy of Connecticut would have preferred that the pamphlet had not been published. It was no help to them in their ministrations; and the laity did not care to see or read anything which appeared like an attack upon the revival system, from the side of the Church. So long as the Congregational ministers confined their labors to their own flocks and refrained from printing any distortions or misrepresentations of personal religion as exemplified in our communion, Episcopalians were content. They knew that the clean page of a good life was better than a whole volume of metaphysical divinity, and in this conviction they were willing to rest. They would leave the Prayer Book to interpret itself, and the Church to speak her own praises in opening a door of refuge for those who were ready to escape from the atmosphere of a rigid Calvinism.

Mr. Rayner, by the publication of his pamphlet, courted a battle, which he was obliged to fight almost alone. He was an unrelenting foe to Calvinistic theology, to fore-ordination, unconditional election and reprobation, and those doctrines which are necessarily connected with them, namely, a partial atonement, irresistible grace, and the final perseverance of the saints. His quick wit and extensive reading supplied the deficiencies of early education, and he became a subtle and fearless polemic, who rarely omitted an opportunity of exposing what he conceived to be heresy and false doctrine. In 1816, the Rev. Nathaniel W. Taylor, pastor of the First Ecclesiastical Society in New Haven, was beginning to make for himself the broad reputation which his talents and peculiar theological views afterwards established. In that year, he preached and published a sermon, entitled, "Regeneration, the Beginning of Holiness in the Human Heart," which with some imperfect extracts from the writings of Bishop Hobart, whose recent visit to New Haven was fresh in the minds of the people, contained an ingenious and unqualified attack upon the doctrines of the Church as inculcated in the Book of Common Prayer. He maintained that outward ordinances are not essential, and that persons once regenerated will certainly be saved; and then referring to the Bishop's idea of the sense in which "as it respects a change of state, baptized persons are regenerated," he said, "I ask again, what difference does baptism make in the state of the baptized? Are not all men in a state of conditional salvation? If they repent and believe the Gospel and are born of God, will they not be saved? If you say, yes, then after all, baptism amounts to nothing as it respects a change of state. If you say, no (and this is the answer given), then no one can be saved without being baptized by one who has received a commission from the Bishop of *the* Church. You see, brethren, it is Episcopacy or perdition!"

He summed up his reflections upon the "delicate subject" which he had discussed, in words that ought to be cited here, — for they show how a good man could be led by his feelings and zeal for his own communion, in a time of religious excitement, to misinterpret the doctrines of the Episcopal Church. "I have thought," said he, "that a scheme fraught with so many and so great errors, a scheme which makes the terms and the promises of salvation palpably inconsistent; which denies that faith and repentance and regeneration are the work of God's Spirit; which places mankind in a state of salvation without a particle of holiness; which vests the power of doing this in the hands of a particular set of men; which includes in this state of salvation all who are baptized by them, and excludes from it, and from final salvation, all who are not; which maintains that a change of heart is not the dividing line between sinners and saints — between the heirs of heaven and the heirs of hell; a scheme too, which with the face of liberality and charity is zealously maintained and propagated — I say I have thought that such a scheme needed exposure. I have felt that I, being set to watch for your souls as one who must give account, ought to show you what that system of error is which you are so often invited to embrace. If any one thinks an apology necessary, mine is, my responsibility to my Divine Master." [1]

The sermon which contained these extraordinary statements was reviewed by Mr. Rayner in a pamphlet of forty pages, and he produced numerous citations from Scripture, from the Westminster Confession of Faith, from the Saybrook Platform and the Catechism of John Calvin, to prove that Mr. Taylor had overlooked the standards of his own order, besides misrepresenting the Episcopal "scheme," and quoting unfairly the writings of Bishop Hobart.

As might have been expected, the review called forth a rejoinder, in which no new light was shed upon the question in doctrinal theology, while the reviewer was treated with a mixture of irony, ridicule and seriousness, that detracted from the dignity of

[1] Sermon, p. 18.

the controversy. Mr. Rayner, in his publications, was accustomed to write himself "Rector" of the parishes of which he had charge, and in the following passage there is an insinuation that he aspired to an office, then vacant in the Diocese, for which his name, among other candidates, had never been seriously mentioned by his brethren: "No sect have at any time set themselves up so high for orthodoxy as the Church of Rome, and her legitimate offspring, the Church of England; and we know of no individual, of late, that has talked louder about *orthodoxy* than the *Rector;* and we doubt not but by his great exertions for Episcopacy, he expects to add another *title* to those he already enjoys, and a better living than the barren rocks of Huntington afford. Indeed it is already a matter of wonder that such sterling talents as those possessed by *the Rector*, should have been so long neglected."[1]

If the notice of this controversy has appeared to be fuller than its merits deserved, it will be seen hereafter that it was the forerunner of events which threatened a more lasting disturbance of the peace of good neighborhood between Congregational ministers and those of the Church. It was narrowed down, at length, to one point of Calvinism, and in the defence of that, another champion was enlisted. The Rev. Bennet Tyler, pastor of the Congregational Church in Southbury, published a sermon in the year 1817, entitled, "Saints' Perseverance Vindicated and Established," which Mr. Rayner was quick to review with his usual ability; and Thomas Thorp, then a Methodist minister in New Haven, came to his assistance in

[1] *The Reviewer Reviewed*, p. 8.

a pamphlet of pungent "animadversions," that had previously received the approval of his clerical brethren stationed in New York. The printers were kept busy for a time by the further discussion of the subject; but in the end metaphysical divinity had lost ground with the people, and Mr. Tyler dropped the doctrine of the "Saints' Perseverance," and turned his thoughts to the preparation of a new scheme for stirring up his chief antagonist.

The General Convention met in New York, May 1817, and the delegates chosen to represent the Church in Connecticut were Rev. Dr. Bronson,[1] Rev. Messrs. A. Baldwin, Searle, and Croswell, and Asa Chapman, Elijah Boardman, Burrage Beach, and Charles Sigourney. Dr. Bronson and two of the lay delegates were not in attendance. Among the resolutions adopted by that body was one which originated in this Diocese, and grew out of the action of the Connecticut Bible Society in issuing a large edition of "the common sized Bibles," without note or comment, but with the corrupt reading of Acts vi. 3, wherein the word *ye* was substituted for *we*,[2] — a reading intended to pervert the whole order of apostolic ordination. The western country was flooded with the copies, particularly Ohio; and at the instance of the Rev. Dr. Smith, then living in retirement at Norwalk, and spending his time in writing treatises on chanting and church psalmody, the delegates to the General Convention from Connecticut were instructed to direct the attention of that body to the propriety

[1] Brown University conferred upon him the degree of Doctor of Divinity, in 1813.

[2] Annals of Trinity Parish, MS.

of establishing "some specific edition of the Old and New Testaments, without note or comment, to be considered as the authentic version or standard, by which the genuineness of all copies of the Holy Scriptures used by the members of this Church is to be ascertained; thereby to secure them against perversions, and the people of our communion from error, either in discipline or doctrine." The resolution was entrusted to the Rev. Mr. Searle, to offer at the proper time, and while it was under consideration, "a lay member, standing in a pew and observing a Bible, took it to turn to the place in question, when he perceived it to be a copy of the edition in which the corruption had been detected."[1] No further argument was needed to secure a unanimous vote for the resolution, committing the whole matter to the action of the House of Bishops. The movement thus begun was followed up at future sessions of the General Convention; and in 1823 a canon was enacted, which is still in force, prescribing "the mode of publishing authorized editions of the standard Bible of this Church."

[1] Bishop White's *Memoirs*, etc., p. 229.

CHAPTER XI.

CONVENTION AT GUILFORD; ADDRESS OF BISHOP HOBART; VISITATION; AND AMMI ROGERS.

A. D. 1817.

Twenty-five clergymen and thirty lay-delegates attended the Annual Convention which met at Guilford, June 4th, 1817. The sermon was preached by Bishop Hobart, a copy of which was requested for publication, and he was invited to take a seat as President of the Convention. One of the first measures adopted was the appointment of a large committee, representing every part of the State, to take an accurate list of the number of souls belonging to each parish; and also the grand levy of each parish in the Diocese. But it is easier to adopt resolutions than to carry them into effect, and this, after being continued from one convention to another, was finally lost sight of, and there is nothing on record to show that the committee ever came together, or acted upon the subject in a formal manner.

It was an encouraging feature, that in no previous year had the parochial reports been so complete. Twenty-two clergymen gave the statistics of thirty-four parishes or cures, and the families began now to be more generally reported, their number in some places having largely increased. It was a period when public attention, in the progress of political events, was turned to the Episcopal Church; and intelligent men in the State, as before noted, found reasons for changing their religious connections.

The matter of electing a bishop appears not to have been discussed in open convention at this time. Doubts had arisen whether such a proceeding would be constitutional, and the clergy in convocation, previously to the meeting, had deliberated for a long time; and finally the only decision reached was an indefinite postponement of the constitutional question. There were those among them who favored an immediate election and were ready to name their candidates — but the subject was not pursued, and the report of the treasurer of the Bishop's Fund, more satisfactory than any hitherto presented, renewed the appeal to the delinquent parishes to pay their respective assessments. Twenty-nine of the seventy-five parishes in the Diocese had recognized their obligation and paid in full or in part; but from the larger number no returns had been received, and these could not be expected to take a very lively interest in the election of a bishop, to whose suitable maintenance they were so indifferent.

"There can be but one sentiment in the Church," is the language of the report, "in relation to the Episcopal office. All will admit its incumbent should be, if they desire the Church should flourish, a man of superior virtues and talents. The Bishop of the Diocese of Connecticut should, if possible, be inferior to no other man in it. Such a man is not to be obtained without an adequate support; nor, if elected from without the State, — as he would probably reside in one of our larger towns, where the expenses of living are great, and where his situation would require from him considerable hospitality, — without such a support as might appear to some, not accurately apprised of the extent of these expenses, to be more than necessary." At that date, the trustees were a close corporation and the charter did not require them to make an annual report to the Convention of the state of the Fund. But in one way and another the subject was kept before the parishes, and they were all continually urged as in duty and honor bound, to "bear their fair proportion of a common burthen for the common benefit."

The Bishop, in his address to the Convention, referred to the past history of the Diocese and to the prevailing spirit of religious inquiry, which was calculated to advance the cause of truth. "The present state of the Church in this Diocese," said he, "as far as I am acquainted with it, affords many causes of congratulation. Obstacles to her advancement from local circumstances are daily removing. Her evangelical doctrines, unmixed with the varying dogmas of metaphysical speculation; her apostolic ministry, unimpaired by those innovations which, displacing her from the only sure foundation, the Rock of Ages, would rest her on the sandy basis of human authority; her primitive worship, free from the unmeaning frivolities of superstition, and the disgusting extravagances of enthusiasm, and exhibiting a simple, sublime, and fervent devotion, are constantly obtaining a stronger hold on the understandings and the hearts of the people. There is reason to hope that she will be that fold of the Redeemer in which the friends of genuine Christianity, long assailed by conflicting systems, and exposed to the attacks of heresy and schism, will at length find rest, in the enjoyment of evangelical truth, apostolic order, and primitive worship.

"This happy result will very much depend on the measures that are pursued to preserve the Church in Connecticut in that purity by which she has hitherto been distinguished. For this purpose too much attention cannot be paid to procuring a pious, orthodox, and learned ministry, by exciting youth of piety and talents to engage in the sacred office, and by assisting them in their preparatory studies."

Connecticut had supplied the Church in other States — particularly in New York — with many clergymen and laymen distinguished for piety, and for zeal, firmness, and perseverance in advocating the principles which pervade our Articles and Liturgy. The inadequate provision, in some cases, for the support of the clergy, was one cause of their frequent removal from the Diocese, and Bishop Hobart suggested to the consideration of the laity, that the only remedy for this inconvenience lay in more zealous exertions and more liberal contributions on their part. It could not be expected that clergymen, pinched by poverty, would refuse to accept, when offered them elsewhere, "situations of equal usefulness and greater temporal comfort." Parishes vacated in this manner, were not likely, in the dearth of ministers, to be immediately supplied with satisfactory services, and hence the increase and prosperity of the Diocese were in danger of being retarded, as they had already been, to some extent, for the same unworthy reason.

One important measure was revived at this Convention and put into effectual operation. Since 1808, a voluntary society had existed — formed in New Haven — for the "Promotion of Christian Knowledge," and composed of gentlemen from various parts of the State who, at the time of subscribing the Constitution, paid one dollar, and one dollar annually thereafter. The Bishop of the Diocese, by virtue of his office, was president of this society; and its object was to publish and circulate at reduced rates, the Bible, Book of Common Prayer, and useful religious works of a doctrinal and practical character. It served a good purpose at that time, for weekly periodicals, devoted to the interests of the Church, had not yet been established. But the organization failed to reach the whole wants of the Diocese, and the Convention, after the death of Bishop Jarvis, initiated a movement to organize a Missionary Society, and adopted a constitution, or articles of agreement, as stated in a former chapter. The management of its affairs and the appointment of missionaries were entrusted to the Standing Committee, — but it was an unfortunate society, that barely struggled into existence and then almost died for the want of proper care. For three years, little or nothing was done under the organization, and the movement to revive it contemplated uniting in the same agency the work of Diocesan missions and the distribution of religious publications. Bishop Hobart had some influence in giving shape to the new plan, and one obstacle was removed out of the way by the members of the voluntary society adopting at their annual meeting in October, 1817, a resolution to the effect that whenever "the Convention of the Diocese shall establish a Society for the Promotion of Christian Knowledge," they would consider themselves dissolved, and pass all moneys remaining in the treasury to "the new society, to be added to the common fund." The plan of operations and the arrangement of details were perfected at the next Annual Convention, and the name of the voluntary organization, which was the title of an English society, was wisely retained. The first article of the constitution read: "The society shall be called 'the Protestant Episcopal Society for the Promotion of Christian Knowledge, by employing Missionaries in the several vacant parishes of the Diocese, and by the gratuitous distribution of the Bible, the Book of Common Prayer, and religious Tracts.'"

Thus the two agencies were blended, and the work of Diocesan missions received a fresh and vigorous impulse. Under God, the Church in Connecticut owes much of her present prosperity to the operations of this Society, for many parishes too small to procure the regular administration of the ordinances were nursed by its protecting care, until they grew into importance and became self-supporting. Scattered families that could not well be gathered and embodied into churches were reached by the occasional visitations of a missionary, and their love for Apostolic order, and attachment to the Liturgy, were rekindled by the interest evinced in their spiritual welfare. Other families at length came among them, and in due time they were united in the formation of parishes that have since had a life of activity and usefulness in the Diocese.

During the session of the Convention at Guilford,

Bishop Hobart confirmed, in the church in that place, twenty persons, and on the last day of the same week he consecrated "the newly erected church" at North Guilford, and confirmed thirty-seven. He arranged at this time for an immediate and extended visitation of the Diocese, and gave early notice of his appointments by publishing them in the secular newspapers of Connecticut. On the 6th of August, 1817, he had entered the State and was in Fairfield County, spending, for the most part, a day in each parish. He passed from New Canaan to Wilton, Weston, Redding, and Danbury, where he officiated on Sunday, and the next day he was at Trumbull, and confirmed in the church at Tashua eighty-two persons, the largest class presented to him on this visitation, except the class at Chatham (now Portland), which numbered one hundred and two. Through the shore towns from Fairfield to New Haven, he bent his course towards Hartford, where he arrived on Saturday in season to admit the Rev. J. M. Wainwright (afterwards Bishop of New York), to the order of the priesthood, and during the services of Sunday, he administered the rite of confirmation in Christ Church to twenty-two persons. After visiting several parishes on the eastern side of the Connecticut river, his appointments took him into New London County and back by a circuitous route to Middletown and New Haven. He was at Woodbridge (now Bethany) on the 30th, and confirmed sixty-nine, and on the following day at Derby, where he confirmed seventy-eight. He consecrated the church at Humphreysville (now Seymour), September 2d, and administered confirmation to sixty-one persons, and on the 3d he consecrated the church at Roxbury, and administered the same rite to forty-three. The total number of persons confirmed during this visitation, which occupied just a month, was twelve hundred and seventy-five, and the record of his previous visits to Connecticut, as far as it has been discovered, gives seventeen hundred and eighty-two. Thus the aggregate list of confirmations in the short time during which he had the provisional charge of the Diocese rose to three thousand and fifty-seven, — only eleven less than the entire number of persons confirmed by Bishop Jarvis in the whole fifteen years of his Episcopate. It was a period of great religious interest, and the clergy partook of the spirit and zeal of their temporary head. They felt the influence of his presence among them, and when he departed they returned to their labors with cheerful toil and steady diligence.

A score of parishes in the Diocese still believed in the sincerity and holiness of Ammi Rogers. He himself may have hoped that, with the death of Bishop Jarvis, the power of his opponents would be broken, and that he could gain a standing among the clergy, which would, in some measure, relieve him from the odium attached to his character. He appeared at the Annual Convention in 1815 with delegates from Hebron and Groton, who were admitted to seats by courtesy, and in consideration that the parishes which they represented had not hitherto been correctly informed relative to the true state of the case; but the personal petition of Rogers was returned to him with the same resolution of the clergy, heretofore repeatedly adopted, that they were "not competent to take cognizance of said petition." He persisted in his attempts to be recognized, and when Bishop Hobart assumed the charge of the Diocese, he wrote him a plausible letter, reciting the history of his ministerial life, and complaining that he was unjustly deprived of his rights and privileges, having never, as he affirmed, "been canonically censured, suspended, silenced or degraded." Such men always gather around them groups of friends and supporters, and at this time, Rogers was travelling to and fro in the northeastern section of the State, preaching and performing service according to the ritual of the Church in nine different parishes, so called — seven of which were purely the result of his officious schemes, and unknown on the journals of the Convention.

Bishop Hobart, while unwilling to countenance these irregular ministrations, or to pronounce upon the canonical steps of his predecessor, was yet desirous of doing his duty to the people of Hebron and other places, and accordingly, about the time of publishing his appointments for that part of the Diocese, he requested the Rev. Solomon Blakeslee, then Rector of the Church at New London, to undertake a mission for him to these places, to hold public services in them, and, if he deemed it expedient, to prepare the way for an Episcopal visitation. Mr. Blakeslee was one of those clergymen who had befriended Rogers, and gravely doubted the correctness of the sentence of degradation issued against him, and when he started upon his journey, he was quite willing to take him into his company, and thus the better side of things was presented to his view, for not only did "genteel families" strengthen the impressions he had entertained of the character of the man and his work, but agreeable incidents marked his progress, and "every toil," to quote his own words, was "sweetened with an endearing recollection."

On completing his missionary tour, Mr. Blakeslee communicated the results of his observation to Bishop Hobart in a long letter, from which a brief extract here will be sufficient. "I have already stated," said he, "that these churches have been reared into life by the care and industry of Mr. Rogers, and to speak with caution, they embrace a number of not less than two thousand souls; many of them have received baptism at his hands, have come to the holy communion through his persuasion and influence, and now wait with a hope and expectation of being presented by their own minister to the Bishop, that they may receive the apostolic rite of confirmation. This is the only point which involves in it any delicacy. . . .

"I should be pleased to accompany the Bishop in his visitation of the Church in Hebron, Jewett City, and Poquetannock (three only of the nine parishes which I visited have churches), should the Bishop be satisfied that it would be consistent with his duty to acknowledge Mr. Rogers' administrations, and to receive from him, as the curate, the subjects of confirmation, and to communicate with him in the offices of the Church; otherwise I do not consider it prudent to hold myself responsible for any consequences that may grow out of your sincere wishes to serve them."[1]

The parishes at Hebron and Poquetannock or Groton, were organized before the Revolution, and the Bishop had included them in his appointments. He travelled upon this visitation in his own carriage,

[1] Life of Rogers, pp. 61–62.

and on the morning of the 20th of August, he was at Marlborough, a town adjoining Hebron, holding a service and administering the rite of confirmation. He had decided that a compliance with the terms stated by Mr. Blakeslee would be an interference on his part with the official acts of Bishop Jarvis, and the news of his intention not to fulfill his appointment reached Hebron in time to take the wardens of the parish and Dr. John S. Peters to Marlborough, to confer with him and make some arrangement whereby the church might be visited and the expectations of the people gratified. It was to no purpose that Rogers accompanied these gentlemen, for the Bishop would neither see him nor listen to any proposal in which he might be supposed to have a share. But he finally consented to visit Hebron, if the wardens would give him a written certificate to the effect that in doing so, they would understand that he was to have no intercourse with this man as a pastor, nor recognize him in any way as a clergyman of the Church. They gave him such a paper, drawn up in language to suit his own feelings, and with it he set forth on the road to Hebron. Upon reaching the door of the church and alighting from his carriage, who should come out to welcome him amid a crowd of spectators, but Rogers himself in full canonicals! The Bishop turned without speaking to him, reëntered his carriage, drove to the public house, and after partaking of some refreshments departed from the town, to the great disappointment and grief of the assembled people, and to the mortification of those who, if they could not control Rogers by their agreement, should at least have ascertained the fact soon enough to save themselves from the appearance of imposing upon a dignified and courteous prelate, yielding to their special request in the matter of a religious service.

The end of this long and unhappy trouble was now approaching. The friends of the degraded priest rallied around him in vain, multiplying their testimonials and redoubling their efforts to vindicate his character. He sought once more to be accepted as a clergyman in the Diocese, and for this purpose transmitted a letter of his own, with sundry documents from his supporters, to the Annual Convention of 1818 ; but no action was taken upon these communications and none was needed, for his case, instead of presenting any new claims for consideration, had, by this time, assumed a sadder aspect. The current of public opinion was bearing him down to depths from which he could never rise, except by the grace and favor of God. He was accused of the most heinous offences, even of crimes committed with a young woman, and arraigned by the State before the Supreme Court of New London County. After a protracted trial, he was found guilty of the charges brought against him, and sentenced to imprisonment in the common jail at Norwich for two years ; the Judge, in mercy to his children, withholding a severer punishment.

From the chamber of his prison he wrote to the Governor of the State, and also memorialized the General Assembly, asking the one to grant him a reprieve as the law permitted, and the other to take his case into consideration and release him from confinement, or allow him a new trial before what he called " an impartial and unprejudiced tribunal." The principal witnesses whose testimony had supported the prosecution were produced at the hearing before the joint committee of the General Assembly, and declared under oath that their former statements were false, and that they had been persuaded to make them, contrary to their inclinations, by those who were concerned in framing the indictment. This contradiction was undoubtedly instigated by the memorialist and his friends. But the perjured witnesses did not avail him, for upon an unfavorable report from the committee, the Legislature declined to rejudge a matter already decided by the proper tribunal. Rogers therefore served out the sentence of the Court, and afterwards published, in a small volume, the "Memoirs" of himself — a bad book, which bears abundant evidence of an insolent and self-righteous spirit, and a corrupt and wicked heart. He went through the country, selling his "Memoirs," and preaching wherever he could gather an audience; but his old adherents now received him with distrust or began to recoil from him, and he gained not even a temporary settlement in any duly constituted parish of the Diocese. His powers to excite an interest in his behalf were at an end. The congregations, which he organized before his imprisonment, broke up, and when he searched for his numerous flocks they were nowhere to be found. He was a pestilent historic character, who was permitted, in the providence of God, to trouble the Church and society for half a century, and died at Ballston, N. Y., in 1852, showing no signs of having "truly and earnestly repented him of his sins," and fighting to the last his sentence of degradation from the ministry.

CHAPTER XII.

POLITICAL REVOLUTION ; CHANGE IN THE STATE GOVERNMENT ; ELECTION SERMON ; AND NEW CONSTITUTION.

A. D. 1817–1818.

WHILE all religious denominations had been tolerated in Connecticut since 1784, pains were taken to keep the control of the government in the hands of the "Standing Order," and to shape things with reference to a right succession. Until Jonathan Ingersoll, an Episcopalian, was chosen Lieutenant Governor in 1816, the State officers from the settlement of the Colony had been Congregationalists, and the ministers of that body were supposed to have great influence in selecting the candidates and accomplishing their election. It is a natural feeling that a religious establishment is entitled to the patronage of the government, and to the honors and emoluments of its offices. But the connection between ecclesiastical and civil power is always dangerous, and the partiality towards the "Standing Order," evinced by the General Assembly in a variety of public acts, and the apparent reluctance to heed the claims of other religious denominations, awakened among a large portion of the people a desire for change and for a more liberal policy. It has already been seen what effect the rejection of the memorial of Episcopalians in regard to the Phœnix Bank Bonus produced; and the "Appropriation Act for the support of Literature and Religion," was a State stratagem which was simply lost upon "the minor sects." If it was intended to be a measure to perpetuate power and appease opposition, it failed of its object, for the new political party that favored "Toleration," rapidly gained accessions from all who were not in sympathy with the Congregational system, and from some who were. The Federalists found arrayed against them those who had hitherto been numbered among their steadiest supporters. Old issues were forgotten, and the Episcopalians of the State almost to a man, though voting heretofore for the existing order of things, now joined the minority, and worked with all the appliances in their power to bring on a political revolution.

Oliver Wolcott, of Litchfield, who inherited from his father — a signer of the Declaration of Independence — the spirit of a patriot and the qualities of a statesman; and who had been a member of the Cabinet under the administration of John Adams, was put in nomination for governor in opposition to John Cotton Smith, then for four years incumbent of the office. He was a Federalist of the old school, "unenrolled in the ranks of democracy on the one hand, and uninfected with the intrigues and plottings of the dominant party on the other." He was therefore an available candidate, and at the annual election in 1817, the "Toleration party," which had taken him up, was victorious, and Wolcott was chosen Governor of the State by a small majority, and continued in the office for a decade of years. At that period the tenure of official station was more permanent than now, and partisan subserviency in the minds of the people had not yet taken the place of better qualifications.

This change in her chief magistracy was the beginning of a new era in the civil and political history of Connecticut. It was rendered more decisive by a corresponding change in the character of the General Assembly, a majority of whose members were counted on the side of toleration, and among them were some of the most influential and capable men in the State. The Episcopal Church was well represented, and prominent in the Council or Upper House were Jonathan Ingersoll, the Lieutenant Governor, Asa Chapman and Samuel W. Johnson, and in the popular branch of the Legislature were Charles Denison, chosen Speaker, John S. Peters and Simeon H. Miner, clerks, all Episcopalians, and zealous for the welfare of the religious body with which they were connected. Governor Wolcott, educated among the Congregationalists, could not be ignorant that his election had turned upon points which required from him some official notice; and hence in his message to the General Assembly, he recommended, among other things, the adoption of measures with a view to a deliberate revision of the ancient system of taxation, but he touched very tenderly upon another matter equally dear to the hopes of the triumphant party. "There are no subjects," said he, "respecting which the sensibility of freemen is more liable to be excited to impatience than in regard to the rights of conscience and the freedom of suffrage. So highly do the public prize their privileges, that they have sometimes ascribed to unfriendly motives towards particular sects or denominations, such regulations as were sincerely intended to secure an equality of rights to every portion of the community. Whenever the public mind appears to be considerably agitated on these subjects, prudence requires that the Legislature should review its measures, and by reasonable explanations or modifications of the law, restore public confidence and tranquillity."

Cautious and measured words like these were not unwise; but the newly chosen Governor was more fearless in departing from a custom which all his predecessors in office had obeyed as implicitly as a law of the land. The General Assembly was then convened semi-annually at Hartford and New Haven in the spring and autumn, and an election for members of the Council and Lower House was held each season, but the State officers were only chosen at the annual Freemen's Meeting in April. The first session and the inauguration of the Governor were always in Hartford, and at the anniversary, a minister of the established faith delivered a sermon "before his Excellency and the Honorable General Assembly," to instruct them in the nature of their duties and in the origin and ends of civil government. The sermon was invariably printed at the public expense, and if the cost of printing had been as great in those days as it is now, the Commonwealth would have paid dearly for its standard theology. The election sermon of President Stiles in 1783, was ninety-nine pages in length, and that of Azel Backus in 1798, from the text, "Oh that I were made judge in the land, that every man which hath any suit or cause might come unto me, and I would do him justice," occupied fifty-four octavo pages. How the legislators had the patience to sit through these long disquisitions is a mystery, but they seem to have prized them more highly than their successors at the present time prize the short prayers of the clergy at the opening of the daily sessions.

Governor Wolcott, on the 30th of October, 1817, the very day on which the Legislature closed its autumnal session, addressed a note to the Rev. Mr. Croswell, Rector of Trinity Church, New Haven, saying, "I have requested President Day to preach the Election Sermon before the General Assembly at Hartford, in May next, but as some accident may occasion a disappointment on his part, I respectfully request you, sir, to attend the election, prepared to deliver the customary discourse on that occasion. Your answer, when convenient, will be acceptable." He immediately acknowledged the flattering distinction, and said it would afford him great pleasure to comply with his Excellency's request. President Day took an early opportunity to make known his purpose not to preach the Election Sermon, and, therefore, as all parties had probably anticipated, the Rector of Trinity Church was left to make the necessary preparation.

So bold a departure from the established custom was calculated to stir up the jealousy of those who fondly imagined that they had a monopoly of all the religious and civil power in the State. The anniversary of the General Election was a high festival with the ministers of the Congregational order. They attended in large numbers the levee of the appointed preacher, and joined in a grand procession under a military escort, with a band of music, to the meeting-house where the sermon was to be delivered. They were also welcome guests at the dinner provided for them at the public expense. To all this ceremony, the Rev. Mr. Croswell, in accepting the appointment, was obliged to conform, and accordingly, clad in his priestly robe, he received the Congregational ministers, as they presented themselves to be introduced and to pay their respects. But it was observed that, on this anniversary, the attendance was small compared with former years, the whole number being less than one hundred. No little curiosity was excited to see how the services would be conducted, for many supposed that the Episcopal form was incapable of being adapted to such a commingling of secular and religious practices, and that it would be necessary to bring in a Congregational divine to offer an appropriate prayer. The Episcopalians were desirous of seeing the Church fully exhibited on this State occasion, and shortly before the time, Bishop Hobart wrote to Mr. Croswell thus: "The preaching of an Episcopal clergyman before the Legislature of Connecticut will certainly be a new and interesting event. It is of considerable importance that as a precedent is now to be established we should exhibit fully the services of our Church. I have no doubt that you agree with me in this, and intend performing the morning service as if it were in your church. It will certainly be proper that you should introduce appropriate prayers; and doubtless none can be more suitable than those drawn up by Bishop Seabury."[1]

The religious services were held in the large brick meeting-house in Hartford, known as the Centre Church, and two of the oldest divines of the Congre-

[1] MS. Letter, May 9, 1818.

gational order were seated with Mr. Croswell in the pulpit, but they were not expected to bear any part in the exercises. By an arrangement with his Episcopal friends, he conducted the service in accordance with the prescribed ritual of the Church, slightly abridged and with only one lesson. The sermon which he delivered was published by the General Assembly, and two or three private editions of it subsequently passed through the press. It was from the text, "Render therefore unto Cæsar the things which be Cæsar's, and unto God, the things which be God's," and the opening paragraphs were calculated to rivet the attention of his audience.

"Holding in high veneration the character of our pious forefathers, feeling every disposition to treat the customs which bear the sanction of their authority with deference and respect, I would not, without good and sufficient cause, depart from a course which appears to have been ranked among the steady habits of my native State; nor would I, from an affectation of singularity, or on any other slight ground, dissent from opinions, which have long been considered by many as incontrovertible. If, therefore, on the present occasion, I shall appear to entertain doubts of the propriety of blending too closely the civil and religious concerns of the community; or if I shall seem more solicitous to maintain the dignity of my profession, than to subserve any particular political interest; or if it shall be found that I am more ambitious to fulfill my obligations as a minister of Christ, than to offer the incense of flattery to any sect or denomination of men; I trust you will do me the justice to believe, that I act under the influence of a solemn sense of duty, and that I am governed by no other motives than a sincere desire to comply with the spirit of the precept which I have selected for my text. Be this, however, as it may, I hope to find a defence of the sentiments which I may advance, and a justification of the course which I may pursue, in the example of our blessed Lord, in the case which drew the precept from his lips."

The conclusion of the sermon, which was addressed particularly to the clergy, is equally decisive and emphatic. He applied the principle embraced in the text to the people collectively; to the civil rulers and magistrates, and to the clerical profession; and then he observed the same classification in his closing remarks. "As there are few occasions," said he, "which call such a number of our profession together, I have deemed this a fit and proper opportunity for expressing, not only my own sentiments, but those held by the Church generally to which I belong. And as we have little reason to hope that we shall all meet again in this world, you will permit me now, on parting, to add a word of exhortation. Let us then, my brethren, endeavor to profit by the precept before us. Aiming to maintain the honor of our profession and the dignity of the Christian ministry, let us not become instrumental in debasing them by worldly mixtures. Let it be our study to stand aloof from those disputes which disturb the peace and harmony of society. Let us not suffer ourselves to be drawn into measures which may tend to promote the spirit of party among our respective flocks. Let us not give any reasonable cause for suspicion that our influence is exerted in those political questions, by which the community is unhappily divided. Let us not put it in the power of the historian to accuse us of descending from our high calling to mingle in those dissensions which are the offspring of human pride and passion. And, above all, let us beware that we do not defraud our Lord and Master of his rightful claims. His kingdom is not of this world. He is jealous of his honor, and will not suffer his unfaithful servants to escape unpunished. We know the nature of our obligations. We know by what solemn vows we have enrolled ourselves under the standard of the Cross. We know that we stand pledged, by everything dear and sacred to man, to preach CHRIST CRUCIFIED. Let us not then incur the dreadful guilt of preaching a religion without a cross. Let us not glory save in the Cross of our Lord Jesus Christ. By this cross, let the world be crucified unto us; and by the same cross, let us be crucified unto the world." [1]

The sumptuous feast provided for the clergy and others at the expense of the State, followed the religious services. In the large dining hall, where the viands were to be served, the table was spread, and at the head of it was placed the appointed preacher, with the two venerable divines who had attended him in the pulpit, seated on either side. One of these was the Rev. Dr. Perkins, of West Hartford — the birth-place of Mr. Croswell — who had been his preceptor and pastor in the days of his childhood, and who seemed very happy to meet his pupil on this festive occasion. "I am always pleased," said he, "to attend these anniversaries, and in forty years

[1] Sermon, pp. 15, 16.

I have never been absent but once from the annual election dinner. But I little thought, when I catechised the children at the South End, that Harry Croswell would become an Episcopal minister and preach the Election Sermon."[1]

The innovation of Governor Wolcott upon the custom of his predecessors did not stop with a single example. The preachers before the General Assembly were subsequently selected not only from the Episcopal Church, but from among the Methodists and Baptists. The clergy, however, were less and less inclined to attend the anniversary; the public interest gradually diminished, and after a few years, the practice, with all its accompanying ceremonies, fell into disuse.

The party which came into power in 1817 was bent on the accomplishment of great changes in the government of the State. From the beginning of the century, there had been much uneasiness among a minority of the people, and several meetings had been held in different places at which the old charter of King Charles the Second was freely discussed, and the way prepared for a political revolution. The spirit of the leaders in these movements was bold and decisive, and one of the pamphleteers of that day said in reference to them, "the peace of families, of neighborhoods, of towns, and of the whole community, has been almost turned into war, and hatred and revenge have succeeded to kindness and mercy."

The complaints of the minority were treated as imaginary, or as the offspring of ambitious demagogues, and many reasons were urged for continuing under a charter which had served the Commonwealth

[1] Annals of Trinity Parish, MS.

so well for more than one hundred and fifty years. The historical associations connected with its preservation in the hollow of an oak at Hartford had their influence upon the Puritan mind, and the established religion was fortified by statutes which had grown up under it, and which, according to the indications, would be set aside in framing a new constitution. Instead of yielding, therefore, to the sentiments of the minority, care was taken to check their advancement, and some acts were passed by the General Assembly which were regarded as arbitrary and oppressive. The "stand up law,"[1] as it was called, touching the elective franchise, was one of these, and it made no friends for the party that procured its enactment. The list of grievances was large, and the first decisive steps to secure a new constitution were taken in the last week of August, 1804, when a convention of men from ninety-seven towns in the State, and understood to represent the sentiments of the Republicans, or Democrats as they were stigmatized by the Federalists, met at New Haven and passed a series of resolutions in favor of the change which they so much desired. This action cost some of the leading spirits of the convention the loss of their humble offices;[2] but two years afterwards another meeting, bolder and more decided in its tone, was held by the same polit-

[1] For example, the Council or Upper House was composed of twelve members, and this law prescribed that votes should be given for one candidate at a time, by the freemen rising or standing, while they were counted, in case of a division; and then the parties withdrew to opposite sides, and this was done twelve times in succession. The law was often the means of designating objects of denunciation; and in many instances deterred the dependent man from voting, or ruined him for exercising that right with more courage than policy.

[2] Hollister's *History of Connecticut*, vol. ii. p. 512.

ical party at Litchfield, and thus things went on until the War of 1812. Connecticut was opposed to this war, and in the disputes that accompanied it the Congregational clergy, as in the struggle for Independence, bore a conspicuous, though different part, and many sermons were preached that helped to strengthen the State government at the expense of the general administration. But the war, which was popular in some sections of the land, gained supporters in Connecticut as it progressed, and closed with better results and a better reputation than its opponents had predicted, and too soon for the Hartford Convention to urge upon the public its schemes for "a limitation of powers which," it was claimed, "had been misused."

It has already been mentioned that at this period in our civil history, the old issues between Federalists and Republicans were forgotten, and the great basis on which the new party achieved their success was that of "toleration." But though coming into power under a new name, the grievances of the minority in the past were remembered and measures at once adopted to provide for their redress. Governor Wolcott, who, with the rest of the people, had learned to reverence the ancient charter, thus spoke of the expediency of some change, in his message to the General Assembly at the May session, 1818.

"Prior to the establishment of American Independence, the charter of Charles the Second of England was viewed as the palladium of the liberties of Connecticut. It surely merited all the attachment it received; for whatever had been the claims of the British crown or nation to jurisdiction or territory, they were all with mere nominal exceptions, surrendered to our ancestors by that instrument; especially there was expressly conceded to them and their posterity, the inestimable privilege of being governed by municipal regulations, framed and executed by rulers of their own appointment. The Revolutionary War, of course, occasioned no change or dissolution of our social system. Considered merely as an instrument defining the powers and duties of magistrates and rulers, this charter may justly be considered as unprovisional and imperfect, yet it ought to be recollected that what is now its greatest defect, was formerly a preëminent advantage, it being then highly important to the people to acquire the greatest latitude and authority with an exemption from British interference and control."

At the same session of the Legislature, it was "*Resolved*, That it be and is hereby recommended to the people of this State, who are qualified to vote in town or freemen's meetings, to assemble in their respective towns on the 4th day of July next, at nine o'clock in the morning, at the usual place of holding town or freemen's meetings, and after having chosen their presiding officer, then and there to elect by ballot as many delegates as said towns now choose representatives to the General Assembly, who shall meet in convention at the State-house in Hartford, on the fourth Wednesday of August next; and when so convened, shall, if it be deemed by them expedient, proceed to the formation of a constitution of civil government for the people of this State."

Further provision was made that a copy of the constitution, when formed, should be transmitted to each town clerk with instructions to lay it before the people of his town, for their approval and ratification. When ratified by a majority of the qualified voters, assembled in legal meeting, it was to become and remain the supreme law of Connecticut.

In this way was adopted the new Constitution, which abolished the established ecclesiastical system, and gave to all the inhabitants of the State equal civil and religious privileges. They were no longer obliged to enroll themselves among Episcopalians or the "minor sects" to escape taxation for the support of the Standing Order. The last restriction upon the consciences of men was now removed, and religion in every denominational form was left to their free acceptance or deliberate rejection. They might be infidels, and yet enjoy the wholesome protection of Christian laws, without contributing a farthing towards the maintenance of Christianity. It was against the plan of the voluntary system that theologians and politicians of that period protested and strove, and some of them spoke of it as a scheme which would open the flood-gates of ruin on the State. But the experience of half a century has proved the groundlessness of their fears; and the promise of our Divine Lord still continues to be the source of all human encouragement amid heresies and false doctrine, that the Church, being built upon a rock, is so strong that "the gates of hell shall not prevail against it."

CHAPTER XIII.

PROSPERITY OF THE DIOCESE; CORRESPONDENCE AMONG THE CLERGY; AND ELECTION OF A BISHOP.

A. D. 1818–1819.

THE adoption of the new Constitution was of no direct or special advantage to the Church in Connecticut. Many, to escape taxation for the support of the Standing Order, and some on political grounds, had already been drawn within her fold and become interested in her services; but the number of parishes remained the same, and the list of the clergy was not immediately increased. Those who, from any cause, after the adoption of the Constitution, became dissatisfied with the religious society to which they belonged, could "sign off," and still continue of the same faith, without being subjected to personal liability for its maintenance. So far the change in the law was rather unfavorable to the Christian bodies that had gained now and then from the necessities of the case.

The power of Congregationalism, however, as a State religion was destroyed, and the future of the Episcopal Church in Connecticut was brighter for the events of the political revolution. Her clergy and leading laymen knew this, and directed their movements with reference to the accomplishment of great and ennobling results. Several of the parishes, particularly in Fairfield County, prior to this date, had established permanent funds, the interest of which was applied annually to the support of their rectors, and thus the odious system — as many termed it — of taxation for church purposes, was in a measure avoided. These funds were raised in some parishes soon after the erection of their houses of worship, and in others at a later period, and in all they were the result of a feeling that it was wise to provide for religious instruction and the regular administration of the ordinances without imposing any burdens upon posterity. Before the voluntary system had been tried, fears were entertained that the interests of Christianity would suffer, if the civil government did not compel all tax-payers to support some form of public worship, and hence, after the repeal of the law, the disposition to create or enlarge the endowments of the parishes was encouraged. The scheme extended to the Congregationalists as well as to the Episcopalians, and ecclesiastical funds at one time constituted no small item in the banking capital of the State. But those who projected and urged this scheme lived long enough to acknowledge that while it might be prudent in certain cases, it was unwise on the whole to make such provision; for people are not apt to esteem very highly that which costs them nothing. The children of each generation have their duties and responsibilities, and in entering upon their inheritance they should understand that nothing done by their fathers can excuse them from bearing the heat and burden of the day in which they live.

The Annual Convention, which met at Bridgeport in 1818, was attended by twenty-five clergymen and thirty-six lay-delegates. Bishop Hobart was present and repeated the Charge which he delivered eight months before to the clergy of the Diocese of New York, entitled, "The Corruptions of the Church of Rome, contrasted with certain Protestant Errors." It reveals the temper of the times, and contains statements which ought always to be remembered. A single extract will show how firmly he vindicated the primitive institutions of our Church from the aspersion that they "symbolized" with the corruptions of the Papal hierarchy.

"Be not intimidated from avowing and defending the Scriptural and primitive claims of Episcopacy, by the reproach, that you are verging to the Church of Rome. The reproach discovers little acquaintance with genuine Episcopacy, and little knowledge of Papal claims. The Episcopacy which it is the privilege of our Church to enjoy, was the glory of martyrs and confessors, centuries before the Papal domination established itself on the depression of Episcopal prerogatives. When you appeal to the Epistles of Timothy and Titus, in proof of the succession of an order of men to the Apostles, in their powers of ordination and supremacy in government, can you be supposed friendly to the supremacy of the supposed successor of St. Peter, in regard to which these Epistles are totally silent? When you quote the command of the martyr Ignatius, the disciple of an Apostle, 'Let no man do any thing of what belongs to the Church without the Bishop,' can you be accused of vindicating a language with which this holy martyr was unacquainted, 'Let nothing be done but in subjection to the Pope of Rome?' When you appeal to a succession of Fathers, in proof of a fact which appears prominent in every ecclesiastical record, that, as is expressed by the judicious Hooker, the 'outward being of a Church consisted in the having of a Bishop;' must you not necessarily oppose a very different dogma, of which the ancient Fathers knew nothing, that the Pope is the visible head of the Church on earth, and that subjection to his supremacy is a necessary evidence of membership in the Catholic or Universal Church? They who suppose that a primitive Episcopacy, such as our Church enjoys, symbolizes with the Roman hierarchy, do not know, or do not consider the facts, that Papal and Episcopal prerogatives are at variance; that the Episcopal tenet of the succession of Episcopal power from the Apostles, and through them from the divine Head of the Church, is incompatible with the Papal claim, that the Episcopal power, as well as jurisdiction, is derived immediately and solely from the Roman Pontiff; and hence, that the history of the Church affords instances of the attempts of the Pope to depress the order of bishops, and of their resistance to his inordinate claims."[1]

There was nothing in the Constitution of the Connecticut Church at this time which defined the number or order of the Standing Committee, and the Convention of 1818, having first resolved that it should consist of five members, three clergymen and two laymen, elected Rev. Dr. Bronson, Rev. Messrs. Shelton and A. Baldwin, and Samuel W. Johnson and Jonathan Ingersoll. But so great was the reverence in Connecticut, for the old practice of choosing into the Standing Committee clerical members alone, that it

[1] Charge, pp. 18, 19.

was resumed the next year, and but for this exception, there would be no record of a departure from it in the whole history of the Diocese.

The important subject which had been before the Church for five years, still rose above all others; and acceptable as was the provisional administration of Bishop Hobart, it was quite evident that the clergy would not long be satisfied with this temporary supply, but would insist on the election of a permanent Diocesan. The very prosperity of the parishes helped to increase the feeling of uneasiness, and the condition of the Episcopal fund was now such as to warrant the steps which some were eager to take. The most perplexing question was that of the candidate, and the policy of choosing from among the resident clergy of the Diocese was again urged, and a brisk canvassing carried on by those who had their favorite ends to accomplish. Fitness for the office, and claims to it on the score of eminent services rendered to the Church, were freely discussed, and few of the more prominent clergymen escaped a searching scrutiny. But there were leading laymen, and rectors occupying positions of importance, who were not inclined to this policy, and who thought it best to settle the question of the Episcopate by looking outside of the Diocese for a candidate. Their course provoked the displeasure of the other party, and their counsel in the matter was not only studiously avoided, but efforts at first appear to have been made to weaken their influence, or to prevent them from exercising it to much purpose.

The Rev. B. G. Noble, then of Middletown, who took a deep interest in the election of a Bishop, from his partiality for a favorite candidate, wrote the Rector of Trinity Church, New Haven, soon after the Annual Convention at Guilford, and confessed that he had opposed his becoming a member of the Standing Committee, though he rejoiced that he was one of the number entrusted with the reorganization of the Missionary Society. He expressed the hope that "no unpleasant feelings" had been excited in his breast on this account, and stated, moreover, that his efforts to "procure an election did not originate from any dislike of Bishop Hobart."

Mr. Croswell, in his reply, recognized his opposition and admitted that he differed with him respecting the expediency of going into the election of a bishop, mainly for the reason that he believed it impossible then to find a candidate, in or out of the Diocese, who would unite their votes. But the burden of his answer bore upon another point in which he was personally involved.

Since the establishment of the Institution at Cheshire, the utmost diligence had been employed to elevate the standard of literary and theological attainment among those seeking Holy Orders, and as far back as 1806, the clergy in Convocation voted, that no person should be considered a candidate in this Diocese, until he had been examined by the Bishop, or such of his presbyters as he might appoint, and that previous to the examination, the person offering himself must have studied with the Bishop, the Principal of the Academy, or some other presbyter in the Diocese at least one year, if he had received the honors of a college or some incorporated academy, and two years, if he had not received such honors. The aim of this resolution was both to encourage sound learning in the Church and direct theological students to Cheshire; and at the time of its adoption, with two or three exceptions, the clergy of Connecticut were graduates of colleges.

Dr. Bronson, the President of the Standing Committee in 1817, and the Principal of the Episcopal Academy, adhered to the sentiments thus deliberately expressed, and he had "declared his unalterable determination never to sign the testimonials of a candidate who had not received academical honors." It was to this rule as being injudicious and extra-canonical that Mr. Croswell objected, and in the letter just referred to he went on to say, "I consider every such declaration on the part of our *great literary characters*, as a slur upon those who have entered the ministry without the classical attainments required by the canon. I can speak feelingly on this subject. I was admitted to orders by an ecclesiastical body as respectable and learned as our Standing Committee. I came in, under the dispensation, humbly trusting that industry and perseverance might, in some measure, compensate for my other deficiencies. There are probably some others much in the same situation, and I assure you that if they are affected as I am by these sweeping declarations of the learned doctor, they will not very readily place him again in his present situation. I am thus plain, because I think plainness becomes my profession. Nor do I say this confidentially. I have no disposition to disguise my feelings. I stand in nobody's way. I aspire to no ecclesiastical honors. Providence has already placed me in a higher and more responsible station than I could have dared to anticipate. I have no other ambition than that of being useful to my fellow men. I would excite no man's jealousy, nor would I feel jealous of others." [1]

The question of filling the vacancy in the Episcopate was openly discussed at the Annual Convention in Bridgeport, and conspicuous in the discussion were Rev. B. G. Noble and Rev. Menzies Rayner, each having his favorite candidate, and both urging an immediate election. But the minds of the majority were not ready for this step, and finally one of the most prominent lay-members put the question to rest for the time, by introducing a resolution, which was adopted, that "it is inexpedient to proceed to the election of a bishop at this Convention." Still there were many who did not feel that the matter should be left precisely in that shape, and in the afternoon, near the close of the proceedings, another resolution was adopted, satisfactory, no doubt, to all parties, "that the Standing Committee be requested to warn a special meeting of the Convention to be holden in the city of New Haven, on the first Wednesday of June next, to proceed to the election of a bishop."

The day thus designated was also the day fixed by the Constitution for the annual meeting, and hence opportunity was given, in the mean time, for fair inquiry and a dispassionate consideration of the claims of the Diocese and of the merits of different candidates. The diversity of sentiment upon this subject was not so great as to be any hinderance to the progress of the parishes. It rather kept alive a spirit of watchfulness, and the gradual inroads of the Church upon the leading denomination of the State were such as to quicken the zeal of its ministers. A

1 Annals of Trinity Parish, MS.

detailed account of the policy pursued to check this current of feeling towards Episcopacy will be given further on in the pages of the present work.

As the time approached for the meeting of the Convention at New Haven, the inexpediency of attempting to choose a bishop from the clergy of the Diocese became more apparent. No one among them could go into the canvass with any prospect of securing a respectable majority, for age or other disqualifications seemed to stand in the way of all. The old were too old for the cares and trials of the office, and the young were too young, and lacked the needed wisdom and experience. A few of the most influential laity in New Haven came to a settled determination, in case the policy of electing a resident clergyman was pressed, to sustain the Rev. Bethel Judd, then Rector of St. James's Church, New London, as better fitted, on the whole, for the office than any presbyter in the Diocese. While his piety was unquestioned, and his views of the ministry and government of the Church perfectly sound, he was especially distasteful to those who had cherished the tone of early Connecticut churchmanship; for he made no secret of differing from his brethren on certain speculative points of theology, and leaned to what he himself was accustomed to term a "moderate Calvinism." Neither his style of preaching nor his manner of conducting the public services of the Church were particularly attractive, but these defects were disregarded by his friends, in consideration of his other qualifications; and those who had brought him forward as a candidate, openly avowed their intention of pressing his election, if the policy of choosing from the Diocese was not relinquished.

Whether the knowledge of this determination affected the result or not, it is certain that the clergy soon changed their ground, and began to inquire for a suitable person abroad to elect into the vacant Episcopate. Their attention was directed to the Rev. T. C. Brownell, Assistant Minister of Trinity Church, New York, and immediately a correspondence was commenced to ascertain from those who might know him best his character and fitness for the high office. Among other letters of a confidential nature was one written by Mr. Croswell to Bishop Hobart, and a short extract from the reply of that discerning prelate will show how far his advice contributed to the end in view. It was right in the clergy to consult him, for he had provisional charge of the Diocese and was concerned about its future prosperity. "My opinion is," said he, "that the person you mention will serve, if he be elected, with provision for his adequate support. And speaking *prudently*, I do think he will answer exceedingly well. The more I know of him, the better I think of him."[1]

The Rev. B. Judd also wrote to the New Haven Rector in strong commendation of the proposed candidate, and added, "If I did not think my want of popularity would prejudice the contemplated election of Mr. Brownell, I would warmly advocate it; but presuming that silent approbation will be most favorable to him, I have thought best to take this course. You are at liberty, however, to say that the election of Mr. Brownell has the approbation of your friend and brother in Christ."[2]

The Convention which assembled at New Haven on

[1] MS. Letter, Feb. 20, 1819. [2] Annals of Trinity Parish, MS.

the morning of the second of June, 1819, was the largest since the organization of the Diocese, being composed of thirty-three clergymen and fifty-four lay delegates. Of the latter, twenty-one were from New Haven County, sixteen from Fairfield County, seven from Litchfield County, five from Hartford, Granby, and Middletown, and the remainder from towns east of the Connecticut River. Bishop Hobart was not present on the first day of the session, and the sermon at the opening services was preached by the Rev. Frederick Holcomb. After the usual recess, the Convention came together at 3 o'clock P. M., in the Senate Chamber of the old State House, and when the preliminary business had been disposed of, the two orders separated for the purpose of proceeding to the election of a bishop — the clergy retiring to Trinity Church. The venerable Dr. Mansfield, of Derby, verging upon a century, met his brethren for the last time on this occasion, and presided over their deliberations during the pendency of the ballot. The Rev. Thomas C. Brownell was duly and unanimously elected; and the result was communicated to the lay delegates, who postponed their action until 9 o'clock the next morning, when they reassembled, and by a unanimous vote concurred in the choice of the clergy.

Thus happily was terminated the long struggle to fill the vacant Episcopate of Connecticut. For six years the subject had occupied the attention of the Church, and though the fund, in the meantime, had been nursed and increased, it was not yet large enough to yield an income which would provide a competent salary for the Diocesan. The committee appointed to wait upon the Bishop elect, consisting of Rev. Messrs. Shelton, B. Judd, Wainwright, and Marsh, and Messrs. Samuel W. Johnson, Daniel Putnam, and Nathan Smith had a difficult and delicate office to discharge. The Convention had not formally instructed them to offer any definite salary. They were to solicit Mr. Brownell's acceptance, "and to adopt such measures as in their opinion should be deemed necessary for his due establishment in the office of Bishop of this Diocese."

But he occupied a prominent position in the city of New York, with an ample income for the reasonable wants of his family, and it was not expected that he would relinquish it for the dignified post tendered him by the Church in Connecticut, without the prospect of an adequate support. After correspondence and a personal interview, the committee stated that fifteen hundred dollars per annum had been secured for his maintenance, and in the name of the Convention, they requested him to accept it, and "take the Episcopal charge of the Diocese, as soon as consecration could be effected." In his communication, signifying to the committee his acceptance of the office, Mr. Brownell added, "With respect to pecuniary support, I do not feel any great solicitude. I have no doubt but the Diocese will cheerfully take upon itself the maintenance of my family; and till the Bishop's Fund is adequate to this object, I think it proper to reserve to myself the right of deriving any necessary aid from the performance of such parish or missionary service as may not be incompatible with my duties to the Diocese at large.

"I shall be ready to enter upon the duties of the

office to which I have been elected as soon after the necessary arrangements for my consecration are completed, as my domestic affairs will permit. And I most fervently beseech the Great Head of the Church to grant his blessing on our humble exertions for the spiritual welfare of the Diocese of Connecticut."

Here it would be proper to introduce some notice of the previous life of the Bishop elect. But an autobiography, in the form of a letter to Bishop Williams, never before published, and kindly given for use in this volume, covers that period so well, that without adding a phrase, or altering a sentence or a word, it will be allowed to stand by itself, as it deserves, and furnish the matter for the next chapter.

On the second day of the session of this Convention Bishop Hobart delivered an address, and admitted Joseph M. Gilbert, a graduate of Yale College, to the order of Deacons. A resolution was adopted, empowering the Treasurer "to call upon the delinquent parishes to pay the sums due from them respectively to the Bishop's Fund, or secure the same with interest annually on or before the 1st day of October." Bishop Hobart had been paid the sum of five hundred dollars as a remuneration for his expenses in visiting the Diocese previously to 1818, and a like amount was appropriated to him for the expense of his visitations in that year. The aggregate of these sums was about the annual income of the Fund, and the Convention could not meet its engagements to the new Diocesan unless the parishes responded with promptitude and cheerfulness to the appeal of the Treasurer, and bore their fair proportion of the common burden.

The vigor with which the work of the Christian

Knowledge Society was undertaken promised success. The receipts from all sources for the past year were about nine hundred dollars, and three itinerant missionaries had been sent on tours of observation into the most neglected portions of the State, and their reports showed the need and utility of their services. "Though the Society," said the Directors in closing the annual account of their proceedings, "is in its infancy, though its receipts have been small, and though its operations have not yet been perfectly systematized, yet it cannot be doubted that its effects have already proved highly beneficial to the interests of the Church and the cause of religion. They indulge the pleasing hope, therefore, that it will still receive the fostering care of the Convention, and that the friends of the Church, both clergy and laity, will afford it their liberal support and encouragement."

It has been mentioned in a former chapter, that, during the progress of political events in the State, some persons were led to declare themselves Episcopalians who proved of no great advantage to the Church. They failed to adorn it with the fruits of piety, though they contributed freely of their means to the support of individual parishes. A vein of secret Universalism ran through the minds of a few of the laity, and it was suspected that one or two of the clergy entertained opinions in sympathy with the same doctrine. The effect was perceptible upon their congregations, and instead of growth, a decline in godliness was the consequence. The statistics of Christ Church, Norwich, as reported in 1819, gave a total of forty communicants only, and yet in that place and "parts adjacent," seventy families had recently conformed to the Church. The Rector, now far advanced in life, had not been present at a convention of the Diocese but once in ten years, and if his views, tending to the opposite extreme from Calvinism, helped to produce this apparent indifference to the deliberations of his brethren, he still remained at his post — a quiet and cheerful sentinel, whom his flock had learned to love and honor for the virtues of a meek, benevolent, and gentle nature. In his own account of the number of his communicants, he said it was always small, "owing to the prejudices of education, which he labored faithfully, but ineffectually, to overcome."[1]

[1] Rev. S. B. Paddock's *Historical Discourse*, 1840.

CHAPTER XIV.

AUTOBIOGRAPHY OF THE BISHOP ELECT.

HARTFORD, May 22d, 1858.

RIGHT REV. AND DEAR BROTHER: In fulfilment of my promise, I now give you a sketch of the principal events of my life, previous to my consecration to the Episcopate.

I was born at Westport, in the State of Massachusetts, on the 19th day of October, in the year 1779. I am the oldest son of the late Sylvester and Mercy Brownell, and the first born of their eleven children — five sons and six daughters.

My father was the fourth in descent from George Brownell, who with a cousin by the name of Graves, purchased from the Narraganset Indians a tract of land lying on the seacoast, extending westward from the Acoaxset River, to the border of the Rhode Island Colony. The farm on which my father resided has continued in possession of the family from the time of its original purchase, to within the last thirty years, when he removed from that place to a farm which he owned in the town of Little Compton, Rhode Island. He died at the latter place, about eighteen years ago, in the eighty-second year of his age. My mother had died about three years earlier, at the same advanced period of life.

Of the lineage of my mother, Baylies in his "Memoirs of the Plymouth Colony" (vol. ii. p. 140), has the following note: —

"Thomas Church, the eldest son of the Warrior (Col. Benjamin Church) left children; one of whom was the late Hon. Thomas Church, one of the assistants of the Government of Rhode Island, and colonel of one of the Rhode Island regiments at the commencement of the Revolutionary War. He was born at Little Compton. In the latter years of his life, he removed to Dighton, in Massachusetts, of which town he was a representative in the General Court. He died there. One of his daughters married the Hon. Sylvester Brownell of Westport, Massachusetts, and is the mother of the Right Rev. Thomas Church Brownell, Bishop of Connecticut."

In my early life, I received, as a farmer's son, a common country school education. At the age of fifteen, when no schoolmaster could be obtained for the district, I consented to act as schoolmaster myself, for several months, and succeeded in securing the respect of my former schoolmates.

About three years after this, with the approbation of my parents, I spent a few months with our clergyman, the Rev. Dr. Shepard, in the study of English grammar, and the rudiments of the Latin language. In pursuance of his advice, and with the approval of my parents, I resolved on obtaining a collegiate education; and became a student of "Bristol Academy," at Taunton, under the Rev. Dr. Daggett, as Principal.

In September, of the next year, 1800, I entered as a member of the Freshman class in the College at Providence, then under the presidency of the Rev. Dr. Maxcy.

In the summer of 1802, at the close of my Sophomore year, the Doctor was appointed to the presidency of Union College, Schenectady; and having formed a strong attachment to him, I accompanied him and his family to their new residence, and became a member of the Junior class in Union College. At the end of two years I was graduated there, at the head of my class, with the "Valedictory."

It had been, for some time, my intention to devote myself to the study of theology, at the conclusion of my collegiate course; and it was the earnest wish of my parents that I should do so. I had, however, begun to find difficulties in the Calvinistic system of theology, in which I had been reared; but resolved to make myself better acquainted with it, before coming to a decision. The Rev. Dr. Nott was then a distinguished clergyman of the Presbyterian Church, at Albany, and kindly consented to take me under his tuition. He had the faculty of presenting these doctrines under a somewhat mitigated form; but advised me to study well the early history of the Church; and for this purpose he put into my hands the "Ecclesiastical History" of Mosheim. After reading a portion of this work, I enquired of my instructor whether there was any more minute history of the *early organization of the Christian Church;* and he referred me to Echard's "History of the first four Centuries," which he had in his library. I read these volumes with deep interest. At the conclusion, I remarked to my instructor that, if the author was correct, the first organization of the Christian Church must have been more like that of the Episcopal Communion, than either the Presbyterian or Congregational denominations. He appeared to admit this fact, but seemed to regard it as a matter of little importance. It was, however, not so with me; and wishing to read further on the subject, I enquired what work he could recommend? He jocularly replied, "Go to Dr. Beasley; he can tell you." I took the advice in earnest; and introducing myself to the Rev. Doctor, enquired if he could recommend to me any approved work on the first organization of the Christian Church? He went to his library, and bringing out the work of Archbishop Potter on that subject, kindly offered me the loan of it. The perusal of this work was like the opening of a new world to me. I read the whole with deep attention. It unfolded to me a new aspect of Christianity. The survey afforded to me unspeakable relief; but it was necessarily attended with many regrets. I had no near relation, and no intimate friend, belonging to the Episcopal Church; and I seemed to be left alone in the world, in regard to my religious sympathies.

It was now autumn; and I determined to return to my home, for the winter, and to take time for a decision in regard to my future course.

About this time, Dr. Maxcy, the President of Union College, had been called to the Presidency of the University at Columbia, South Carolina, and the Rev. Dr. Nott was elected to fill his place. Soon after he had accepted, and entered on his new duties, I was appointed tutor in the Latin and Greek languages, in the institution. After due reflection, I decided to accept the station, and entered on the discharge of its duties on the 5th of April, 1805.

To sustain myself reputably, in my new position, I was now obliged to devote all my leisure hours to the study of the ancient classics.

At the Commencement of 1807, I was elected Professor of "Belles Lettres and Moral Philosophy." A new department of learning was now opened to me, which necessarily occupied the greater portion of my thoughts and of my studies.

Two years later, I was again requested to change my professorship, and course of study. The sciences of Chemistry and Mineralogy were then in their infancy in this country. But Professor Silliman, of Yale College, had now returned from Europe, with an imposing chemical apparatus. A fine cabinet of minerals had been procured for that institution from Colonel Gibbs; and these acquisitions had given to Yale College an imposing position, which could not fail to stimulate the exertions of kindred institutions. Accordingly, a department of Chemistry and Mineralogy was established in Union College, at the Commencement, in 1809, and I was appointed the first Professor; with leave to spend a year in Europe, in the examination of kindred institutions.

In the autumn, I sailed for England; having been appointed, by President Madison, as "Bearer of Despatches" to Mr. Pinckney, the American Minister in London, and to General Lyman, the United States Consul General. It was during the famous Embargo; and the only conveyance to be obtained was by the *British Packet* from New York to Falmouth. It was also during the famous "restrictive system" of Bonaparte, and there was allowed no communication between England and the Continent of Europe.

My travels and researches were, therefore, necessarily confined to Great Britain and Ireland. I had taken letters of introduction to Sir Humphrey Davy,

Dr. Singer, Dr. Babington, Dr. Marcet, William Allen, and other distinguished scientific gentlemen in London, and found a free access to their cabinets, laboratories, and lectures. My winter was thus spent very industriously in London.

In the spring, I had resolved on a tour through the interior of England, Scotland, and Ireland; and a well-educated young gentleman of New York, who had been my fellow-passenger on ship-board, and fellow-boarder in London, volunteered to accompany me. Our object was not so much to see the large towns, as to examine the agricultural, manufacturing, and mining operations of the country; and to effect this end we resolved to travel on foot. Though such a mode of travelling, by gentlemen in our situation, was then a novelty, we found no reason to regret our decision. On one occasion, indeed, in an obscure part of Scotland, and when separated from our credentials, we were arrested for a robbery and murder which had been committed in the vicinity; yet we found but little difficulty in making our real character understood, and were speedily released.

We spent a considerable time in exploring the caverns and mines of Derbyshire; and in visiting the manufactories of Worcester, Manchester, and Birmingham; and in admiring the lake and mountain scenery of Cumberland and Westmoreland. We passed through the southern part of Scotland to Port Patrick; and from thence crossed over to Donahaddie, in Ireland. After visiting Lough Neagh, and the Giant's Causeway, we returned by the eastern coast of Ireland to Belfast, and thence by packet, again to Port Patrick, in Scotland. From the latter place we pursued our way along the western coast to the city of Glasgow. In this latter place we spent two or three weeks, during which time I had free access to the laboratories of Dr. Ure and Dr. Cleghorn. From Glasgow we proceeded to the city of Edinburgh. Here we spent a few weeks in examining the most interesting objects of the city and its environs. I found every facility in visiting the laboratories, and attending the lectures of the distinguished chemists and mineralogists, who have added so much to the fame of the ancient capital of the kingdom.

Our peregrinations on foot terminated in this city. It had come to be time for our return to America. We took the mail stage for Liverpool; from whence we embarked in a merchant ship for New York. After a pleasant passage to that city, I reached my home at Union College, just in time to commence my course of chemical instruction at the opening of the Fall term.

I had brought with me a considerable cabinet of minerals, and sufficient chemical apparatus to enable me to illustrate the principles of chemical science to advantage. Thus had passed one of the most busy and eventful years of my life; and I now entered on my course of instruction with zeal and industry.

The year after my return from Europe, on the 6th of August, 1811, I was married to Charlotte Dickinson, of the city of Lansingburgh, N. Y. She was daughter of Tertullus Dickinson, once a partner in mercantile business with Col. Beverly Robinson, of New York, and her mother was a daughter of Dr. Huggeford, an eminent physician of the same city.

My wife, and nearly all her connections, were of

the Episcopal Church; and we were married by the Rev. Dr. Butler, Rector of St. Paul's Church, Troy. I was thus, for the first time, brought into intimate relations with Episcopalians.

Previous to this, I had become convinced of the historical and Scriptural grounds of Episcopacy, yet I had not felt the necessity of changing my church relations. But I was now led to give a more particular examination to this subject. At the ensuing Easter, I took a pew in St. George's Church, Schenectady, under the Rectorship of the Rev. Dr. Stebbins. On the 5th of September, 1813, I was baptized in that church by the Rector. Shortly afterwards I was confirmed by the Bishop, and was admitted to the Holy Communion of the Church.

It will seem strange that I had not received Christian Baptism at an earlier period. The fact of the delay is to be accounted for, though not justified, by the state of society in which I was reared.

The community in which my early years were passed, were either Quakers, or Calvinistic Congregationalists. My parents attended public worship with the latter denomination; and though they had a distance of five miles to travel, and over bad roads, they were very punctual in their attendance, and were careful to provide a conveyance for a good portion of their family. Though always exemplary in their moral character, they were not technically "members of the Church." But when they came to be about forty years old, an extensive "revival" prevailed in their vicinity; they became subjects of it, and were then baptized, with all their younger children. I was at that time some thirty miles from home, at Bristol

Academy, and on the point of entering college. I may add, too, that it was then considered almost an unheard of thing that a person twenty years of age should receive baptism, unless he was the subject of some prevailing *revival*, and had, as it was termed, "experienced a change of heart;" a change which was supposed to be sudden, if not instantaneous, and wrought by the irresistible operation of the Holy Ghost.

Soon after my baptism, confirmation, and admission to the Holy Communion of the Church, I began to devote my leisure hours to the study of theology, as it is taught in the standard Church works — not, however, with a view to the relinquishment of my college avocations, but in the hope that I might add to my usefulness by receiving Holy Orders, and affording a Sunday supply to some vacant parishes in my vicinity.

On the eleventh of April, 1816, I was admitted to the Holy Order of Deacons, in Trinity Church, New York, by the Rt. Rev. Bishop Hobart; and soon afterwards, in the same place, I was admitted by him to the Holy Order of the Priesthood.

During the ensuing summer and autumn, I officiated every Sunday in vacant parishes within twenty miles of Schenectady. In the early part of the following spring, I was attacked with a severe disease, which settled on my lungs, and disqualified me for labor through the ensuing summer. In the autumn, my physician advised me to spend the coming winter in a milder climate, and I determined on a journey through the Southern States. Accordingly, I proceeded, by easy stages, as far south as Georgia; spending a few days in each principal city by the way, and devoting four or five weeks each to Charleston and Savannah. My health was, all the time, steadily improving, and I found myself able to preach at least a portion of nearly every Sunday.

Returning to New York in the spring, with recovered health, I spent a Sunday there, and preached in Trinity and St. Paul's Churches. There was then a vacancy in the ministry of Trinity parish, occasioned by the recent defection of the Rev. Dr. How. Shortly after returning to my home in Schenectady, I received an invitation to fill that vacancy. The overture was altogether unexpected. But as I received private letters from the Bishop, who was Rector of the parish, and also from his two assistants, assuring me that my acceptance would be agreeable to them personally, I decided on a change of occupation, after the ensuing College Commencement, if my health should then appear to be sufficiently reëstablished.

Accordingly, in the ensuing month of August, I entered on the duties of Assistant Minister of Trinity Church, New York, and removed my family to that city on the following October.

My residence in the city of New York was of brief duration, but was, in all respects, agreeable. I was received with great cordiality by the Bishop, and by my brethren of the clergy, and with all kindness by the people among whom I was called to minister. I supposed I had then entered upon the labors of my entire subsequent life.

But, in the following June, I was waited on by a delegation from Connecticut, informing me of my election to the Episcopal charge of that Diocese.

Such an event was altogether unexpected by me. I had received no previous intimation of it; and having entered the sacred ministry so late in life, there would have been but little probability that I should ever be called to one of its highest stations. But though such an office was not to be sought, nor expected, it was not to be hastily declined.

After seeking the Divine direction, after consultation with my Bishop and other friends, and under assurances of the unanimity of my election, I decided on accepting the solemn responsibilities of the office to which I was called.

I was accordingly consecrated to the Episcopal office, in Trinity Church, New Haven, on the twenty-seventh day of October, in the year of our Lord one thousand eight hundred and nineteen, by the Rt. Rev. William White, D. D., Bishop of Pennsylvania, the Rt. Rev. John Henry Hobart, D. D., Bishop of New York, and the Rt. Rev. Alexander Viets Griswold, D. D., Bishop of the Eastern Diocese.

With what degree of faithfulness, and with what success, I have fulfilled the duties of the sacred office, it becomes not me to speak. I entertain a most grateful sense of the indulgence and kindness with which my imperfect services have been received by the Diocese.

Commending the people of the Diocese, and yourself, as my assistant and successor, to the keeping of Almighty God,

I remain your affectionate friend and brother,

THOMAS CHURCH BROWNELL

RT. REV. BISHOP WILLIAMS.

CHAPTER XV.

THE CHURCH DEFENDED; COVERT ATTACKS; "SERIOUS CALL;" AND "SOBER APPEAL."

A. D. 1819.

It was natural for an opponent to watch with some degree of alarm the prosperity of the Church. But the part they sustained, during the high political excitements through which the State had just passed, rendered Episcopalians particularly obnoxious to the Congregational ministers, and new attempts were made to weaken or destroy their influence. "An association of gentlemen" was formed professedly for the purpose of "inculcating the doctrines which have ever prevailed in the great body of the Congregational and Presbyterian Churches;" but really, as one of its members incautiously avowed, "to write down the Episcopal Church in Connecticut." The question of Orders was revived, and among the first fruits of this association was a doctrinal tract entitled, "Plain reasons for relying on Presbyterian ordination." It was the third in the series and extensively circulated, and triumphantly put into the hands of churchmen as an unanswerable argument. Though written with some degree of cant and bitterness, mingled with much affected candor and liberality, the tract advanced everything that could be embraced in so short a compass, in favor of Presbyterian ordination, and the subject of it was regarded by the author, who withheld his name, as of "the highest practical importance." He labored to show among other things that the succession in the Episcopal Church is Presbyterian; that all ministers of the Gospel are successors of the Apostles, and that any claim on the part of bishops to "a superior rank is nothing less than usurpation."

The pamphlet was a reproduction of the same reasonings which had often been met, but like every former attempt of the kind, it was destined to enjoy but a temporary triumph. It called forth a very able and conclusive answer from an Episcopal clergyman in Connecticut,[1] under the title of "Presbyterian Ordination Doubtful," in two parts, the first of which contained the Scripture evidences on the matter in controversy, and the other the historical testimony. The Society for the Promotion of Christian Knowledge had already published an address on the primitive government of the Christian Church as proved by the Holy Scriptures, in which the difference between Episcopalians and Presbyterians was fairly stated, and the claims of a threefold ministry modestly but firmly vindicated. Mr. Judd's work, two thousand copies of which were published and distributed by this society, was clear in its reasonings and courteous in its style. In no single instance was he drawn by the provocation of his opponent into any undue warmth or the least degree of asperity.

The learning displayed in this controversy was not so great, and the researches made by the respective

1 Bethel Judd. The author of the doctrinal tract to which he replied was Luther Hart, the Congregational minister at Plymouth.

authors were not so extensive as in the earlier and more notable controversy on the same subject between Dr. Miller, a Presbyterian divine of the city of New York, and Dr. Bowden. In the latter case Dr. Miller challenged to the onset, and wrote his " Letters concerning the Constitution and Order of the Christian Ministry," at his leisure and in his best and most fascinating style. He assailed Episcopacy in a way well fitted to satisfy those who had rather lean on others than think and search for themselves. At that period the writings of the Fathers were but little known in this country, and their testimony was locked up in Greek and Latin, where few were able to find it or to verify another's citations. Dr. Bowden was a master in patristic learning, and stepped forward to vindicate an abused and calumniated church, as well as to show how much there really was in the history of the first and second centuries to disprove the doctrine of ministerial parity. In replying to these " Letters," he sometimes exceeded the bounds of a gentle nature and wrote with severity, especially when he detected his opponent in mutilating and misrepresenting the Fathers, and making them to say things they never dreamed of, and to bear testimony against truths which they had spent their whole lives in defending.

Reference to Dr. Miller's work, as authority for the historical evidence in favor of ministerial parity, was made by the writer of the doctrinal tract, in a rejoinder to " Presbyterian Ordination Doubtful," and at a later period zealous champions arose in other quarters and lent their support to the common cause of crushing " Episcopal claims." In 1822, five years after the author had gone to his rest, and nearly twenty since the controversy was first started, James Wilson, a Congregational minister in Providence, R. I., published in a pamphlet of one hundred pages, an elaborate "Review of the Letters of the late Rev. John Bowden, D. D.;" and though not fully concurring in the Presbyterian idea of ordination, he left as much unsettled as ever, the question of what he was pleased to call "Congregational Episcopacy."

The friends of the Church in Connecticut were puzzled at this time to know precisely on what ground the Congregationalists meant to rest. In seeking shelter under the standard of Presbyterianism, they virtually abandoned their own system in regard to a valid ministry, for according to this no lineal succession from the great Head of the Church is necessary. According to this system, our Lord's commission to the Apostles confers full and complete authority to preach the Gospel and administer the sacraments, on every person who is set apart for that purpose, either by "delegated brethren," or "ruling elders." The earliest divines of New England, as it has already been seen,[1] were troubled about the matter of lay-ordination. Dr. Stiles, President of Yale College, referred to this in his Election Sermon before the General Assembly, May, 1783. He seems to have used *Congregational* and *Presbyterian* as synonymous terms; and visions of the future greatness of the body with which he was connected floated before his mind, and emboldened him in his ecstasy to make assertions which do not place him among the most sagacious and far-seeing men of his age.

[1] Vol. i. p. 40.

"When we look forward," said he, "and see this country increased to forty or fifty millions, while we see all the religious sects increased into respectable bodies, we shall doubtless find the united body of the *Congregational, Consociated, and Presbyterian* Churches, making an equal figure with any of them; or to say the least, to be of such magnitude as to number, that it will be to no purpose for other sects to meditate their eversion. This, indeed, is enterprised, but it will end in a sisyphean labor. There is the greatest prospect that we shall become thirty out of forty millions, and while the avenues to civil improvement and public honors will here be equally open to all sects, so it will be no dishonor hereafter to be a Presbyterian, or of the religious denomination which will probably ever make the most distinguished figure in this great republic. And hereafter when the world shall behold us a respectable part of Christendom, they may be induced by curiosity, with calmness and candor to examine whether something of Christianity may not really be found among us." [1]

From this statement, President Stiles went on to say, "Our churches are as completely reformed and as well modelled as can be expected till the millennium." He devoted ten pages of his extraordinary sermon to the matter of ordination, and in the history of it in New England, which it came within his province to give, he made some admissions or confessions that would be spurned by those who do not believe a lineal succession from Christ and His Apostles necessary to a valid ministry.

"The invalidity of our *ordinations* is objected against

[1] Sermon, pp. 57, 58.

us, and so of consequence the invalidity of all our official administrations. And now that we are upon the matter, give me leave to exhibit a true, though summary state of it, as the result of a very full, laborious, and thorough inquiry. It was the mistaken opinion of some of our first ministers in New England (than whom there never was a more learned collection, for they embosomed all the theological and ecclesiastical erudition of all ages), it was, I say, their opinion, that the power of ordination of all church officers was in the church, by their elders. They well knew, from ecclesiastical and Scripture antiquity, that the power of election was there; and they judged ordination the lesser act; but their great reason was, that the church might not be controlled by any exterior authority, whether Episcopal or Presbyterial, and so no more be harassed by Bishops' courts, or any other similar tribunals. . . .

"Immediately upon publishing the Cambridge platform, 1648, our brethren in England remonstrated against allowing lay ordination. They alleged that we had no example in Scripture, and not only that it was safest to proceed in this way, but that it was the only Scriptural ground. These arguments convinced our fathers, and they immediately set about to remedy the practice, which had hitherto, providentially, wrought no mischief, as the body of the pastors had been ordained by the Bishops." [1]

Lay ordination, in the judgment of President Stiles, "was almost the only error of moment," which the ministers of New England fell into, in the first century of its settlement; but he seemed to think that even

[1] Sermon, pp. 59, 62.

this irregularity was not to be condemned, since it "was done by the advice and under the inspection" of those whom English bishops had ordained to the work of the ministry. These bishops did not intend, however, according to his own admission, to "communicate ordaining powers," and every presbyter of the Church of England, in his vow of submission to Episcopal authority, made when he answered to the questions in the Ordinal, gave a very solemn pledge that he would exercise no such powers. The theory, therefore, of a lineal succession from Christ and the Apostles, maintained in this way, was a virtual surrender of the principle of lay ordination. It was worth nothing to the cause of Congregationalism, and it did not help the Presbyterian idea of ministerial parity. But Wilson in his "Review of the Letters" of Bowden, adhered to it, and denied what he found stated in the work which he was criticising, that "In New England, there have been numerous instances of lay ordination." Speaking of her Independent Churches, he said, "Nor does it distinctly appear,[1] that more than two lay ordinations, actually such, ever occurred in those churches; the first was at Woburn, Massachusetts, in 1642, and the last at Stratford, in Connecticut, in 1665. This last instance was the lay ordination of Israel Chauncey."[2] At the same time, he frankly admitted that appearances sanctioned in some degree the statement of Dr. Bowden, because the installment or the introduction of ministers, al-

[1] *Review*, etc., p. 89.

[2] "His ordination was in the Independent mode. It has been the tradition that Elder Brinsmaid laid on hands with a leather mitten. Hence it has been termed the leather mitten ordination." — Trumbull's *Hist. of Conn.*, vol. i. p. 464.

ready ordained, into the pastoral charge of a particular congregation, was performed by lay-brethren, and this, from the beginning, was termed ordination. In establishing their rules of ecclesiastical polity, the Puritans could not quite forget the obligation due to English bishops, and still they acted as if there could be no true religion unless they kept themselves "out of sight of mitres and the purple."

The controversy upon the subject of the ministry was not yet closed, when another attack was made upon the Church, different from all former ones, and encouraged by men of the highest standing and responsibility in the Congregational ranks. A pamphlet of twenty-four pages entitled, "A Serious Call to those who are without the Pale of the Episcopal Church. By a Consistent Churchman," was printed and freely circulated in Connecticut, where it was designed to produce its sinister effect. It was not one of the doctrinal tracts referred to in the beginning of this chapter; but it was read to the "associate gentlemen," who relished it highly and advised its publication. No imprint was given, and the hypocrisy of the title-page was in keeping with the misrepresentation and irony of the whole pamphlet. The author professed to be a "Consistent Churchman," though he was a rigid Congregationalist,[1] and penned his work with the deliberate intention of misleading his readers. He addressed it to Presbyterians, Congregationalists, Baptists, Methodists, Quakers, and all of every denomination who do not belong to

[1] Rev. Bennet Tyler, then the Congregational minister at South Britain, in Southbury, and afterwards the first President of the Theological Institute of Connecticut, located at East Windsor Hill.

the Episcopal Church; and he began in this startling manner: —

"Fellow travellers to eternity: I come to you on a momentous errand; and I beg your patient and candid attention to my message. You may, perhaps, wish to know who I am, and what claims I have to your regard; but this is not the time to gratify an idle curiosity. If I were passing your dwellings in the dead of night, and saw them in flames, while you were quietly reposing in sleep, I should not stop to tell you my name or place of abode, till I saw you safe from your danger. This is but a faint emblem of the danger from which I am now to exhort you to flee. Let it suffice, then, to say (and here let your curiosity cease), that I am a member of the EPISCOPAL CHURCH, the only Church on earth; and my message is, to inform you, that you must become members of the same, or be lost for ever. You may be startled at such a suggestion; but count me not your enemy because I tell you the truth. The most unwelcome is sometimes the most friendly message; and if what I say shall cause pain, it is the pain inflicted by a faithful surgeon, who wounds only to heal. If you are all in the broad road to destruction, it is certainly high time that you knew it; and he who sounds a timely alarm in your ears, acts the part of the most unfeigned friendship. If it be a fact, that while you remain out of the Church you are aliens from the commonwealth of Israel and strangers from the covenants of promise, having no hope, and without God in the world; surely, no means should be left untried to effect your conversion."

The author professed to derive support for his

premises from two sources — the Word of God; and the writings of Bishop Hobart, Rev. Thomas Y. How, D. D., and Rev. Menzies Rayner. When he had made all his citations and been liberal in pathetic appeals, he was not content until he added an appendix, containing animadversions upon the conduct of inconsistent churchmen. The conclusion of the pamphlet accords with the spirit of the introduction.

"Let the syren song of charity, then, be sung no longer. Let all the ministers of our Church assume a tone of consistency. Let them no longer crouch to their adversaries, nor tremble at the epithet of bigot. Let them not be afraid or ashamed to proclaim upon the house-top, that out of the Episcopal Church, there is no salvation. Let the pulpit thunder and the press groan, 'EPISCOPACY OR PERDITION.' Let the sound ring from house to house, from neighborhood to neighborhood, from town to town. Let it be wafted upon every breeze, and echo from every hill. Let it be proclaimed in the highways and hedges, in the street and at the market, in the tavern and the grog shop, 'EPISCOPACY OR PERDITION;' and no doubt the poor Presbyterians and Baptists and Methodists will be frightened out of their wits, and rush into the Church by scores and by hundreds. The Saybrook Platform will be cast to the moles and the bats, no man will dare have a Bible without a Prayer-Book by its side, and at no distant period, as Dr. How predicts, Episcopalians will be the predominant sect in Connecticut."

The vein of irony, running through the whole production, was so well concealed, that a careless reader, dipping into its pages here and there and not examining the authorities cited, might be led to think the

"Consistent Churchman" was in sober earnest. Some persons[1] were undoubtedly deceived in this way until the scheme was exposed.

By a chain of providential circumstances the Rector of Trinity Church, New Haven (Rev. Mr. Croswell), became acquainted with the fact that the proof sheets had been revised and corrected by his neighbor, the Pastor of the First Ecclesiastical Society, and that the publisher was a Congregational deacon, who sustained intimate relations to this pastor. Scarcely had the work come from the press before he was ready with an answer in the shape of "A Sober Appeal to the Christian Public." Called out on this occasion by a sense of duty to the interests of religion, he spoke with severity of the obvious design of the pamphlet, which was "to slander and defame the ministers and members of the Protestant Episcopal Church — to misrepresent its principles and doctrines — and to ridicule and disparage its ordinances." He vindicated the reputation of Bishop Hobart both as a divine and a man, and pronounced the extracts from his publications to be "garbled, distorted, or disjointed," and not warranting the inferences drawn by a writer who "opened the first page of his work with an egregious falsehood." He characterized the following paragraph relating to baptism as "a vulgar profanity — a cold-blooded mockery in its style and manner, which none but the worst of infidels have ever equalled." And surely it is something beyond mere burlesque.

"No doubt hell is paved with the skulls of infants, for

1 The story is told of a poor post-rider — a zealous churchman — who thinking the *Serious Call* was meant to be serious, filled his saddle-bags with the pamphlets and scattered them along on his route into the country, in the full belief that he was doing the Church good service.

no other reason but because they were never sprinkled by an Episcopal Priest!! Oh! it is enough to chill one's blood in his veins, and to make every tender hearted mother *run crazy*, to think how many poor infants must be eternally miserable when they might have been so easily saved. O ye parents, how can you suffer your children to remain unregenerate! Fly with them to the Church. Have them baptized without delay. Then, they will be *children of God and inheritors of the kingdom of heaven.*"[1]

Mr. Croswell referred to the rules of the Congregational order, prohibiting the baptism of infants, except in certain cases, but in his opinion, they did not justify the ridiculing of those, "who, acting as ministers of Christ, conceive themselves bound by *his* command to baptize all who are presented for that purpose, agreeably to the rules of the Gospel."

He might have turned back to a period when there was a diversity of opinion among Congregationalists about the proper subjects of baptism. One hundred years before, the "half-way covenant system," as it was called, had occasioned strife and contention in the colony, and even towards the end of the eighteenth century, some ministers of the Standing Order, with their churches, fell under the censure of their brethren for adhering to it and inclining to the merciful side of the question. But the views of those who favored admitting only "professors of piety" to the communion, and only the children of such persons to baptism, were now beginning to triumph, and soon the "half-way covenant,"[2] which had caused so much trouble

[1] *Serious Call*, p. 16.

[2] This provided that baptized persons of good moral character, solemnly

in various churches, was generally abandoned in Connecticut and throughout New England.

The pious fraud, if it could be thus described, was so well answered that it is not known whether "A Consistent Churchman" made any further public demonstration. Mr. Croswell concluded his "Appeal" with an allegory intended to match the startling paragraph already cited from the first page of the "Serious Call." "If I were to awaken in the dead of night, and find my dwelling in flames, and should discover a person skulking away in some dark corner, muffled

owning or renewing the covenant before the Church and publicly professing their assent to the doctrines of faith, yet without furnishing credible evidence of any Christian experience, might not only have the privilege of presenting their children for baptism, but "be admitted and accounted members of the Church, and under the care and discipline thereof as other members," the communion excepted. Fitness for this ordinance was to be determined by future trial and examination.

So late as 1795, when Dr. Dwight was a candidate for the Presidency of Yale College, the system had its advocates; for objections growing out of the "half-way covenant" were raised against him, and in a letter to the Hon. Jonathan Ingersoll, who favored his election, a passage occurs which should be quoted in this place for the history it contains.

"The admission of children to baptism on what is commonly called the *half-way* plan, has never appeared to me a sufficient reason to refuse communing with a church; nor, indeed, do I consider it as having anything to do with the subject of communing. I have *repeatedly administered the Lord's Supper to the Church at Stamford*, in which that practice has always existed. You will make the necessary conclusion.

"It appears to me poorly worth the while for any man to employ himself in circulating such reports with reference to the appointment proposed; and (shall I say) almost equally so for my friends to employ themselves in obviating them when spread. I thank my friends, however, and heartily; and you, in particular, for this instance of your good will.

"But I do not court the appointment. Let those who do, take it. I am already happily settled, and in a station little exposed to envy or obloquy. To build up a ruined college is a difficult task. It is a pity the man who wishes for it should not be gratified. I am not that man." — MS. Letter, June 24, 1795.

up in a clumsy disguise, with a torch in his hand, and a dagger concealed under his jacket, and withal refusing to disclose his name, — I should certainly be justified in considering him (whatever might be his professions) as a thief and incendiary; as an assassin and plunderer; and, as such, should think it my duty to hand him over to public justice. I leave it to a candid public, and, indeed, to the ingenious author himself, to determine which of these similitudes best suits his case. Let justice be done and I shall be content."

The "Sober Appeal," like its predecessor, had a wide circulation, and produced not a little sensation in the community where it was published. While the original assailant lay concealed, two pamphlets appeared, addressed to the Rev. Mr. Croswell, and evidently designed to provoke personal controversy. The authorship of one of these was "imputed at the time to an ambitious shoemaker, who laid claim to extraordinary piety, and who, subsequently, in a great revival season, gained considerable celebrity as a lay-preacher. He unfortunately lived long enough, as his brethren asserted, to fall from grace."[1]

The other was from the pen of an officer of Yale College (Prof. Goodrich), and was in the form of a letter which began thus: —

"Rev. Sir: As a member of the Church of Christ, and a citizen of this town, I have witnessed with deep concern the asperity of feeling created of late by a pamphlet signed 'A Consistent Churchman.' From the first I have regretted its publication. The irony is in some instances unwarrantably severe; and how-

[1] Annals of Trinity Parish, MS.

ever legitimate its deductions may be, the citizens of this town will, I fear, consider even the most decisive proofs of rashness and weakness in the reasonings of Dr. Hobart and Mr. Rayner as a poor compensation for the pain inflicted on a large and respectable class of the community. Mingled as we are by our interests and our relations in social life, it is deeply to be lamented that jealousy and discord should be kindled up between different denominations of Christians."

This was a soothing and courteous introduction. But in the heat of his zeal to defend the pastor of the First Ecclesiastical Society, in New Haven (Rev. N. W. Taylor), and to deny that he was the author of the pamphlet in question or had any "share in its composition," personalities and syllogisms and special pleadings were resorted to, which ill became so accomplished a mind and so graceful a pen.

No rejoinder was made by the author of the "Sober Appeal," and the controversy ended, but the effects of it did not readily pass away. Its natural tendency was to provoke further inquiry; and books, setting forth the claims of Episcopacy, were eagerly sought after and read; so that prominent instances of subsequent change of opinion and of conformity to the Church were easily traced back to circumstances connected with this incident. The case of Hector Humphreys,[1] the son of Congregational parents, and early imbued with all the sectarian prejudices, so prevalent

[1] He graduated at Yale College in 1818, with the highest distinction, and had but just entered on his theological studies when these pamphlets made their appearance and fell into his hands. They seem to have awakened in him an apprehension that if men of learning and piety, whom he had always been taught to hold in the greatest veneration, could resort to such "base expedients to build up their cause, there must be something radically

at that day, throughout New England, may be selected as a type or representation of those brought under the indirectly converting influences of "A Consistent Churchman."

defective in their system. Be this as it may, he could no longer conscientiously pursue his theological studies under a system so apparently marked with deformity; nor did he at that time even dream that he could ever bring his mind into conformity with the conflicting system of the Church. He began therefore, to turn his attention to the study of the law. But in the meantime he made an earnest and thorough investigation of the whole subject in dispute between the Church and the sects. And the result of this investigation was precisely what might have been expected. He was not long in coming to a full conviction of the soundness of the claims of Episcopacy, and this conviction was followed up by his embracing, openly and unreservedly, the doctrines and worship of the Church." — *Annals of Trinity Parish, MS.*

The Rev. Dr. Humphreys died on the 25th of January, 1857, having been President of St. John's College, Annapolis, Maryland, for twenty-five years. He preserved to the last the "Serious Call" and "Sober Appeal," which were the instruments of his conversion to Episcopacy, and used to say that there were no volumes in his library which he valued more highly.

CHAPTER XVI.

SPECIAL CONVENTION; CONSECRATION OF DR. BROWNELL; GENERAL THEOLOGICAL SEMINARY; AND REVIVAL OF THE CHURCHMAN'S MAGAZINE.

A. D. 1819–1821.

THE Standing Committee, in compliance with a resolution of the last Annual Convention, summoned the presbyters, deacons, and lay deputies from the several parishes to meet in Trinity Church, New Haven, on the 26th of October, for the transaction of ordinary business; and "on the following day to receive and recognize the Bishop of the Diocese, who was then to be consecrated." Forty-two clergymen, including eight from other dioceses, and forty lay delegates were present, together with a large number of churchmen, drawn to New Haven by the interest of the occasion.

The first day was chiefly occupied with the affairs of the Episcopal Academy. A special committee, appointed at the previous Annual Convention to investigate the state of the funds, and all the facts connected with the interest and prosperity of the institution, made their report, accompanied by a fuller statement from the Principal, concerning the "course of studies." He gave sixty as the average number of students in each term, during the last thirteen years, and said: "Of those educated at the Academy since its institution, twenty-eight have taken Holy Orders, three are now candidates, and about ninety have been qualified to enter the various colleges. The number of those who have been qualified for the professions of law and medicine is considerable, but cannot be correctly ascertained."

The Convention met on the second day of the session in the old Court-house, and after the transaction of some routine business, and the election of delegates to represent the Diocese in the next General Convention, an adjournment took place to attend the consecration. The presbyters, deacons, and lay delegates, with the visiting clergymen, then formed a procession from the house of Lieutenant Governor Ingersoll to Trinity Church, accompanied by the Bishop elect and Bishops White, Hobart, and Griswold. The clergy, in those days, were accustomed to appear in the black gown on such occasions. Morning Prayer was read by the Rev. Reuben Ives, and Bishop White, who acted as the consecrator, preached the sermon. Towards the conclusion of it, he addressed himself particularly to his reverend brethren of the Diocese, and referred to his long intercourse with those who had filled the Episcopate among them.

"With your first Bishop, he [the preacher] was connected in preparing and establishing the Book of Common Prayer. The Bishops of our Church were then three in number, and one of them, owing to indisposition, was absent from our counsels; so that the business was gone over in familiar conversation between your Bishop and him who now addresses you; who has ever since retained a pleasing recollection of the interviews of that period, and of the good sense and the Christian temper of the person with whom he was associated.

"After his decease, it was in this city, about twenty-two years ago, when the present speaker was the principal agent in the consecrating of a successor. Many have been the subsequent occasions, when we took sweet counsel together, and walked in the house of God as friends. His memory will be precious to his surviving brother, until he shall follow to the rest that remains to the people of God, when the labors of life shall be over; if, through divine mercy, he shall attain to such a termination of his pilgrimage.

"With your Bishop, who has sustained a provisional charge of the Episcopacy among you, the intercourse of your preacher has been longer and more intimate, in consequence of a knowledge of him from his infancy; and while the sense of his active usefulness among you is cherished throughout this Diocese, it is here associated with many recollections which give a personal interest to the issue."[1]

The closing duties of the Convention involved a formal relinquishment by Bishop Hobart of his provisional charge, and a recognition of the new relation in which the services of that day had placed the Diocese. In the few farewell words which he addressed to his brethren of the clergy and laity, he bore witness to their love and zeal for the pure and primitive doctrines of the Church, and to numerous acts of attention, kindness, and hospitality which could never be forgotten.

"A connection thus consecrated and endeared," said

[1] Sermon, pp. 20, 21.

he, "I cannot consider as now dissolved, without emotion. But I should be selfish indeed, if I did not check the feelings of regret, by those of congratulation at the auspicious event which this day places over you a Bishop, who, in the fidelity and the talents that have distinguished him in the stations which he has hitherto filled, has inspired our sanguine expectations of his great usefulness in the important relation which he will now sustain to you."

The Convention was not ungrateful to him for his eminent services in the Diocese, and the words used by the committee appointed to draft an address of thanks, show well enough that he and his work would long be remembered. Speaking of his sacrifice and labors in adding the care of the Church in this State to the arduous duties of his own Episcopate, they said: —

"When we consider that this sacrifice was made, and these labors undertaken, without any view to pecuniary interest, and when we call to mind the eminent services which you have rendered; the new impulse which your visitations have given to our zeal; and the general success which has attended the exercise of your Episcopal functions, we feel bound to offer to the great Head of the Church and Supreme Disposer of all things, our sincere and heartfelt acknowledgment of the distinguished blessings which he has been pleased to confer upon us through the medium of your services."

But the Rev. Dr. Bronson, president of the Standing Committee, presented, in behalf of the Convention, a longer address to Bishop Brownell, recognizing him as their Diocesan, and anticipating an increase of zeal and unanimity in promoting the interests of religion, and in drawing men "by gentle persuasives to be reconciled to the Divine Saviour of the world, and to walk in love and peace together." Their memories lingered around the struggles of the past, and they could not refrain from alluding to them on an occasion when their hearts were filled with so much joy.

"Looking back to the time when that venerable man, Bishop Seabury, the first Protestant Bishop in America, took charge of this Diocese, and reflecting on what we this day have witnessed, we see abundance of reason for thanksgiving and praise to the Great Head of the Church. Under his prudent, yet energetic administration, and that of his dignified successor, we have increased greatly in numbers; we have become a consolidated and uniform body; as far as is consistent with fallen human nature we are united in doctrine, in discipline, and the service we render to Almighty God. By the liberality of our civil rulers, and the joint contributions of the Church at large, we are now able, we hope, to disencumber the Episcopal office of parochial services, that it may be wholly dedicated to its peculiar duties. For the accomplishment of this so desirable an object, much has been due to the exertions and unremitting recommendations of those two eminent characters in our Church."

And in replying to this part of the address, Bishop Brownell said: "In the performance of my duties, it shall be my endeavor to imitate that prudence and zeal which characterized the earliest Bishop of this Diocese and of this country, and to cultivate those virtues which distinguished his immediate successor. These venerable men have gone to their reward, and we now enjoy the fruit of their labors. While we cherish their services and their worth in grateful remembrance, we cannot be unmindful of the zealous and disinterested services of a bishop now present, who has, for two years past, performed the Episcopal duties of this Diocese, under the XXth Canon of the General Convention. Having lived under his Episcopal jurisdiction ever since the Church has enjoyed the benefit of his labors in this present station, and having been for the year past associated with him in the intimate relation of assistant in his parochial labors, I should do violence to my feelings if I neglected, on the present occasion, to acknowledge my obligations to his personal friendship, or to express my sense of his services in this Diocese, and to the Church at large."

These addresses of welcome and congratulation closed the solemnities of the day, and all returned to their respective homes with new hopes and raised expectations. Bishop Brownell removed his family to Hartford, and he was chosen to the temporary charge of Christ Church in that city, which the Rev. Mr. Wainwright resigned to accept the station of assistant minister of Trinity Church, New York, made vacant by his own elevation to the Episcopate of Connecticut. He began his official duties with an ordination to the Diaconate at Middletown, on the 17th of November; and, a week afterwards, he consecrated the new church in Sharon, built of brick, and the church in Kent. He also administered the rite of confirmation in both these churches the same week, in the former to forty-six persons and in the latter to thirty-five. Between the date of his consecration and the meeting of the Annual Convention in June of the next year, he had confirmed in all, three hundred and fifty-two, and visited twenty-three parishes.

His first tour was chiefly one of observation, and in travelling through different portions of the State and witnessing the number of vacant cures, and the depressed and feeble condition of churches which were only supplied with occasional ministrations, he could not but feel that the most pressing wants of the Diocese were missionaries and missionary work. The "Society for the Promotion of Christian Knowledge" had already accomplished enough to entitle it to confidence, and he therefore publicly urged more liberal collections in aid of its benevolent object of "advancing the interests of religion and the prosperity of the Church."

The candidates for Holy Orders were beginning to increase at this time throughout the country; and Bishop Brownell, in 1820, gave the names of seven under his jurisdiction, two of them only being graduates of a college. The General Convention, which met at New York in 1817, had decided that it was expedient to establish a general theological seminary for the better education of these candidates, and a committee of nine, composed equally of bishops, priests, and laymen, was intrusted with the business of perfecting the plan and setting it in active operation. The institution was to be located in the city of New York, and agents were appointed by the Convention to visit the several parts of the United States and solicit contributions towards its endowment. When the scheme was originally proposed in the General Convention, Bishop White, who was afterwards placed at the head of the committee of nine, differed from the majority of both houses as to the expediency of the measure, and he was supported by his own Diocese in suggesting a plan which would have left to local seminaries the whole matter of theological education. His reasons for the views he entertained, are given at length, in his "Memoirs of the Protestant Episcopal Church,"[1] and the progress of events has shown some of them to be of more practical importance than the majority were disposed to think at the time.

But while Bishop White, on principle, was against the establishment of a general theological seminary, he acted earnestly with its friends after the question was settled, and took special pains to overcome the prejudices of those "who," as he said, "laying due stress on the religious qualifications called for by the ministry, and being laudably desirous of fencing the sanctity of its character in this respect, entertain the opinion that it requires but a slender furniture of intellectual information."

The Seminary, as originally organized, did not flourish in New York. Difficulties inseparably connected with all new undertakings surrounded it, and the efforts to establish the institution in that city not proving as successful as had been anticipated, the General Convention, which met at Philadelphia in 1820, resolved that it "be transferred to and located within the city of New Haven, in the Diocese of Connecticut." The Bishops, in communicating to the House of Clerical and Lay Deputies their concurrence in this action, deemed it proper to declare that they did not mean to interfere with any plan then contem-

[1] Page 237 *et seq.*

plated, or that might "hereafter be contemplated, in any diocese or dioceses, for the establishment of theological institutions or professorships."

On the 14th of July, nearly two months after the adjournment of the General Convention, Bishop Brownell, by order of the Board of Trustees, presented to the Christian public a plan for the organization of the Seminary, preceded by an address, and followed by resolutions. The institution was publicly opened at New Haven on the 13th of September, with an inaugural discourse by the Rev. Samuel H. Turner, D. D., at that time the only professor; and ten students, to whom four others were soon added, were present on the occasion. Bishop Brownell had tendered his services gratuitously till the state of the funds would warrant the appointment of another professor, and in the ensuing month he removed to New Haven, and aided Dr. Turner by meeting the students once a week, and instructing them in the delivery of sermons and the department of Pastoral Theology. He was deeply interested in its prosperity, and favored measures to endow a professorship in memory of the first Bishop of Connecticut. An extract from his address to the Annual Convention of 1820, will show his sense of its importance to the Church: —

"Without a learned, as well as a pious ministry, it is impossible that her character can be maintained, or her boundaries enlarged. The state of our country now demands higher theological attainments than our candidates have an opportunity of acquiring. In the institutions at Andover and Princeton, examples are presented to us of what a communion is capable of effecting, when its zeal and resources are concentrated on a common object. I feel confident that neither ability nor liberality are wanting in our Church, to establish such an institution as her exigencies require, and I trust there will not be wanting either unanimity or zeal to bring her resources into the most efficient operation. The high salaries necessary to support competent professors in New York, and the inability of most young men to support themselves, during a three years' course of study, in so expensive a city, rendered necessary an amount of funds altogether beyond the reasonable expectations of the friends of the Seminary; especially while there existed, in various parts of the Union, such strong objections to its location. Influenced by these considerations, and by the consideration of the more moderate habits which the students would be likely to form in such a place as New Haven, as well as by various other motives of preference, the vote of the Convention for transferring the Seminary to Connecticut, was almost unanimous. While this removal appears likely to prove highly beneficial to the Church at large, it seems especially calculated to be useful to the Church in this Diocese, and throughout New England, where so large a portion of the clergy of the Episcopal Church have been born and educated. But a great responsibility is thrown upon this Diocese; as both its clergy and laity will naturally be expected to take the lead in the patronage and support of the institution. I trust that neither will be found wanting in their duty in so important a matter."

The Seminary had been in operation scarcely a year at New Haven, before the number of students had risen from ten to twenty-two. But, in the meantime, discussions were going on, and conflicting statements were put forth in other quarters, which were calculated to interfere with its prosperity, and check the collection of funds for its endowment. Bishop Hobart, in a pastoral letter to his Diocese, reviewed the history of the General Theological Seminary, and then considered the right of every diocese to make provision for the education of students in divinity, the expediency of this provision being made by New York, and the mode in which it should be effected. The result of the Pastoral was the establishment of a "Protestant Episcopal Theological Education Society of the State," with the principal school located in the city of New York, and a branch of it in the village of Geneva, each under its respective professors.

Nor was this all. Mr. Jacob Sherred, a vestryman of Trinity Church, New York, died in that city, March, 1821, leaving by his will, dated some thirteen months before, about sixty thousand dollars to a theological seminary to be established within the limits of the State, under the direction or by the authority of the General Convention "or of the Convention of the Protestant Episcopal Church in the State of New York." The bequest was thus in the alternative as it regarded the two conventions, and the question was raised whether a seminary to be established within the limits of the State by the General Convention, would be entitled to the legacy in preference to a seminary established by the Convention of the Diocese. Legal opinions were taken, and some of the most distinguished lawyers decided that the right to the legacy under the conditions of the will, was vested in the Theological Institution already established in the State, and that it was not in the power of the General Convention to deprive the existing institution of the title thus acquired. But with a view to settle the difficulty, a special meeting of that body was held in Philadelphia on the 30th day of October, 1821, when it was agreed by the parties in interest, "all in the spirit of conciliation and mutual concession," that the Seminary should be removed from Connecticut, where it had been incorporated by an act of the Legislature, back to New York, and a new institution organized by uniting it with the local school of that Diocese. This merging of the two into one was the formation of the present General Theological Seminary, which secured the legacy of the benevolent testator.

For several years the "Churchman's Magazine," which met with misfortunes after it was taken out of Connecticut, had ceased to be published. It was felt that its revival, under suitable management and control, would greatly promote the interests of the Church; and the Annual Convention of 1820 requested Bishop Brownell to call in the assistance of such of the clergy and laity as he might think proper, to arrange with some persons for its publication in the Diocese, and to take the superintendence of the same, "provided, however, that the whole risk and responsibility of the work shall devolve on the publishers, without any direct or indirect obligation, on the part of the Convention, to make up losses or deficiencies." At this date, periodical literature of every kind was beginning to be more liberally encouraged, and churchmen saw with what assiduity other denominations circulated their magazines, and propagated their peculiar views of religious truth. The Bishop, with five of his clergy and one layman, acted gratuitously as editors in issuing the work for three years, but at the end of that period, the patronage having been barely sufficient to defray the expenses of printing, they terminated their responsibility, and the publication which had thus been "recalled from the tomb and reanimated by its legitimate parents," was again suffered to fall asleep. The Convocation, however, which met at Cheshire on the 24th of November, 1824, revived it once more, and elected the Rev. Dr. Bronson editor, under whose auspices it continued to be published till the day of his death.

The Church in Connecticut had now entered on a new epoch, and her prosperity, like that of the Christian denominations about her, was henceforth to be affected by great changes in the customs of society and the modes of administering to personal comfort. In the milder climate of England, from which our ancestors came, no artificial means had been employed for warming the sanctuary, and the first settlers naturally brought with them the practice of the mother country, and built their meeting-houses here without reference to the rigors of a northern winter. Generation succeeded to generation, and still the churches, as if run in the same mould, were constructed on the principle that no heating apparatus was necessary or to be tolerated. The worshippers from a distance might gather in their rude "Sabbath-day houses,"[1]

[1] These were small structures, divided into two rooms for the accommodation of the sexes, and erected by individuals, usually on the public

during the intermission, and kindle their fires and consume their refreshments, but in the great temple there was to be nothing but the crowded assembly to take off the chill of an almost Arctic atmosphere. The little foot-stove was occasionally a luxury; but with the thermometer at zero, worship must have been a sort of moral martyrdom. We may feel a cold shudder as we sit amid the comforts of these days and think of our forefathers, facing the wintry blasts and going up to the house of God, often perched on some bleak hill, and there, wrapped in furs and homespun coats, waiting devoutly through the long prayers and sermons of the minister. For nearly two hundred years after its settlement, the practice of warming churches was unknown in Connecticut, and when it began to be introduced there were prejudices to overcome, which in some places cost many a hard battle. A few of the smaller parishes in the Diocese provided themselves with stoves at an earlier date; but Trinity Church, New Haven, had not the means of being warmed in the winter season, until 1822,[1] and by that time all the denominations in New England

ground around the meeting-house; the authorities of the town granting them permission.

[1] Dr. Turner, speaking of his residence in New Haven, as Professor of the General Theological Seminary, says: "In the summer season I frequently visited some neighboring vacant parish and officiated; but generally I attended Trinity Church, of which Dr. Harry Croswell was rector. In the winter the building was excessively cold, as the practice of warming places of worship had not then been introduced in Connecticut."— *Autobiography*, p. 105.

The vestry of Trinity, in the autumn of 1806, "allowed liberty to put up a stove in the church, provided it was done without expense to the parish," a liberty which seems not to have been used, or if used in the old wooden structure, the new stone edifice was occupied for six years, before decisive steps were taken to warm it in the winter.

were gradually adopting the practice. No house of worship was thenceforth erected without reference to the comfort of those who were to occupy it, and a stove or a furnace soon became as much a necessity in the church as in the private dwelling.

CHAPTER XVII.

MANNER OF PERFORMING DIVINE SERVICE; SUNDAY SCHOOLS; CHARGE OF THE BISHOP; AND PROSPERITY OF THE DIOCESE.

A. D. 1821 – 1823.

The prejudices of a community in which Puritanism prevailed led to some laxity in the rubrical observances of the clergy. They and their people thoroughly understood all questions pertaining to the ministry and doctrines of the Church, but in matters of the ritual they were not so careful or so tenacious of uniformity. The order of architecture, followed by parishes in the construction of their churches, had been for the most part a New England meeting-house, and arched windows were the principal mark to distinguish the edifices of Episcopalians from those that belonged to the sects. Chancel arrangements were made without regard to the convenience of the clergyman or to the proper manner of conducting divine service, and frequently in the smaller churches in rural districts a spacious pulpit, built next to the wall, and nearly midway between the apex of the roof and the level of the main floor, was used both for the prayers and the sermon. Sometimes lower down in front of the pulpit a high breast-work was raised for a reading desk, and outside of this stood the Lord's Table, which the priest never approached except on Communion Sundays. A recessed chancel was not to be seen, and where a surplice was worn, the clergyman generally passed the whole length of the church to reach the vestry-room and change it for the black gown.

The gradual advance in architecture brought with it many improvements, but at the time when Bishop Brownell entered upon the duties of his office, this description would apply, with a few exceptions, to all the churches in Connecticut. In the absence of any artistic skill, popular opinion governed, and the same authority affected the practices of the clergy, who had then nowhere in the land been accustomed to a ritual relatively above the prevailing style of ecclesiastical architecture. At a Convocation held in Cheshire, September 6, 1821, a committee was appointed to take into consideration "such known diversities of practice as may exist among the clergy of this Diocese, and to suggest those particulars on which in their judgment it is desirable that there should be uniformity." The resolutions growing out of this action, and adopted by the Convocation, were in substance as follows: That the clergy use the ante-communion service every Sunday in the year, except under those circumstances which necessarily prevent, and that it be read from the chancel on Communion Sundays; that the congregations be dismissed previous to the communion service with a collect and the shorter benediction; that the Lord's Prayer be omitted before the sermon and a collect only used; and that the clergy instruct their choirs to close every psalm and hymn with the doxology.

The due performance of the music of the Church received early attention in Connecticut. One of her clergy — Dr. Smith, formerly Principal of the Episcopal Academy at Cheshire — addressed a petition to the General Convention which met at New Haven in 1811, relative to a volume of music composed by him, entitled "The Churchman's Choral Companion to his Prayer Book." The object of the work was to favor the introduction into our churches of "chanting and the singing of anthems;[1] and though it was decided to be inexpedient to take any action thereon, yet according to Bishop White,[2] the book was well esteemed; and "it was not from any dissatisfaction with it that the application was rejected, but because the request to enjoin the use of the chants and tunes exclusively of all others was thought unreasonable," and to have granted it would have been a high exercise of power. Still Dr. Smith persevered in his efforts, and in 1816 published a smaller work to aid the first, of which he thus spoke in the introduction: "As the experiment has been made, and almost all our churches show an increasing disposition to adopt this primitive and once universal way of setting forth the most worthy praise of Almighty God, it hath become incumbent on the author to ameliorate his former publication by means of the present."

Not more than half a dozen churches in the Diocese supplied with organs could be found at the beginning of the century, and their number was not

[1] At the annual meeting of Trinity Parish, New Haven, Easter Monday, 1802, an organist was appointed with a fixed salary, and required to substitute always an anthem for the voluntary, which "has been usually played."

This vote had no reference to the voluntaries before and after divine service, but to a practice which had long prevailed of playing a voluntary after the second lesson of the Morning and Evening Prayer, in conformity with an English custom.

[2] *Memoirs*, etc. p. 213.

much increased for twenty-five years. A few rectors, skilled in music, took great pains to cultivate a taste for chanting, even where there was no instrumental accompaniment, and soon volunteer choirs, composed principally of the young, grew familiar with the practice, and congregations learned to crave something beside the metrical psalms and hymns. The old choristers were at first the greatest obstacles in the way of introducing the chants, and in some parishes troubles arose on this account which extended into many families and lasted long. But intelligent churchmen stood by their rectors, who simply adhered to the plain construction of the rubrics, and only "said or sung" the anthems and doxologies as the Prayer Book prescribed. If the people anywhere objected to chanting, it was not so much from a feeling that it was a Popish innovation, as from the want of a suitable number of competent persons to lead in it and render it really an offering of praise. Sacred music differs from all other kinds of music in that it is an act of devotion. Found in all ages and associated with all forms of Christian faith, it is the most subtle and powerful collateral influence connected with the offices of public worship. Instead of being a matter of mere entertainment or vain show, it is a mysterious and potent agency, having the same silent aim as religion, and awakening the heart, concentrating the thoughts, and elevating and enchanting the soul. The theory of the Protestant Episcopal Church is, that her members should join in the song of praise as well as in the act of prayer; but the churchmen of Connecticut, who fifty years ago were unable to do this, were no worse off than their descendants of the present day, who find quartette choirs and operatic performers practically depriving them of all participation in singing or chanting.

Bishop Brownell, in his primary address to the Convention in 1820, called attention to the subject of Sunday-schools, and urged their establishment in all the parishes. "I believe," said he, "that they are already very generally established throughout the Diocese; and much praise is due to the clergy, and others who have promoted them, as well as to those generous individuals who have taxed their charity with the labor of instruction. To withdraw the young from profane amusements, or a thoughtless indolence on the Lord's day; to assemble them together for religious worship; to store their minds with the elements of Christian knowledge; to excite in their hearts devout affections, and to familiarize them to the pious and evangelical services of our liturgy, are objects which may well call forth the charities of the friends of religion."

It was then only forty years since the system of Sunday-schools had been first instituted, and they owe their origin to a pious and philanthropic layman of Gloucester, England — Robert Raikes, a printer and the son of a printer. He saw in the state of the population by which he was surrounded, the necessity of something more than the ordinary teachings of the parish minister to check the progress of vice in the lower classes, and the deplorable profanation of the Lord's day. His benevolent heart, therefore, turned to some means of gathering together and teaching the poor and neglected children, and with the aid of a clergyman of the Church of England he planned this system and set it in operation. It was originally very simple. Mr. Raikes had distinguished himself by various efforts for the relief of human misery, and he stipulated for a shilling a day with a few well-disposed women, living in those suburbs of the city where the lowest of the people dwelt, to receive as many children as he should send on Sunday, and instruct them in reading and the Church Catechism. The clergyman of the parish engaged, for his part, to go round to the schools in the afternoon for the purpose of examining the progress that was made, and enforcing "order and decorum among such a set of little heathens." It was really an effort at civilization, and the originator of it often derived great pleasure from discovering genius and innate good dispositions among the children, which he called "botanizing in human nature."

The system thus conceived and operated commended itself to the minds and consciences of all, and soon Christians every where welcomed it with zealous approbation; and wondering that it should never have been devised before, they "seemed determined to repair, as much as possible, the mischief of past neglect, by applying with the utmost diligence the benefits of this new discovery in the world of morals and religion." The wealthy bestowed on it their contributions, noblemen lent their influence to its extension, and the labors and prayers of all, as well as the energies of the press, were freely enlisted in its behalf, so that within two years from its origin, it was computed that 250,000 children in our mother country were every Sunday receiving instruction in this way.

It has been seen that the first Sunday-school teachers were hired, and this practice was continued until about the beginning of the century, when voluntary gratuitous instruction became general in Great Britain, and the pecuniary expense otherwise entailed upon the system ceased to be an objection. The first Sunday-school in the United States was commenced in Philadelphia by the "First Day or Sunday-school Society," in 1791, and the name of Bishop White appears among the founders of the institution. The movement of Connecticut towards its adoption was not prior to that of other Dioceses. Her system of common schools, from which religious instruction had not been entirely discarded at so early a date, rendered it difficult to find any of mature age who were unable to read and write. Knowledge was brought within reach of the masses, and ignorance—the parent of vice—fled before the demands of a virtuous and intelligent people. As far as the Sunday-schools, upon their first establishment in Connecticut, were confined to instruction in the rudiments of secular knowledge and the fundamentals of religion, they were undertaken by benevolent Christians without regard to denominational differences. But the times were charged with excitement, and Episcopalians, who had nothing to gain but much to lose by such a union, chose to organize their own Sunday-schools, and they made them at once a prominent feature in parochial work, especially during the summer months.

It has not been ascertained precisely how early they came in, but they had been organized in several parishes while the Diocese was under the provisional jurisdiction of Bishop Hobart. Bishop Brownell spoke of them in his address to the Annual Convention of 1822, as established in nearly all the parishes, with the most salutary results, both to the children and their instructors. "The munificent provision of the State," said he, "for the support of common schools, and the disposition which prevails among all classes of the community to derive the greatest benefit from them, have caused elementary education to become so universal among our youth, that we have no occasion to devote any portion of the Lord's day to this species of instruction. This is a peculiar advantage which we enjoy, and which enables us to apply our Sunday-schools directly to their legitimate object — *religious instruction.* It is a most gratifying circumstance, that there has yet been no want of pious and well-disposed persons ready to assist their clergymen in this charitable labor." Some difficulties were experienced at first in procuring proper books, and much diversity prevailed in the modes of instruction; and hence the Convention of that year, through a committee, recommended that the children be instructed in the Church Catechism and Explanation; and also that they be required to commit to memory passages of Scripture and "exercised in questions in the Bible, and on the Rubrics in the Book of Common Prayer." In 1826 the "General Protestant Episcopal Sunday-school Union" was established during the session of the General Convention at Philadelphia — a scheme which the clergy of Connecticut in Convocation had already formally approved, and requested the delegates from the Diocese to aid in accomplishing. Its main object was to remedy existing evils and to provide an adequate supply of the several grades of books needed in Sunday-schools, and which would impart no other religious views than such as are consistent with "the truth as it is in Jesus" — exhibiting that truth in the fullness and integrity in which it is revealed in the Holy Scriptures, and faithfully conveyed in the standards of our Church.

The Annual Convention for 1821 was held at Waterbury, when thirty-two clergymen and thirty-eight lay delegates were present — a number somewhat larger than had assembled the previous year at Hartford. Bishop Brownell gave his primary charge to the clergy, and the leading consideration to which he called their attention was to "keep constantly in view the great object and end of their ministerial profession," namely, "to induce sinful men to embrace the way of salvation by Jesus Christ, and to build up the Church in the most holy faith." After dwelling on piety and learning as qualifications requisite to the due discharge of the sacred office, he directed their thoughts to the manner in which its duties may be most successfully performed. He spoke of private monitions and parochial visits in the scenes of sickness, adversity, and affliction, as among their most useful labors, and then passed to their public ministrations — to "the service of the desk and the altar, and the service of the pulpit." In defending the true faith against "all erroneous and strange doctrines contrary to God's word," and in proclaiming the distinctive principles of the Church, a delicate duty was involved, requiring as much prudence as Christian charity. Under this head he put forth counsels which are applicable to all times and too good not to be quoted here.

"In this spirit, my brethren, and on these principles, it will be your duty on all proper occasions to hold up to view the *distinctive principles of your Church.* This is a privilege freely exercised by other denominations of Christians, and one which we freely concede to them. It is not unreasonable, then, that we require the like privilege in return. Indeed, it is only by a free declaration of the truth, and a zealous defence of it, that it can ever be propagated, or even maintained.

"It is by these means that the Episcopal Church in Connecticut has acquired her growth. A century ago she numbered not more than eighty families within the State. She can now count as many regularly organized congregations. And during this time she has had almost every thing to retard her prosperity, and no single circumstance to advance it, except the excellency of her principles, and the frank avowal and firm support of them. Were she to cease from this course, situated as she is in the midst of a respectable and much larger denomination of Christians, she would soon cease to exist. Her clergy, as well as the laity, would soon become ignorant of her peculiar doctrines, and then indifferent to her distinctive character. Under these circumstances, there would be nothing to counteract that universal law of nature by which smaller bodies gravitate towards larger ones, and the Church would soon be merged in those religious communities with which she is surrounded.

"Loving your Church, then, my brethren, and attached to her distinctive principles from a conscientious conviction of their excellency and importance, you will not think you have faithfully discharged your duties to your flocks, unless they are fully instructed in them. Nor will you be deterred by any false delicacy from publicly avowing and firmly defending these distinctive principles, whenever it may be done with propriety and advantage. In pursuing this course, you will not be led of necessity to make any direct or gross attack upon the sentiments of other religious denominations: the simple display of truth is generally the best antidote to error. Much less will you feel yourselves called upon to impugn the motives — the sincerity or the piety — of those who may conscientiously differ from you. By the manifestation of a Christian temper, and the exercise of a judicious moderation, you will evince to the world that you are not merely contending for the dogmas of a sect, but for essential doctrines of that faith once delivered to the saints.

"Liberality of sentiment upon religious subjects is amiable and commendable in the sight of all men, and is, moreover, a high Christian duty. But there is an erroneous principle which usurps its name, and which would confound all distinction between truth and error. This spurious liberality pretends to consider as of no importance all those varieties of opinion which prevail among different religious denominations, and seems to demand that we should regard with equal estimation the widely differing creeds of all who profess the Christian name. Such a latitudinarian principle, if carried to its full extent, would go to the utter destruction of Christianity itself. There is one denomination which rejects its external ordinances, and another which obliterates its most distinctive features — the divinity and atonement of the

Saviour. Deprive Christianity of these characteristics, and there is but little to distinguish it from modern Deism."[1]

He contended that an enlightened charity would not exhaust itself in futile attempts to "abolish sectarian distinctions," but would rather direct its efforts to the promotion of kindly feelings and a mutual toleration of opinions among those who profess a common Christianity. "With regard, then," said he, a little further on in this charge, "to our union with other religious denominations, we may cordially associate and coöperate with them in all secular affairs; in all humane, literary, and charitable objects; nor should differences of faith create any difficulties in the way of social intercourse and good neighborhood; but in objects *purely religious* we can form no union with other denominations with which we are surrounded, without either abandoning important principles, or incurring, if we adhere to them, the imputation of sectarian bigotry. While, therefore, we concede to others the same right, let us pursue our religious and ecclesiastical affairs according to the regulations and institutions of our Church, without any mistaken attempts to compromise in matters of conscience. Nor let us think that we are violating any principle of Christian charity, when we freely avow and firmly maintain our distinctive principles."

It was in such a spirit that the newly consecrated Bishop of the Diocese entered upon his official duties, and directed the labors of his clergy. Under its influence the Church moved on "in quietness and confidence," and the signs of her prosperity were every-

1 Charge, pp. 16 – 18.

where visible. During the year which ended with the Convention of 1821, the rite of Confirmation had been administered in thirty-four parishes, to eight hundred and thirty-six persons: the candidates for Holy Orders had been doubled, one had been advanced to the Priesthood, and two had been admitted to the Diaconate. Edifices begun several years before were completed, and of these St. Paul's Church, Ripton, and St. John's, Washington, had been duly consecrated to the service of Almighty God.

The names of the venerable Dr. Mansfield and Dr. William Smith disappear from the list of the clergy at this time — the first of whom died a few days preceding Easter, 1820, and the other twelve months later, leaving behind them in the Diocese only one clergyman, Rev. John Tyler, who received his Orders in the Church of England. Mr. Tyler soon followed his aged associates, and died at Norwich on the 20th of January, 1823, having been fifty-four years Rector of Christ Church in that city, — and Dr. Mansfield, from the date of his ordination to the time of his decease, a period of nearly seventy-two years, had continued in the rectorship of St. James's Church, Derby.

At the Convention of 1821 a committee, appointed the previous year to revise the Constitution and Canons of the Church in the Diocese, reported a new Constitution, which, after sundry amendments, was adopted and ordered to be printed, and submitted to the several parishes for their approval. The new Constitution contained an article which gave to the Convention the power of future amendment without submitting propositions to the parishes, but so fixed were the churchmen of that period in their views, or so indifferent to the advantages of any change, that four years elapsed before the requisite returns were received so as to make this revised Constitution the law of the Diocese.

Bishop Brownell found time, amid his other engagements, to compile his valuable "Commentary on the Book of Common Prayer," which was published early in 1823, and was the first work of the kind prepared in this country. He had then made thorough visitations of the Diocese and become acquainted with the zeal of the clergy, and the spirit and wants of the laity. "Everywhere," said he in his address to the Convention of 1821, "I have been received with a kindness and an interest highly gratifying to my feelings. Concerning the general prosperity of the Church, it may be difficult to decide with confidence; but from the best observations and inquiries which I have been able to make, her friends have no reason to despond. She seems to be gradually enlarging her borders and strengthening her stakes, while at the same time there appears to be an increasing degree of piety and zeal among her members. Her clergy are everywhere zealous and faithful. I make this observation with the more satisfaction, as I have formerly heard them charged from abroad with coldness and indifference. Nothing but ignorance, or gross prejudice, could have suggested the imputation. It is my full conviction that if there exists, in any part of our country, a body of clergy who by their labors and privations, their industry and fidelity, approach to the model of the primitive ages of the Church, such men are to be found among the Episcopal clergy of Connecticut. To insure the continued prosperity and advancement of the Church, nothing is wanting, with the blessing of Heaven, but the continued zeal and perseverance of her friends. There is nothing in the circumstances of the times which can warrant a relaxation of either. On the contrary, the excitement with regard to religion, which seems to prevail through the greater part of the State, furnishes ground to the friends of the Church for the exercise of a more especial degree of vigilance. From the clergy, in a particular manner, it calls for increased watchfulness and zeal. The present is certainly a period when people in general are more disposed than usual to attend to the concerns of religion. Not that we have reason to believe there is any special effusion of the Spirit of God in any particular region, but the excitement which has been raised in the community, has led people to give more heed to those ordinary influences of the Holy Spirit, and to those ordinary means of grace which are at all times dispensed in such measure as to enable all who will coöperate with them, to work out their salvation through the merits of the Redeemer. But if the people are disposed to hear, and to inquire, whatever may be the cause, it is the especial duty of the clergy to warn and to instruct. More especially is this their duty, at the present period, that they may guard their flocks from the delusions and errors of ignorant teachers, and lead the inquiring mind to just and rational views of that way of salvation revealed in the Gospel."

CHAPTER XVIII.

CHARTER OF A COLLEGE; OPPOSITION TO ITS ESTABLISHMENT; CHANGES IN THE CLERGY; AND DEATH OF DR. BRONSON.

A. D. 1823-1826.

THE project to establish a college in Connecticut, which should be under the auspices of the Protestant Episcopal Church, was now revived, after having slept for seven years. The return of the General Theological Seminary to New York, was the signal for fresh efforts to obtain a charter, and eighteen clergymen, specially convoked, met at the house of Bishop Brownell in New Haven a week before Christmas, 1822, to take the preliminary steps. The Bishop, with two of the brethren and three laymen, were appointed to draw up a memorial to be circulated in the Diocese for signatures, — praying "the General Assembly to grant an act of incorporation for a college, with power to confer the usual literary honors, to be placed in either of the cities of Hartford, Middletown, or New Haven, according to the discretion of the Trustees." The act of incorporation was to take effect whenever funds should be raised for an endowment amounting to thirty thousand dollars, and not before. And the committee, in preparing the memorial, asked leave to appropriate towards the endowment such portion of the funds of the Episcopal Academy at Cheshire, or the income thereof, as might be thought expedient, "provided the consent of the Trustees of said Academy be first obtained, and that no portion of the funds contributed by the inhabitants of Cheshire be removed." This part of the petition was denied, or withdrawn, but the recent political changes in the State, and the breaking down of the old dynasty, had prepared the way for hearing the memorialists, when they said: —

"We are members of the Protestant Episcopal Church,— a denomination of Christians considerable for their numbers and resources in our country,—and we beg leave to represent, that, while all other religious denominations in the Union have their universities and colleges under their influence and direction, there is not a single institution of this kind under the special patronage and guardianship of Episcopalians. It cannot be doubted but that such an institution will be established in some part of our country, at no distant period; and we are desirous that the State of Connecticut shall have the benefit of its location.

"As Episcopalians, we do not ask for any exclusive privileges, but we desire to be placed on the same footing with other denominations of Christians."

That nothing might be done to peril their petition, the memorialists allowed a name, dear in the military and civil history of the land (Washington), to be inserted in the proposed act of incorporation, rather than the name of the first Bishop of the Diocese. The charter was granted on the 16th of May, 1823, and the event was welcomed in Hartford, where the General Assembly was holding its session, with demonstrations of great rejoicing. Cannons were fired and bonfires lighted. Though given upon the prayer of Episcopalians, and contemplating their management, the charter, as the petitioners wished, required that the college should be conducted on the broad principles of religious liberality, and about one-third of the original corporators were taken from outside of the Church. It contained a provision, prohibiting the Trustees from passing any ordinance or by-law that should make the religious tenets of any officer or student in the college a test or qualification of employment or admission. And here it may be observed that, up to the very day before the petition for this charter was presented to the General Assembly, the statute of Yale College, in reference to tests, — modified upon the accession of Dr. Stiles to the Presidency from consent to the Westminster Catechism and Confession of Faith into an assent to the Saybrook Platform, — was still in force. That day, at a special meeting of the corporation, held in the city of Hartford, the obnoxious test-law was repealed. There were those who thought the time was thus critically chosen for its repeal, that an influence might be brought to bear upon the minds of the liberal Legislature, touching the memorial for a second college. But be this as it may, no sooner was the charter granted, than its friends, who had been so long contending with the evils of popular prejudice, were now compelled to contend with poverty and other discouraging causes. The amount necessary to secure the provisions of the act of incorporation was, indeed, over-subscribed, for, within one year from its date, nearly *fifty thousand* dollars were raised by private subscription towards an endowment. This subscription was obtained by offering to the larger towns in the State the privilege of fair and laudable competition for its location, and Hartford, never wanting in public spirit and generous outlays, secured, in this way, the honor of being its seat.

The erection of the college buildings was commenced in June, 1824, and the business of instruction in September of the same year. But the funds subscribed were barely adequate to this beginning. The Trustees had already deputed one of their number[1] to visit England and solicit donations towards the supply of a library and philosophical apparatus. He carried with him an address or general letter of introduction, officially signed, and directed to the Bishops, Clergy, and Laity of the Church of England. It does not appear to have been the original intention to give much publicity to the object of this mission, but on the arrival of the agent, he found himself in the way of other applicants[2] from this country for similar aid, and he was induced to print the letter, together with a statement of his own, setting forth the necessities of the Church here, and the more important facts in regard to the condition of the two oldest New England colleges.

The agent returned to this country, with the donations which he had received, soon enough to be a conspicuous and fearless actor in that war of pamphlets which arose from "Considerations suggested by the Establishment of a Second College in Connec-

[1] Rev. N. S. Wheaton, Rector of Christ Church, Hartford.

[2] Bishop Hobart, for the General Theological Seminary; and Bishop Chase, of Ohio, to found the Institutions at Gambier.

ticut."[1] Not only had zealous endeavors been used in various sections of the State, to prevent the subscription papers from being filled up in order that the charter might take effect, but even after the college had been organized and located, attempts were made to interfere with its success, to disparage its usefulness, and to produce an impression that it was "an instrument of sectarian aggrandizement," a "scheme fraught with the seeds of discord," and calculated to "entail on distant generations a source of implacable jealousies and feuds." It was claimed that, while one institution of learning in the State was certainly demanded by the interests of literature, a second was not; and "that Washington College could rise into distinction and usefulness only by depressing Yale to the same extent." Events have proved that fears of this sort were wholly groundless. The institution survived the early hostility to its establishment, and it did not sicken and die when the State afterwards refused to feed it with a tithe of the bounty which had been bestowed upon the venerable sister. So late as 1822, the President and Fellows of Yale College, recognizing "the past liberality of the State," recited their necessities in a memorial to the General Assembly, and cheerfully left it to that body, "the constituted guardian and patron of the College, to direct to such relief, either by grant from the treasury, or in some other way, as might be deemed most consistent with the public good."

[1] This was the title of the first anonymous pamphlet, which received an anonymous reply, and then a rejoinder followed. The reply, entitled "Remarks on Washington College and on the Considerations Suggested by its Establishment," was written by the Rev. Mr. Wheaton.

The first President of Washington College[1] was he who scarcely needed a formal vote to be placed in that office. He was the Bishop of the Diocese, and had been charged with the presentation of the petition to the General Assembly. He had watched its progress with solicitude, and witnessed its success with delight. Long experience in academic discipline had made him acquainted with the responsibilities of the office, and when he removed to Hartford to enter upon his enlarged duties, he brought to his aid some of the best minds of the Church, and had among the Faculty, Rev. George W. Doane — afterwards Bishop of New Jersey — and Rev. Hector Humphreys. The great object in establishing the college was to provide a place where the sons of Episcopalians might obtain a classical education without having their early religious predilections tampered with by sectarian teachers. The necessity for some such institution was felt by the General Convention in 1823, when resolutions were adopted by that body, instructing a committee, among other things, to inquire into the privileges afforded to Episcopalians in the existing colleges of the land, and also to report on the practicability of establishing a seminary or seminaries for the education of youth, which should be under the influence and authority of the members of the Protestant Episcopal Church. At that time, too, an increase in the ranks of the ministry

[1] Upon the memorial of the Trustees, showing that there were sundry other colleges in the United States bearing the name of *Washington*, the General Assembly, at the May session, 1845, changed the name of the corporation to that of "The Trustees of TRINITY COLLEGE;" — a name which "will attest forever the faith of its founders, and their zeal for the perpetual glory and honor of the one holy and undivided Trinity."

was especially needed to meet the pressing demands for the services of the Church, both in the old and newly settled States. There were about six hundred organized parishes in the whole country, and scarcely more than one-half that number of clergymen actually engaged in parochial duty. The General Convention, in 1820, adopted a constitution for the Domestic and Foreign Missionary Society, which was amended at later dates, and admitted as members all the bishops of the Protestant Episcopal Church, the House of Clerical and Lay Deputies for the time being, and such persons as subscribed money annually or for life to the objects of the organization. In 1823, the House of Clerical and Lay deputies, in concluding their report on the general state of the Church, invited the attention of the Bishops to the following facts: that many parishes were without pastors; that, in the West, there existed a large body of Episcopalians who were as sheep without a shepherd, and that, for want of missionaries—for want of laborers—the plenteous harvest, as respected our Church, could not be reaped. The College at Hartford became one of the natural sources of supply to this spiritual destitution, and almost immediately received a respectable number of students, sixty-five being reported as connected with it in 1826. A good proportion of these and of the early graduates took Orders in the Church, and radiating in all directions of the country, they have done for her worship, as ministers and missionaries, what the friends and founders of the college predicted and hoped would be done. Many charities are consumed while they are used. They are like the annual flowers of the field, which leave little behind them save the recollection of their beauty and grateful fragrance. But the endowment of a seat of learning, and especially of Christian learning, is the planting of a tree whose fruits are perennial, whose roots strike deeply into the soil, and whose branches, spreading over the earth, and shooting upward into the skies, continue from year to year, and from age to age, to reproduce and to commemorate the benefaction.

Frequent emigrations from the State deprived many of the parishes of their most active members, and kept them weak and depressed. This led to frequent changes in the location of the rural clergy, and to a feeling in the depleted parishes that they were unable to make permanent arrangements for the ministrations of the Church. The contributions to the Society for the Promotion of Christian Knowledge, which had now become the missionary agency of the Diocese, would not yet warrant sufficient appropriations to render the connection between pastors and their people less slight and transient, and consequently much of the benefit that arises from long attachment and mutual intercourse was foregone and lost. The best that the weak parishes could do under such circumstances was to unite and form themselves into convenient cures, but even this did not prevent the evil of frequent clerical changes, nor faintness from sometimes coming upon the spirit of the people. In 1825, when the clergy of the Diocese numbered forty-six, and the congregations seventy-four, Bishop Brownell said to the Annual Convention, meeting at Hartford: —

"A great portion of our parishes are small and

weak, when compared with the other religious societies with which they are surrounded. Many of them are, consequently, but partially supplied with ministerial services, and the burthen of support falls heavily on individuals. In addition to these considerations, it need not excite our wonder that some should be unwilling to hazard their popularity, by connecting themselves with a body, which is regarded by many of those around them as but a minor sect of Christians. But religious prejudices still constitute the most formidable obstacle to the growth of our Church. There is no part of our country where these prejudices might be expected to exist in greater force than in Connecticut. Settled originally by Puritans, who abandoned their native country, in abhorrence of Episcopacy, and at a time when the principles of religious liberty were but little understood, they naturally regarded the introduction of any opinions different from their own, as an intrusion upon the asylum they had chosen. Their early institutions were calculated to foster these sentiments, and it is no way extraordinary that some traces of them should have been perpetuated to the present generation. In short, the preponderance of public sentiment has been hostile to our Church, and the tendency of the civil and religious institutions of the State has naturally been adverse to its interests. Under these circumstances, we have less cause to wonder that it advances so tardily, than that its growth should have been so rapid; and we have less reason to complain of the prejudices, and other obstacles which have impeded its growth, than we have to admire the successful progress of what we deem to be truth, and the excellency of those doctrines and institutions which could overcome such difficulties, and surmount such obstacles. Time is the great remedy for all prejudices and errors. Possessing our souls in patience, and doing whatsoever our hand findeth to do, we may abide with confidence its salutary operations. The prejudices to which I have alluded, are, moreover, so intimately connected with the frailties of our common nature, and have resulted so naturally from the position in which our Church has been placed, that we ought to regard them rather in sorrow than in anger."

The pastoral relation was sundered in a few cases where no plea of inability to support public ministrations could well be set up. When age has crept upon the servants of God, and they cease to be attractive as preachers, a mere love of novelty will sometimes induce parishes to seek a change by pensioning their venerable rectors in retirement, or leaving them to provide for their own wants in the best way they can. Two presbyters, who were among the four candidates admitted to Holy Orders by Bishop Seabury at the first Episcopal Ordination held in America, after having served their churches, the one for more than forty years, and the other for more than thirty, withdrew to smaller fields, and left the posts they vacated to younger men.

The Rev. Philo Shelton, in 1824, resigned the Rectorship of St. John's Church, Bridgeport, and henceforth confined his services entirely to the parish in Fairfield, which had always formed a portion of his cure; and the Rev. Ashbel Baldwin, in the same year, relinquished the charge of Christ Church, Stratford, and found employment elsewhere. They were neighbors and intimate friends, and had long been associated together as members of the Standing Committee. They had labored faithfully in the Diocese during its darkest periods of depression, and, through the progressive stages of its advancement, they had taken a leading and important part in its councils, as well as in the councils of the Church at large. Besides being frequently delegates to the General Convention, both of them had held office in that body, Mr. Shelton having been chosen Secretary by the House of Bishops in 1811, and Mr. Baldwin Secretary by the House of Clerical and Lay deputies at the same time, in which office he was continued until his resignation in 1823. The latter was also Secretary of the Diocesan Convention for nearly thirty years, and retired with cordial thanks for his services during the eventful period he had thus officiated. His self-possession and readiness in clearly expressing his opinions, gave him great advantage, in a deliberative assembly, over many of his brethren who were not inferior to him in sound judgment and general information.

With other changes in the clergy, came those which were made by death. Mr. Shelton, whose latter days were embittered by severe trials, did not long survive the sundering of his pastoral relations. He was the founder of the church in Bridgeport, "and for forty years the continued promoter of its best interest, by the soundness of his doctrines, the zeal of his preaching, and the primitive simplicity of his conversation." He died on the 27th of February, 1825, and no words of eulogy were ever better deserved than those which Bishop Brownell spoke concerning him in his address at the ensuing Convention: "For simplicity of character, amiable manners, unaffected piety, and a faithful devotion to the duties of the ministerial office, he has left an example by which all his surviving brethren may profit, and which few of them can hope to surpass."

His departure was soon followed by that of another whose name stood high up on the list of the clergy, and the wisdom, prudence, and moderation of whose counsels had contributed, in no small degree, to preserve the peace and promote the prosperity of the Church in Connecticut. Warned by the advance of years and the approach of bodily infirmity, Dr. Bronson addressed a letter to the Annual Convention which met at Newtown on the 7th of June, 1826, and, as it shows the man and outlines the history of his ministerial experience, it is quoted here entire.

"Next October will complete forty years that I have been in the ministry. During the whole of which time I have been blessed with such a measure of health as never to have been absent from Convention through bodily indisposition; rarely from any other cause, and never more than on three or four occasions from the public service of the Church, until within a few weeks past. At this time, there is but one clergyman in these States whose letters of orders from the American Episcopate are dated earlier than mine. During twenty years past, just one half of my clerical life, I have been honored with the confidence of the Convention in their choice of Standing Committee. It is thus full time I should wish to retire from the trust. To this I am loudly admonished by increasing years, and more by a bodily infirmity which threatens to render me incapable of discharging the incumbent duty. It is, therefore, my earnest desire no longer to be considered as a candidate for any appointment in the gift of the Convention. With all proper sentiments of respect and gratitude for the past, I beg the acceptance of my best wishes and prayers for the harmony, peace, and prosperity of the Church and Diocese, in which I have so long ministered. May the spirit of Divine Grace pervade all the deliberations of the Convention, to the breaking down of Satan's kingdom in men's hearts, and the enlargement of the Redeemer's reign upon earth. And may the Church in this Diocese continue, as heretofore, a sound member of the Church universal, until the time shall come when all the nations of the earth shall bow submissive to the heavenly kingdom of the Lord Christ. Though absent in body, believe me present in mind and desires."

To this communication, a suitable answer was returned, and in just three months from its date, after repeated attacks of paralysis, the venerable man passed to the reward of his labors. The light of his virtuous and holy life was some consolation to his friends, for the dark cloud which was thrown over his last moments. A few years later, his pupils and personal friends, bearing in affectionate remembrance his character and long continued services, marked his grave by an appropriate monument.

Dr. Bronson was a man of delicate sensibilities, and he would often weep like a child while reading publicly those appointed lessons in the Calendar that detail the history of Joseph and his brethren. As a scholar, his reputation was deservedly high. He was profound and correct, without being brilliant or polished. His love of the classics increased with his years, but his favorite studies were mathematics and natural philosophy, and to these he would devote himself for hours, unconscious of external things and unmindful of his bodily comfort. He delivered to his pupils a series of lectures on the "history of the Manual Arts," which, begun at an early period of his labors as an instructor, were perfected as the advancement of science and his own researches furnished materials. Detached parts of these lectures appeared in the "Churchman's Magazine," of which he was editor at the time of his death. The last numbers of the volume which was in hand when the messenger came to call him, were compiled by a friend for the benefit of his family, and then the publication ceased to exist, and the "Episcopal Watchman," a weekly periodical, appeared in its place.

There was need of more frequent approaches to the people by the way of the press. A religious revival was sweeping the State, and out of it was springing, in many places, an uncharitable spirit towards the Church. More vigilance, too, was demanded on the part of the clergy, to check the progress of error and the abuses of religion. Two years before this time, Bishop Brownell had said to the Convention: —

"Among the prevailing errors of the day, you cannot fail to have observed the pernicious effects of *universalism, of fatalism, and of fanaticism.* The denial of all future punishment relaxes the morality of the gospel, rejects its most awful sanctions, and gives the reins to every licentious passion. The doctrine that all the thoughts and actions of men are precisely fixed and determined by an eternal necessity, destroys all sense of accountability, and leaves men to the sole guidance of their own corrupt propensities. And a fanatical reliance upon imaginary revelations and impulses, supersedes and sets aside the revelation which God has given us in his Gospel. Thus do these errors create a tendency to infidelity in those that embrace them, while, by being held up to the world as a part of the Christian system, they produce, in the minds of the unreflecting, a strong prejudice against the truth of Christianity itself. It is true, indeed, that, in some of the scenes of the late French Revolution, the world has received such a lesson upon the effects of infidelity as should not soon be forgotten; yet, though disgraced, it has not ceased to exist, and its principles are so congenial to the corruptions of the heart, so flattering to human pride, and so pleasing to the natural love of novelty, that they cannot be too strongly deprecated, or too strictly guarded against.

"It is our part and duty, my brethren, to guard ourselves and our flocks against the prevailing errors of the times, to exhibit Christianity as it is in the gospel, and to see that its real spirit and temper be wrought in our own hearts."

CHAPTER XIX.

SUPPORT OF THE EPISCOPATE; ACADEMY AT CHESHIRE; MENZIES RAYNER; AND HIS SUSPENSION FROM THE MINISTRY.

A. D. 1826 – 1828.

THE Diocese stipulated to pay Bishop Brownell an annual salary of fifteen hundred dollars, and the Fund, with the additions which were made to it soon after his consecration, was nearly sufficient to yield this income. But misfortunes befell it, and, in the autumn of 1825, the Eagle Bank at New Haven, in which the Trustees had invested five thousand five hundred dollars, failed, and the failure involved other banks in the State, and diminished, for a while, the dividends from those in which the remainder of the Fund was chiefly invested. The consequence was that the annual deficiency in the sum which the Diocese bound itself to raise for the support of the Bishop, was considerably increased, and the several deficiencies amounted, on the first of July, 1828, to two thousand seven hundred and thirty dollars, without computing the interest thereon, which was justly due. The inconvenience to the Bishop was less felt, for the reason that, at this time, he was receiving a salary from the College as its President, but the Convention was dissatisfied with the constant deficiency, and took frequent steps to provide for it and perform to the letter the terms of the original obligation.

Agents were appointed and authorized to settle equitably, according to their present circumstances, with those parishes which had failed to comply with the assessment laid upon them in 1813, in exact proportion to the several amounts of their grand list. That assessment rested solely on the recommendation of the Convention — a body which possessed no power to enforce a performance of the obligation, so that, after all, the payment of it was nothing more than a voluntary gift on the part of those who had at heart the best interests of the Church. Many of the parishes submitted to the assessment with cheerfulness, and paid promptly and without hesitation their respective dues, but others, weak, without the stated services of ministers, and unrepresented, perhaps, in the Convention which imposed the tax, found themselves in no condition to meet the full claims upon them, however willing they might be to bear their proportion in the support of the Episcopate. A few parishes that possessed ample ability, under the influence of illiberal advisers, declined to recognize any obligation, and these, with the other delinquent parishes, were badgered for years by acts and agents of the Convention until 1823, when the Rev. Stephen Jewett, then Rector of the Church in Derby, was appointed to visit them and "make a settlement of their arrearages." He was indefatigable in his negotiations by letters and repeated visits, and made a final settlement with about twenty of the parishes, thus adding to the Fund nearly one thousand dollars. After the failure of the Eagle Bank, the remaining delinquents were again importuned to assist in restoring the loss, but the result was unsatisfactory, and provoked some irritation without drawing forth much money. The proceeds from the lottery grant, referred to in a previous chapter, came in about this time, and helped to relieve "the present distress," but the Trustees, with all their economy and diligence in endeavoring to collect the old assessments, could not raise the income of the Fund to an amount equal to the annual salary pledged to the Bishop. The charter under which they acted made them a close corporation, and they filled their own vacancies, and only reported to the Convention by courtesy, and as exigencies seemed to require. This was unfavorable to a completion of the endowment of the Episcopate, and tended to produce uneasiness in the minds of those who always dislike anything that savors of secrecy in the management of public funds.

Besides involving in loss the various parishes which had made permanent investments therein, the failure of the Eagle Bank impaired the endowment of the Episcopal Academy at Cheshire. The Trustees of that institution held stock in the bank to the amount of several thousand dollars, which thus became valueless, and the death of Dr. Bronson occurring soon after, and the College at Hartford being now established and in full operation, the Academy languished, and, for a time, its doors were shut. The Convention originally had the power of appointing the Principal, and Bishop Brownell, alluding in his address for 1827 to the vacancy, said: "It will be a matter of no small difficulty to find a person suitably qualified to fill this important station. If it should be hastily and improperly filled, the evil cannot be easily remedied; and if no candidate can be found who shall receive the decided approbation of the present Convention, I would recommend that the Trustees of the institution be requested to procure some proper teacher to supply the vacancy till the next Annual Convention."

His suggestion was followed, but the temporary provision was uncertain, and failed to attract students and to produce that benefit to the Church which those who contributed towards the endowment of the institution had a right to expect. The desire to increase the members in the classes of the new College, and the feeling that the centre of education for the Church in the Diocese was changed, may have led, for the time, to some apparent, if not real neglect of the venerable seminary which the Episcopalians of a preceding generation had founded. The parish in Cheshire, also, was too ready to seize upon the Principal, whoever he might be, and elect him its rector. Bishop Brownell called special attention again to the matter in 1829, and remarked: —

"Whether, under present circumstances, the Academy can be put in successful operation, seems extremely doubtful. The expedients which have been adopted by the Trustees, have hitherto failed of success. The funds of the Academy were raised for the education of youth under the auspices of the Church, and it is obvious that they ought to be sacredly applied to this object. They cannot be diverted to the support of a parish minister, nor to constitute a sinecure for a nominal Principal. It therefore becomes a question of no little embarrassment, how this Convention and the Board of Trustees shall best fulfil their duty to the founders of the institution, and especially to those inhabitants of Cheshire who contributed towards the endowment. If no better resources can be devised, I recommend the continuing the funds at interest till the sum lost by the failure of the Eagle Bank shall be restored."

The remarks of the Bishop were referred to a committee, who made a report of considerable length, meeting the various points of the case, objecting to the scheme of leaving the funds to accumulate, and concluding in these words: —

"Under the conviction before expressed of the ill consequences resulting from the union of the Academy and church, your committee respectfully and unanimously recommend the adoption of the following resolution: *Resolved*, That, in the opinion of this Convention, it is inexpedient that the same gentleman should fill the office of Principal of the Episcopal Academy at Cheshire, and pastor of the Episcopal congregation in that place."

This resolution, which the Convention adopted, was good on paper, but the year had not ended before both its spirit and letter were violated in the appointment of the Rev. Christian F. Crusé to the united charge of the Academy and the church. His connection in this capacity was of brief continuance, for he removed from the Diocese early in the winter of 1831, having been invited to a more congenial field of labor. His successors and the changes in the organization and management of the institution will be noted hereafter in their proper places.

An effort to revise the Canons and establish a more specific code was begun in 1821, and continued through a period of five years. The progress of events in the Church seemed to render some legislation of this kind necessary, and the call for fuller parochial statistics, and for more care in the maintenance and regulation of cures, could be met in no way so directly as by a canonical provision. Since the accession of Bishop Brownell to the Episcopate, the number of the clergy had increased from forty to upwards of fifty — but some of these were infirm, and others, perhaps from insufficient support, were inclined frequently to change their positions in the Diocese without due regard to the welfare of the parishes, or without consulting the ecclesiastical authority. The worldly inducements to enter on the office of the Christian ministry, never a matter of temptation in this country, were in no part of it more humble than in Connecticut. The salaries of rectors, from the establishment of the Church, had been small, especially in the rural districts, but with the prosperity of the State and the contributions to the Christian Knowledge Society, came a better provision for their support.

The Annual Convention which met at Norwalk in 1828, arranged all the parishes into forty-four cures, and enacted a canon making it "the duty of the Convention, from time to time, to examine and declare the limits of the several cures within the Diocese, and, in the settlement and maintenance of clergymen," the parishes were required not to depart from "such arrangement except in cases of imperious necessity, and with the advice and consent of the ecclesiastical authority." This legislation was intended, while the dearth of clergymen continued, to reach, with stated ministrations, the destitute portions of the Diocese.

The "Church Scholarship Society," founded in pursuance of a communication by the Bishop to the

Annual Convention of 1827, offered its first report the ensuing year, in which the Directors said: —

"Many members of the Convention had long seen the need of an Education Society, to be formed on principles somewhat varying from others then in being; and the interest which they took in its establishment has received substantial approbation in every portion of the Church where its claims have been presented. If the object were one of doubtful utility or success; if, while promoting the good of our fellow-men, it did not exercise and improve some of the best of human feelings, or if it did not promise, in some good degree, to advance the interests of true religion, the Directors would hesitate to urge its further consideration. But if there be truth in the maxim that *knowledge is power*, and if it be important to enlist this power in the cause of the Church, surely we cannot falter in our endeavors to procure the means for so desirable an end. That meritorious young men, members of the Protestant Episcopal Church, studying under the embarrassments of poverty, may be assisted and prepared for usefulness, either as members of our laity or clergy, the friends of the Church Scholarship Society hope, by the blessing of Heaven on their labors, abundantly to accomplish.

"It will be recollected that the Constitution requires no restraint on the choice of a profession at so early a stage in education as to render an unbiassed decision difficult or improbable. It will not be disguised that we may earnestly desire to educate many ministers for our altars, but we would put no such bond on the conscience of any, and, least of all, would we apply to any mind an unworthy motive to a choice, which, however deliberately formed by a young and ardent spirit, a further knowledge of the world, and a deeper insight into the hidden things of the heart, might make it desirable to rescind. We would not that any individual, however much his talents might promise, should become a candidate for the sacred office from motives of mere gratitude to his patrons, or, indeed, without feeling himself, on the deepest and most rational convictions, moved thereto by the Holy Ghost.

"The cause of this society, then, is the common cause of learning and religion, and it will be successful in proportion as men of real worth and talents shall be aided to surmount the difficulties of poverty, and to occupy useful stations in the learned professions. It is true that genius will, at some rate, work its own way in spite of all obstacles, and we would be far from lending encouragement to inaction, and from sparing any young men in straitened circumstances the salutary necessity of *making themselves.* Such a scheme would be unnecessary and unwise, if not positively hurtful. We would have no drones fattening upon the fruits of our labors. Our wish is to extend only a partial support — enough, however, to enable our young friends to toil their arduous pathway up the hill of science without lagging under the lengthened chain of debt, by which many generous spirits are dragged down and lost to that sphere of usefulness, which a little succor would have empowered them to reach. They whom we would aid, should learn to rely on themselves, to put forth all their energies, and they should seek no indulgence but that of equal privilege for study with those whose collegiate course is uninterrupted."[1]

The Society was the child of the Convention, and the foregoing extract from the first Annual Report of the Board of Directors will show the spirit and design of its founders. The Constitution limited assistance to the form of loans, and to students in the College at Hartford, and these loans were to be repaid, without interest, within three years from the time of leaving college. By his own note the student became responsible for the sums received, and, when returned, they were to be used again in aiding other meritorious young men, members of the Episcopal Church, in the attainment of a collegiate education. Though a loaning society, it has been the means of doing much good, and the lengthening the list of the clergy of the Diocese, shortly after its organization, was due in no small measure to its beneficent agency. It is still in existence, modestly continuing its work, and, by a canon of the Diocese, each parish is required to make an annual collection in aid of its funds.

Among the canons that underwent the revision of 1821, were those which declared the offences for which a clergyman may be brought to trial, and the manner of his trial. The constitution of the ecclesiastical court, the notification to the offender, the charges made against him, and the form of proceedings, were all detailed by the new Canon with a minuteness which left no room for doubt or misunderstanding. Under the old law, it was provided that an indefinite number of persons, accusing a minister of offences for which he might be tried, should apply in writing first

[1] Journal of Diocesan Convention 1828, pp. 38, 39.

to the Standing Committee, and if it appeared to them that there was ground for the charges, they were to report to the Bishop, who thereupon "called a convention of the clergy (not less than seven), and, after a full and fair examination, the Bishop, with the advice of the clergy present, should pronounce sentence against him."

The new Canon was specific, and required two persons, one of whom must be a presbyter of the Diocese, to bring the charges, under their own signature, to the Standing Committee, and if the Committee deemed them properly made, they notified the Bishop that there was sufficient ground for presenting the offender for trial, and they prepared to act as prosecutors before the court of nine presbyters subsequently designated to hear the case.

The first clergyman who fell under the operation of this Canon was the Rev. Menzies Rayner. He had been conspicuous in the councils of the Diocese for a quarter of a century, had used his pen freely in controversy, and participated in some of the sharpest theological disputes of the day. Quick-witted, as shown in a former chapter, and rather belligerent in his temperament, but deficient in the refinements of literary culture, he was a bold assailant, and thought little and cared less about the storms that might arise from encountering the prejudices and opposing the views of Christian people from whom he widely differed. Calvinism was the ghost that constantly disturbed him in his religious dreams, and he fought it like a tiger. Whenever it rose before him, he instantly prepared himself for battle, and with a feeling of conscious ability, and flattered by the praise of men who love the prophets that "speak unto them smooth things," he overlooked the principles of the Church, and fell into the habit of countenancing and disseminating opinions contrary to her doctrines and discipline. He sprung to the opposite extreme from Calvinism, and the dissertations in dogmatic theology which he uttered, both from the pulpit and from the press, finally awakened the fears of his friends and parishioners, and led them to charge him with holding and teaching the doctrine of Universal salvation. Instead of quieting their suspicions, and convincing them that he was sound in the faith and accepted the generally received and Scriptural view of the future punishment of the wicked, he grew bolder in the utterance of his opinions, and complied with invitations from Universalists to preach in school-houses, public halls, and private residences, where the rubrics and liturgy of the Church were, for the most part, disregarded, and the impression produced that he was a great champion, in the priestly office, of the cause of Universalism. His controversies, about this time, were not wholly confined to religious matters, for at a Convocation of the clergy held in Newtown, June, 1826, he "obtained liberty to make a statement in relation to a lawsuit in which he was interested." This was a suit brought by himself against a fellow townsman for defamation. It grew out of his defence of Universalism, and although it was decided in his favor, and he recovered damages to the amount of seven hundred dollars, yet he was unable to regain the confidence and affections of his people, and the parish in Ripton speedily devised measures to terminate his rectorship. Other suits followed, one with a physician in Ripton, a prominent churchman, who had been his fast friend, and for some time Mr. Rayner gave more attention to the civil courts than was consistent with the office of a priest, appointed to serve "in the courts of the house of our God."

Until 1823, the Episcopalians in the town of Huntington formed one incorporated society with two churches, and the worshippers in these were not to tax each other for repairs, or any "expense except for the support of a clergyman." But in that year the Episcopalians in the part of the town then called New Stratford (now Monroe), petitioned the General Assembly "to be incorporated into a separate and distinct ecclesiastical society," and also asked that the fund and other property belonging to the whole in common, might be divided and apportioned between the two parishes of Ripton and New Stratford, so that each should have the power to manage its own concerns, and possess and control that portion of the fund which was subscribed within its particular limits. The petition was granted, and the division peaceably consummated according to a mutual understanding of the two parishes, but it involved no change in the pastoral relations of Mr. Rayner. He continued his residence at Ripton and officiated as before in the two churches, but there was a growing discontent among the people of that place, which came to a head in midsummer, 1826. Then the difficulties between himself and the parish at Ripton were carried before the Bishop and Standing Committee of the Diocese, and upon their recommendation, the connection was soon after dissolved. Mr. Rayner transferred his residence to Monroe, and the parish there — whether desiring them or not — had, for a time, the full benefit of his ministrations. He claimed a settlement for life, and the people, learning wisdom from the dear experience of Ripton, quietly waited the action of the ecclesiastical authority to dispose of his case.

On the 7th of November, 1827, the Standing Committee met at Stratford, and the following document, duly signed, in conformity with the Canon, by two persons, one a presbyter and the other a layman of the Diocese, was received and considered: —

"Whereas it is commonly reported and believed, that the Rev. Menzies Rayner, a presbyter of the Protestant Episcopal Church in the Diocese of Connecticut, is in the habit of countenancing and disseminating opinions which are contrary to the doctrines of the Protestant Episcopal Church in the United States; and also, that the said Rayner is in the habit of public preaching, without using the Liturgy of the Church, and further, that his conduct, for some time past, has been unbecoming the character of a Christian minister: —

"Now, therefore, we, the undersigned, earnestly desirous that the truth of the said reports should be investigated, agreeably to the fourth Canon of the Convention of the State of Connecticut, do hereby charge the said Menzies Rayner with the above recited offences, and present the same for the consideration of the Standing Committee."

In consequence of information received from the Bishop that Mr. Rayner had assured him that "he would immediately make the declaration required by the seventh Canon of the General Convention of 1820, to enable the Bishop to suspend him from the ministry of the Church without trial," the Committee decided to postpone all proceedings on the charges until further informed, and when they met again, two months afterwards, he had relinquished his ministry in the Episcopal Church, and been suspended from the exercise of its office.[1]

This was not the first change which he had made, having been, in early life, a Methodist preacher. It was evidently no sudden step with him, and in preparing for it he watched his opportunities well, and obtained from the Universalist Society in Hartford overtures tantamount to a call, before finally leaving the fold which had enclosed him in love for so many years. He removed back to the city where he first began his Episcopal ministry in Connecticut, but his old friends did not welcome him in the new capacity of a Universalist preacher. Whatever regard they had for the man, they had more for the Church of Christ, and the same might be said of those who sustained him to the last in the cure where Providence permitted him to sow seed that sprang up and yielded a plentiful crop of religious doubt and indifferentism.

This is not the place to record his history in the new pastoral relations to which he devoted the remainder of his days. Enough will have been said when it is mentioned that he lived on, beyond the time of his renunciation of the Episcopal ministry, a score of years or more, leaving Hartford after a brief connection with the Universalist Society there, and residing in different places out of the State, according as he could find the best support for himself and his family. He made occasional visits to his

[1] Appendix C.

former friends in Connecticut whom he had indoctrinated with his sentiments, and sometimes he taxed the courtesy of his Episcopal acquaintance to aid him in procuring a hall or school-house to preach in; but these visits could not have afforded him much satisfaction, when he saw the communion which he had forsaken growing everywhere with such fair proportions, and the sect, to the bosom of which he had fled, still struggling to plant its foot firmly upon the soil.

CHAPTER XX.

NEW PARISHES; PROPOSED CHANGES IN THE LITURGY; VISIT OF THE BISHOP TO THE SOUTHWESTERN STATES; AND LACK OF CLERGYMEN.

A. D. 1828 – 1831.

For a period of ten years the outward prosperity of the Diocese had been seen, not so much in the formation of new parishes as in the vigor and growth of those already established. Several of them had erected larger and better edifices to take the place of the rude structures built before the Revolutionary War, and in 1828, the parishes of Christ Church, Hartford, and Christ Church, Norwich, proceeded each to the erection of a stone edifice in the Gothic style of architecture. That at Hartford was the design of the Rector (Rev. N. S. Wheaton), and was modelled mainly after Trinity Church, New Haven. Standing on the corner-stone, which was laid May 13th, 1828, and referring to the superstructure, Mr. Wheaton, among other things, said: —

"We build this house in Faith. We have the divine assurance that the gates of hell shall not prevail against the Church; and it is therefore with no feelings of distrust that we strengthen our hands for the work.

"We build this house in Hope. We are animated by the expectation that many sons and daughters will here be born to God, that many sinners will be reclaimed and fitted for eternal glory. For ourselves, we anticipate, if such is God's pleasure, the enjoyment of many days of holy communion with Him in this house, and when our voices have ceased to roll along its walls, and our heads are laid low in the dust, it is our confidence that a generation will not be wanting to perpetuate our hymns to Christ, the King of Glory.

"We build this house in Charity. While we conscientiously differ from some of our Christian brethren, and on points not unimportant, we desire to be united with all who love the Lord Jesus in sincerity, in the bonds of Christian love. Most devoutly do we pray, also, that the harmony of feeling which pervades the parish in relation to our undertaking may continue and increase. It will be the surest pledge of our prosperity, that our Jerusalem is built as a city that is at unity in itself. O pray then for her peace, that it may be found within her walls, and knit all hearts together in the bonds of a close and holy fellowship."

The church was consecrated the next year, two days before Christmas, by Bishop Hobart, in the absence of the Bishop of the Diocese.

An edifice of stone in the Gothic style was also built at Kent, and consecrated late in the summer of 1827, — being "the fourth church erected, in four adjoining towns, under the auspices of the Rev. George B. Andrews." The other three were in Sharon, New Preston, and Salisbury, and were constructed of brick. Still earlier than this, a new brick church at Hebron had been consecrated, in the autumn of 1826, which

Bishop Brownell, in his address to the Convention the next year, thus described: "In point of beauty and design, and excellence of workmanship, it may probably rank as the second church in the Diocese, — Trinity Church at New Haven being the only edifice which is superior to it."

But now new parishes were beginning to be organized in places where, hitherto, there had either been no call for the services of an Episcopal clergyman, or where they had been only occasionally rendered. The church in the eastern part of the State, built before the revolution on the confines of Pomfret, Canterbury, and Plainfield, did not suit the convenience of the Episcopalians residing in Pomfret, and they formed themselves into a parish, which was admitted into union with the Convention at its session in Norwalk, 1828. The next year an organization was effected in Hitchcocksville (now Riverton), Litchfield County, under the direction of a missionary of the Society for the Promotion of Christian Knowledge, and an expensive stone church was begun, and, after a while, completed with the aid of contributions from other parts of the Diocese. But the prosperity of the village suddenly declined, and the enterprise proved unsuccessful, though more recently the parish has been revived, and the hope is now entertained that it will ultimately flourish.

The parish of Trinity Church, New Haven, received such accessions from the increase of the city and other causes, that it was found necessary, in 1828, to call an assistant minister (Rev. Francis L. Hawks), and to adopt measures to erect a chapel in another part of the city for the better accommodation of the worshippers. It was a spacious Gothic edifice, the fifth of our churches in the Diocese built of stone, and was consecrated April, 1830. It was the first instance of erecting a second Episcopal church in any city of Connecticut, and the plan pursued to raise the money to meet the expense was the same as in the case of building the mother church. Bishop Brownell, in his address for 1829, said: —

"Since the last Annual Convention, I have visited more than half the parishes in this Diocese, and, owing to its compactness and the facility of intercourse, have had opportunities for receiving information from most of the others. While a few of these parishes continue to languish, through adverse dispensations of Providence, or from a want of zeal in the people, the general aspect of the Diocese is calculated to inspire us with hope, and to fill us with gratitude. Most of the congregations appear to be increasing in numbers and strength, and in several instances, where a few years ago the united exertions of two neighboring congregations could hardly support a clergyman, each one is now in the full enjoyment of the regular ministrations of the gospel. Some new parishes have recently been organized, and I have lately received pressing calls for missionary services, with a fair promise of usefulness, in places where the ministrations of our Church have never yet been dispensed. Since my removal to this Diocese, little more than nine years ago, I have consecrated eleven churches, nearly all of which have been built within that period. It gives me peculiar satisfaction to add that active exertions are, at the present time, in progress for the erection of ten new churches, three of which are in parishes newly organized. Within the period above alluded to, the number of the clergy belonging to the Diocese has increased from *thirty-four*[1] to *fifty-nine*, and there are, at the present time, five vacant parishes capable of supporting settled clergymen, besides one vacant missionary station. If the spiritual state of our Church should have advanced in improvement, in the same ratio with its external growth, we should, indeed, have great cause for mutual felicitations. Within the last few years, a decided revival of Christian zeal seems to have pervaded the great body of our Church, and may we not hope that this Diocese has participated, in no small degree, in its animating spirit?"

Among the "ten new churches," referred to in this extract, were those at Windham, Chatham (now Portland), and Middletown. The two latter were in a style of Grecian architecture, and constructed of the brown sandstone, taken from the celebrated quarries in the neighborhood. The church at Windham was built of granite, and the parish there was a new organization. An Episcopal Society was started in the town as early as 1804, but "after maintaining worship about a year, the members voted to join the First [Congregational] Society in the support of the gospel ministry." A new parish was organized at Saybrook — a place where sixteen men, twelve of them Congregational ministers, met in September, 1708, and adopted a platform which, receiving, a month later, the approbation of the General Assem-

1 This was the number recorded as present at the consecration of Bishop Brownell, but six clergymen "belonging to the Diocese" were absent at that time, among them Mansfield and Tyler.

bly, became the legal ecclesiastical establishment in Connecticut. It was natural that some feeling should be exhibited when steps were taken to introduce the Episcopal form of worship[1] into a town around which clustered, for the Congregationalists, such peculiar historic associations.

The Convention of 1829 appointed a committee to take into consideration the state of the Church in the Diocese, but nothing of importance was elicited in this way. A brief extract from their report will show that the spiritual building was, as it always should be, the main concern of the clergy.

"To secure the future prosperity of the Church, the harmonious efforts of both ministers and people must bring into action the feelings of the heart, the powers of the mind, and the devotedness of the soul to God. The externals of religion may be beautiful and splen-

[1] "Now we turn the leaf, and see a page altogether different — a page blotted by disunion and the rendings of deforming schism. As early as the beginning of February [1830], the month anterior to the great accession to this Church, and in the midst of a full flow of revival feelings, and the all-thrilling sympathies of religious excitement, some of our opulent citizens invited an Episcopal clergyman to officiate in private dwellings, and hold a weekly evening service. These meetings continued, week by week, either in those mansions or the school-house, till, on April 9th, they observed a public day of worship, on Good Friday. On May 31st, as I understood, they organized their church, and elected their wardens and vestrymen. On the 9th of August, 1830, the corner stone of the Episcopal church was laid, and, in the next year, Aug. 16th, 1831, the church was consecrated. Public worship has been sustained by them to the present time, and we have now two houses of worship within our local boundaries. All this constitutes a new era in my ministry, and in the religious history of Saybrook." — Rev. F. W. Hotchkiss' *Half Century Sermon*, 1833, pp. 13, 14.

The clergyman who held the "weekly evening services" was the Rev. Ashbel Steele, a Missionary of the Society for the Promotion of Christian Knowledge.

did, and the form of godliness may spread far and wide; but what are these when its power is not deeply felt, or when the holy truths, sealed by the blood of apostles and martyrs, are rejected or coldly assented to? The sinfulness of the human heart must be felt, faith in the atoning blood of Christ must be consented to in the affections, and all the duties of Christianity practiced, to render the spiritual building of God *all glorious within.* Sacrifices must be made, and the standard of the cross must be raised over the ruins of pride and selfishness and vanity, for the safety of our own souls and the souls of our fellow men."

Up to this time Bishop Brownell had administered the rite of confirmation to three thousand three hundred and seventy-four persons.

Since the revision by the General Convention of 1789, the Book of Common Prayer had undergone no changes. Some dissatisfaction was occasionally expressed with the length of the morning service, but, for the most part, the members of our communion were entirely contented with the Liturgy, and opposed to alterations.

At the General Convention of 1826, the House of Bishops, then composed of ten members, and all being present except two, unanimously recommended certain changes in the order for reading the Psalter and Lessons, in the office of Confirmation, and in the rubric at the end of the Communion service. These changes were proposed by Bishop Hobart, and the preamble which accompanied his resolutions stated that the House of Bishops were "deeply solicitous to preserve unimpaired the Liturgy of the Church, and yet desirous to remove the reasons alleged, from the supposed length of the service, for the omission of some of its parts, and particularly for the omission of that part of the Communion office which is commonly called the Ante-communion." The resolution which related to the reading of holy Scripture, provided that "the minister may, at his discretion, instead of the entire Lessons, read suitable portions thereof, not less than fifteen verses. And on other days than Sundays and holy days, in those places where Morning and Evening Prayer is not daily used, he may read other portions of the Old and New Testament, instead of the prescribed Lessons." An alternative preface was to be inserted in the Order of Confirmation, and also another collect, which might be used, at the discretion of the Bishop, instead of the first collect.

The resolutions were not concurred in by the House of Clerical and Lay Deputies, and submitted to the consideration of the different dioceses, without strenuous opposition. Of the four clerical and two lay delegates present from Connecticut, three of the former and one of the latter voted against them, and Bishop Brownell, in his address to the Diocesan Convention of 1829, thus stated his objections:—

"The consideration of the proposed alterations in the Liturgy of our Church was postponed to the present Convention. I had purposed to avail myself of this occasion fully to express my views on the subject, but the sense of the Church appears to be so decidedly averse to the alterations, that I think there is no probability of their receiving the approbation of the General Convention. Under these circumstances, a discussion of them would be superfluous. Although, at the last General Convention, I voted in favor of submitting these alterations to the consideration of the Church, it was partly in deference to the opinions of others, and on the intimation that such a measure would tend to promote harmony in the Church, and uniformity in the ministrations of the clergy. For myself, I desire to see no further attempts made for changes in the Liturgy, and I believe this to be the general sentiment of this Diocese. I might, indeed, fancy myself able to make improvements in it, if it were left to my discretion. Many others would probably enter on such a work with greater confidence than myself. But I am persuaded that there is no part of the Liturgy but has become endeared to so many pious people, that nothing could be altered or expunged without doing great violence to feelings which every ingenuous mind should respect. I rejoice in the decided expression of opinion which has been evinced in regard to the proposed alterations, and consider it as more auspicious to the integrity of the Liturgy, than any enactments of the General Convention which could possibly be devised."

He was right in his opinion of the general feeling of the Diocese, for the same Convention, to which he spoke these cautions, expressed its sense of the proposed alterations by unanimously rejecting them. The clergy of Connecticut, some years before, had agreed among themselves to a use of the Ante-communion service every Sunday, and they did not wish any modification or new construction of the rubric on this point. In dioceses, too, where the greatest liberties had been taken with the Liturgy, opposition was raised to the changes — and when the General

Convention assembled at Philadelphia in August, 1829, a resolution was adopted, offered by Bishop Hobart himself, to the effect that, "under existing circumstances," it is inexpedient to approve of the propositions, "and they are, therefore, hereby dismissed from the consideration of the Convention."

Bishop Brownell preached the sermon at this meeting in Philadelphia. His subject was "Christian Zeal," and in the treatment of it, he referred to the work of the "Domestic and Foreign Missionary Society," considering its prosperity as inseparably connected with the prosperity of the Church, and the piety of her members. A vast territory of our Union, spreading to the West and to the South, was not then under the jurisdiction of any Protestant bishop, and the Directors of the Society requested him to visit it, and "to perform such Episcopal offices as might be desired, to inquire into the condition of the missions established by the Board, and to take a general survey of the country, for the purpose of designating such other missionary stations as might be usefully established." He was the youngest of the American prelates, and the best situated, it was thought, to undertake a journey which must separate him from his Diocese for many months, and involve him in the perils of a traveller by sea and by land. He left Hartford on the 5th of November, 1829, being escorted to the steamboat by the officers and students of the College, whom he bade an affectionate adieu, and at New York he was joined by the Rev. William Richmond, his faithful companion on the whole visitation.

The general direction of their tour was from Philadelphia to Pittsburgh, and thence down the Ohio and Mississippi rivers, to New Orleans, — the latter city being the utmost point of their destination. Welcomed wherever they passed, and taking advantage of all opportunities to make known the objects of their mission, they succeeded in reviving an interest for the services of the Church, where the people had become discouraged, and in facilitating the organization and support of new parishes. The Bishop exercised his Episcopal functions in Kentucky, Mississippi, Louisiana, and Alabama, and, besides consecrating six churches, admitting one candidate to the priesthood, and confirming one hundred and forty-two persons, he preached, or assisted at divine service seventy-four times, administered the sacrament of the Lord's Supper on several occasions, and baptized twenty-two children and twelve adults. In the course of his visit to Louisiana and Alabama, he presided at conventions held for the regular organization of the Church in those States. Speaking, in his report to the Directors, of the future character and aspect of the country through which he had travelled, he said: —

"The great Valley of the Mississippi, which is so interesting to the statesman and the philosopher, has not failed to attract the attention of the Board I address, to its spiritual wants. This immense region, extending from the Alleghany ridges to the Rocky Mountains, and from Lake Erie to the Gulf of Mexico, was, a few years since, but a vast wilderness, inhabited by wild beasts and a few tribes of wandering savages. At the present day, it comprises a vast empire, and contains nearly five millions of inhabitants. In twenty years to come, it will probably contain twelve millions of souls, which will then be a majority of the whole population of the Union.

"There is a grandeur and solemnity in this march of population, which cannot fail to arrest our attention, and dispose us to reflect on its results. What is to be the religious, the moral, and the intellectual state of these increasing millions? Who, that regards their temporal welfare, would not wish to see them blessed with the religion and the ministrations of the Gospel? But, from the manner in which this country was settled, it is unreasonable to expect that competent provision should yet be made for the support of literary and religious institutions. The emigrants did not take with them their pastors and their schoolmasters, like the Pilgrim Fathers of New England. And, though their enterprise and industry have made the wilderness to bud and blossom as the rose, there have not been the same inducements, nor the same opportunities for religious culture."

On returning homeward "through Alabama, the Creek Nation, and the Atlantic States," Bishop Brownell paid a friendly visit to his brother in the episcopate at Raleigh,[1] North Carolina. He at length reached his home in Hartford on the 14th of March,

[1] "Here we remained a day, for the purpose of rest, and to see the Rt. Rev. Bp. Ravenscroft, who, we had learned, was dangerously ill. We found the Bishop in a very feeble and emaciated state, affording scarcely a hope of his recovery, and awaiting the time of his departure with the most perfect resignation and composure. He had caused a door to be cut in the floor of the chancel of the church and his grave to be dug there, and had caused a plain pine coffin to be made to contain his body." — *Bp. Brownell's MS. Notes.*

On the 5th of March, 1830, ten days after the visit of his brother, Bp. Ravenscroft entered into his rest, "without a struggle or distorted feature," at the age of nearly fifty-eight years.

having been engaged in missionary services for the Church four months, accomplishing a tour through the West and South of about six thousand miles, and rivalling in extent the far-famed visitation of the lamented Heber in India. It is worth while to cite, from his own note-book, the words in which he records his gratitude: —

"I have been graciously preserved from every danger to which I may have been exposed. Nothing has occurred to mar the satisfaction of my journey, or to frustrate the benefits to be expected from it, and I have been permitted to join my family and friends again, under circumstances of the richest mercy. May I be suitably grateful for these unmerited favors, and may the great Head of the Church pour forth abundant blessings on my unworthy labors."

The spiritual destitution seen on this visitation, impressed the beholder with the necessity of an increase in the number of the clergy. The growth of the Church was greater than the supply of faithful laborers, and duly qualified missionaries could not be obtained, to meet the wants of the West and the South, so long as the older parishes in the Eastern and Atlantic States claimed all the active men in Holy Orders. The complete list of the clergy at that time in the country, as shown by the Journal of the General Convention, numbered only five hundred and seven. Bishop Brownell, therefore, once more invited attention to a subject, which he had frequently placed before the Convention of his Diocese. "It is obvious," said he in 1830, "that the principal efforts of Episcopalians should be directed to the education of young men for the sacred ministry." Nothing but a strong sense of religious duty would lead any to devote themselves to a calling which, in this land, offers so few worldly inducements, but there were young men whose piety inclined them to enter the ministry, and whose talents qualified them to adorn it, but who had not the pecuniary means of obtaining a suitable education; and such must be sought out and assisted.

It was to create a feeder for the College, and, in some measure, a nursery to the ministry, that the churchmen of Hartford established an academy in that city, and induced the Rev. Reuben Sherwood to relinquish his pleasant parish in Norwalk, and accept the charge of it, Easter, 1830. Whether he sighed again for the full pastoral work, or felt disappointment at the prospects of the Academy, he ceased his connection with it at the end of a year, and removed from the Diocese, and the buildings, after some fruitless attempts to accomplish the original design, passed into other hands, and were used for other purposes.

Because it speaks of an evil, partly springing from the scarcity of clergymen, and yet directly connected with the misjudgments of the people, this chapter will be closed with an extract from Bishop Brownell's address in 1831:—

"The Convention will not fail to notice the numerous changes in the location of the clergy, reported from year to year. This is not peculiar to Connecticut, but is a common complaint in almost every Diocese. It is occasioned, in a considerable degree, by the inadequate number of the clergy. Vacant parishes will not fail to make overtures to settled clergymen, when no others are to be obtained. These importunities, together with prospects of better support, or of more extensive usefulness, must lead to frequent changes. Another cause, of considerable influence in this Diocese, will be found in the condition of our parishes. Many of these are yet in so feeble a state, that two or three of them are obliged to unite for the support of a clergyman. Under these circumstances, they will generally be averse to the formation of permanent arrangements, in the hope that each will be able to secure the exclusive services of a clergyman at no distant period. But there is still another cause for these frequent changes, for which no justification can be urged. I allude to that love of novelty, and that admiration of mere popular preaching, which, I fear, is too much a characteristic of the present times. It is not thought sufficient that the minister is sensible, discreet, and pious; that he visits the sick and the afflicted, and discharges all his pastoral duties with fidelity. He must, moreover, be an orator, attract the admiration of the multitude, and draw crowds to hear him preach. A good elocution is certainly a very desirable qualification in a public speaker, but it may be doubted whether splendid displays of eloquence contribute greatly to Christian edification. It sometimes happens that men's minds are so engrossed by their admiration of the orator, that they think little of any practical application of the truths which he delivers. But what is called popular preaching, is too often but frothy declamation, set off by some of the graces of delivery. Such popularity is of short continuance. It ceases as soon as the novelty is past, and the unfortunate parish that relies on it, will be grievously disappointed. This eagerness for popular preaching is especially the propensity of the young, whose ardent feelings expose them to the influence of showy and imposing qualities. I have known more than one pastoral connection broken up, where the clergyman possessed undoubted talents and piety, and all those substantial qualifications which go to form the character of the faithful and useful pastor, but was thought deficient in a popular elocution. The temporal condition of the parish did not prosper so remarkably as some of its sanguine members could desire — for though men may plant and cultivate, it is for God to give the increase, and he does this in his own good time. Reports are circulated of the ephemeral growth of some neighboring parish, under the auspices of a popular preacher, and it is fondly imagined that mere popular preaching will produce the same effects in every parish, and that these effects will be permanent. The ardent and restless members of the parish become uneasy. Dissatisfaction and complaints increase, till the clergyman finally deems it expedient to relinquish his station, and seek for service in some other part of his Master's vineyard."

CHAPTER XXI.

RETIREMENT OF THE BISHOP FROM THE PRESIDENCY OF THE COLLEGE; CHARGE TO THE CLERGY; AND GENERAL MISSIONARY SOCIETY OF THE CHURCH.

A. D. 1831 – 1835.

THE Diocese became somewhat restless under the partial supervision of the Bishop, and adopted measures, in 1831, to separate him from the presidency of the College. The combined duties of the two offices were too much for one man to discharge well, and there was a feeling in some quarters that each would suffer, if they continued to be united in the same person. The College was the favorite institution of the Bishop, not less as a nursery of learning than of the ministry of the Church, and around it hung his affections and his prayers. The movement to withdraw him from the immediate administration of it was a delicate one, and the Convention, in making it, bore grateful testimony to the important services rendered by him in founding it and advancing its interests. But, in the same resolution, the earnest hope was expressed that, while so many parishes were destitute of settled ministers, he would devote his labors exclusively to the pastoral care of the Diocese, as soon as a suitable gentleman could be provided to fill the presidency of the institution, and a competent support secured for his family.

He met the request of the Convention without hesitation, and entirely concurred with the members in regard to the expediency of the step which they asked him to take. The question that now rose before them, was, What salary shall be paid to the Bishop? and a committee of five laymen was appointed to devise and report a plan for immediately increasing it to eighteen hundred dollars. This, with the amount of arrearages due to him, which had been accumulating for years, constituted a sum so large, that many feared it would not be raised. The poor parishes, still delinquent in the matter of the old assessments of 1813, were again stirred up, and vigorous efforts made to increase the permanent fund. But they were far from being successful, and the next year a new scheme was adopted, in the shape of the following preamble and resolution: —

"Whereas, at the last Convention of this Diocese, it was voted to grant the Bishop an annual salary of eighteen hundred dollars, and whereas, the funds for the support of the Episcopate yield at this time only about thirteen hundred dollars, therefore, —

Resolved, that, for the purpose of making up the deficiency, the Convention earnestly recommend to the several parishes in the Diocese, to raise an annual contribution of two and one-half per cent. per annum on the amount paid to their clergymen respectively, and to remit the same annually, on or before the first day of August, to the Treasurer of the Bishop's Fund, until the interest of the Bishop's Fund shall amount to the sum of eighteen hundred dollars."

And the members of that Convention, by another

resolution, "individually pledged themselves" to use due diligence to further the object thus recommended.

The Bishop resigned the presidency of the College, in the course of a few months, and his successor was the Rev. N. S. Wheaton, Rector of Christ Church, Hartford. His "Farewell Address" to the students on the occasion of his retiring, delivered in the College Chapel, December 16th, 1831, opens with a passage rich in tender historic associations: —

"The time is at hand when I am to retire from the immediate charge of this institution. It is an event which I cannot contemplate without some emotion. Having made the first movements for the establishment of the College; having been engaged, with great solicitude, in all the measures for procuring its charter, for raising the funds for its endowment; having presided over the instruction and discipline which has been dispensed in it, from its origin to the present time, it is naturally to be expected that my feelings should be strongly identified with its interests and its prospects.

"These feelings of general interest, derive peculiar force from the acquaintances I have formed, and the attachments I have contracted with the young men who have passed under my charge. About *eighty* youth have already received the honors of the institution. They have carried forth into the world a measure of talents and worth of which its friends may well be proud."

A large proportion of these youth entered the sacred ministry, and of the twenty candidates for Holy Orders named by the Bishop in 1832, thirteen were graduates of the College at Hartford. The number increased from year to year, and the Church in Connecticut and other Dioceses received, from this source, many accessions to her educated clergy.

Withdrawn now from other cares, the Bishop devoted himself exclusively to Episcopal duties, and, in 1832, stated that he had visited, since the last Convention, sixty-six parishes, and administered, in fifty-four of them, the rite of confirmation to twelve hundred and ten persons. In the same period he consecrated five new churches, and preached one hundred and thirty-nine times, notwithstanding a "severe lameness," from which he suffered during the early part of the year. Activity in the overseer of the vineyard, as well as in all its workers, was specially demanded. Public attention was now very much directed to the subject of religion in Connecticut, and Bishop Brownell, in his "Second Charge" to the clergy, counselled them how they might best fulfill the ministries with which they were intrusted, and have a due regard to the circumstances of the times. In the heats of religious excitement, charity is often forgotten and misapprehensions propagated, and hence no cautions are more proper than those which relate to the message of salvation and its right acceptance.

"As members of the Protestant Episcopal Church," said he, "we believe that her articles and formularies present a correct view of the true doctrines of the Gospel. That they do so, is generally conceded by all the orthodox denominations of Christians in our country. But we are sometimes charged with holding these doctrines, subject to some mental reservation, and of really entertaining erroneous and defective views of the great doctrines of the Cross. I feel assured that this charge, as applied to the clergy of our Church at the present time, is utterly erroneous and groundless. In retracing the history of the Church of England, we may, perhaps, find a period, when the discourses of her divines were directed too exclusively to the enforcing of social obligations, partly because they considered the peculiar doctrines of the gospel to be generally understood, but chiefly because the sectarian preachers were accustomed to dwell exclusively on high points of faith, to the neglect, and often to the disparagement, of the common duties of life. It may be that the imputation in question has been handed down from these times, in the traditions of dissenters, and transferred from our parent Church to our own. But, however we may feel the injustice of the reproach, it will ultimately be put to shame, if we continue faithfully to preach the great doctrines of grace and salvation through Jesus Christ; and if, when we are called upon to inculcate the relative duties of life, we enforce them by Christian motives and Christian sanctions.

"The whole economy of the gospel supposes mankind to be, by nature, in a state of sin and guilt, subject to the just displeasure of God, and utterly incapable of extricating themselves from misery by their own unassisted powers. This fact constitutes the basis of the scheme of salvation unfolded in the Scriptures, and the foundation of all our efforts to seek the mercy of God, through the merits of the Redeemer. It should be faithfully set forth and enforced by every minister of Christ."[1]

This whole charge, spoken in 1832 to a Conven-

[1] Second Charge, pp. 6, 7.

tion of forty clergymen and forty-three lay delegates, is full of the soundest instruction, and many extracts from it might be made to reflect the religious history of the times. One more, however, of considerable length, is as much as the limits of this chapter will allow.

"The times in which we live, require that we should take especial heed to ourselves and to our doctrine; that we should be abundant in our labors, vigilant in our care of the Church of God committed unto us, and faithful and zealous in the performance of all our duties. Never was there more need of a strict observance of the precept of the Saviour: 'Be ye wise as serpents and harmless as doves.' The subject of religion occupies an unusual share of the public attention. There has been no period since the Reformation, when such zealous exertions have been put forth for its advancement. This auspicious characteristic of the times has been gradually developing itself for more than twenty years, and as the era was preceded by a period of comparative apathy, the present has, not inaptly, been called a season of revival. It is highly important, brethren, that we participate in this characteristic of the age. It is, therefore, incumbent on us, not only to take peculiar heed to our own religious state, and to the spiritual welfare of those who are committed to our charge, but we are called upon to take an active part in the common efforts that are put forth to extend the Redeemer's kingdom through the world. We are called upon to afford our aid in the dissemination of religious knowledge, and in sending forth the gospel of salvation, with its ministry and ordinances, not only to the destitute of our own country, but to the benighted heathen in other lands. And we are emphatically called upon to contribute our aid in elevating and sustaining the tone of religious piety in the communion to which we belong, according to that unerring standard prescribed in the Gospel.

"But, brethren, our times are marked by other characteristics, less auspicious to the cause of divine truth. While these zealous exertions have been put forth for the promotion of the Christian religion, we cannot fail to have observed that this holy cause is bitterly assailed, both by open and covert enemies, and that it is sometimes lamentably injured even by its professed friends. The success of the Redeemer's cause seems to have called forth the most active and subtle opposition of the adversary. Infidelity has arisen from the dust, into which it was humbled by the events of the French Revolution, and once more stalks boldly through the land. The plenary inspiration of the Scriptures, and the divinity and atonement of the Saviour, are now denied by those who bear the Christian name. And even among those who imagine themselves the best friends of religion, its doctrines are sometimes so distorted, the modes of advancing it are sometimes so injudicious and extravagant, and the course of duty it prescribes is sometimes so revoltingly misrepresented, that one is at a loss to determine whether the sacred cause is most injured by its professed friends, or its avowed enemies. The misrepresentations and perversions of infidel writers have, indeed, done incalculable mischief to the cause of Christianity; all the powers of sophistry, sarcasm, and ridicule, have been exhausted by them, and appeals have constantly been made to the worst passions and prejudices of human nature; yet it is still problematical whether it has not been as deeply injured by the erroneous views and mistaken efforts of those who have professed the Christian faith. The history of the Church is full of instructive lessons on this subject. During the period emphatically designated the Dark Ages, the errors and the absurdities of the Romish faith became the occasion of a wide spread infidelity on the one hand, and of the grossest hypocrisy and superstition on the other. The glorious event of the Reformation was soon marred by the metaphysical subtleties intermixed with the Christian faith, in Geneva, Germany, and Scotland. And these perversions have probably been the occasion, in later times, of more pernicious and fatal errors, which sap the very foundation of the Christian faith. There is too much reason to fear that the same theological views have led to the same dangerous errors, in some sections of our country. In the south of Europe, where the abuses of the Romish Church still maintain their sway, a secret infidelity is cherished by large portions of the community. A distinguished Congregational divine has expressed the opinion that, 'In England, the extravagances of the pious, in the time of Cromwell, threw back the cause of vital piety for two centuries.' And he warns the churches of his communion, in New England, and certain portions of the West, against the consequences to be apprehended from the encouragement of similar excesses."[1]

A scheme to convert the Episcopal Academy at

[1] Pages 14, 15.

Cheshire into a self-supporting school, proposed at the previous Annual Convention, and intrusted to a committee, was rejected in 1832, as "inexpedient, if not impracticable." Since the removal of Mr. Crusé from the Diocese, the office of Principal had been vacant, but it was decided to fill it at this time, and, before the ballot was taken, a resolution was adopted, requesting the Trustees of the Academy, in fixing the salary and duties of the Principal, to take into consideration "the expediency of making some provision whereby a portion, or the whole of the students, might contribute something towards their own expenses, by the performance of suitable manual labor." The Rev. Bethel Judd, D. D.,[1] who was the originator of the self-supporting scheme, was chosen Principal. The election relieved the parish at New London of a venerable rector, whose services had ceased to be acceptable to a majority of the members, but it carried no vigor or prosperity to the church and institution in Cheshire. From 1828 to 1835, but two meetings of the Board of Trustees were held, and one only during the administration of Dr. Judd, and that to fix his salary and determine the conditions of his appointment. He tried the visionary project of providing for the support of necessitous young men, by adopting in part the manual labor system, but he failed to create any interest in his work, and, with the infirmities of age upon him, he could do little for the parish of which he was also the Rector. Not meeting,

[1] The College at Hartford, in 1831, conferred the degree of Doctor of Divinity upon Rev. Daniel Burhans, Rev. Harry Croswell, and Rev. Bethel Judd. They were the first American clergymen upon whom the corporation conferred this honor, but since that date, many of our bishops and presbyters have received it from the same source.

therefore, with the success that he anticipated, Dr. Judd resigned to the Convention his office of Principal, in October, 1835, and afterwards removed from the Diocese. He had not, for some months previous to this, resided in Cheshire, or interested himself in the concerns of the parish or the management of the institution. The building, which had gone into decay, was then extensively repaired and remodelled, and a whole year was suffered to elapse, before the right man could be procured to fill the vacant post.

For half a century the Annual Convention had assembled in different parishes, according to the determination of the Bishop, on the first Wednesday of June, but, in 1831, a proposition was made to substitute for this date, the second Tuesday of October, and, the next year, the amendment was approved by the concurrent vote of both orders, and became a part of the Constitution of the Church in the Diocese. It carried the meeting to a season, when it was thought a better attendance of lay delegates might be secured, especially from parishes in the agricultural districts. The first Convention to be held under the amended Constitution, was appointed at Chatham, now Portland, but no quorum assembled, for it appeared to be the general impression that all necessary business had been transacted at the previous meeting in June. The next year, 1833, it was appointed at Norwich, and as railroads had not yet taken the place of stages and private carriages, it was unfortunate, for testing the expediency of the change, that a place should have been selected so much out of the way, and in a part of the State where there were but few parishes.

The clergy and laity met in Christ Church, in that

city, at the time appointed, and after morning prayer, and a sermon from President Wheaton, the roll was called, and twenty-one clergymen answered to their names, and then an adjournment followed till the afternoon. Upon reassembling, only seventeen lay delegates were found to be present, — not enough for the transaction of business, the Constitution requiring twenty of this order. The parochial reports, however, were read, and an informal discussion was had upon a communication from the Secretary of the General Convention, relative to certain alterations in the rubrics, but the evening was very stormy, and an adjournment took place till the next day. Wednesday came, and there was still no quorum. Another public service was held at eleven o'clock, and a sermon preached by the Rev. Dr. Croswell. In the afternoon, notwithstanding the nearest unrepresented parishes had been specially requested to send in delegates, two were yet wanting to enable the Convention to organize, — a number which would have been supplied but for a melancholy accident that occurred early that morning, and destroyed the lives of several persons, and among them two laymen, who were on their way from a remote section of the State to attend the Convention.[1] Numerous meetings of the clergy were held, and the occasion was by no means without interest and profit, but the business of the

[1] The steamboat New England, on her passage from New York to Hartford, having on board seventy-one persons, burst both her boilers near Essex, about 3 o'clock Wednesday morning, and eight persons were immediately killed, and thirteen seriously injured. Among the fatally injured were Mr. John M. Heron and Dr. Samuel B. Whiting, lay delegates from Redding, and they were within a mile of their landing-place at the time of the accident.

Diocese was necessarily postponed, and the members finally adjourned, sorrowing over the intelligence which had reached them of the terrible disaster on the Connecticut River.

Bishop Brownell left New York, in a ship for New Orleans, November 18th, 1834, with a view to his wife's health, and at the request of the vestry of Christ Church in that city. He was absent during the winter and a part of the spring, and spent most of the time in New Orleans, collecting together the scattered congregation of Episcopalians, and encouraging them to erect a new church and elect a permanent rector. Alabama had been placed under his provisional charge, and he was present at the Annual Convention, held at Tuscaloosa on the 19th of January, preached the sermon, and presided over its deliberations. He was also present at a special Convention of the Diocese of Mississippi, held at Natchez on the 23d of February, and took great interest in the steps which led to the formation of the Southwestern Diocese.[1]

The General Convention, which met at Philadelphia in 1835, took a long step forward in the work of Domestic and Foreign Missions. It was the last Con-

[1] This was composed of the "Dioceses of Mississippi and Alabama, and the churches in the State of Louisiana," organized under a special Canon of the General Convention of 1832. Before Bishop Brownell left for the North, the Rev. Francis L. Hawks, D.D., had been elected Bishop of the Southwestern Diocese, and rector of the parish in New Orleans. But he declined the offices to which he was thus chosen, and "other untoward events" happening, the organization failed, and was soon broken up.

Bishop Brownell, during this visit to the South, confirmed sixty-two persons — thirty-eight in New Orleans, seventeen in Mobile, and seven in Tuscaloosa, where he also consecrated the church.

vention at which Bishop White presided, for he died the ensuing year; and, having witnessed the first efforts of the Church, in 1792, to "support missionaries to preach the Gospel on the frontiers," and the establishment, in 1820, of a voluntary society, composed of contributors to its funds, that the work might be done more effectively, he now saw, in the progress of Christian zeal, the primitive ground taken, that the Church, as such, is our great Missionary Society, and that every person who is admitted within her pale by baptism, becomes by that act a member of the Missionary Society in the highest sense of the term. As the organ and representative of the Protestant Episcopal Church in the United States of America, the General Convention of 1835 openly, in the face of all Christendom, recognized this principle, and assumed the corresponding duties. And thus our Church publicly pledged herself henceforth to fulfil, according to her ability, the divine injunctions of the Saviour, — "Go ye into all the world, and preach the Gospel to every creature; go, make disciples of all nations, baptizing them in the name of the Father, and of the Son, and of the Holy Ghost; teaching them to observe all things whatsoever I have commanded you; and, lo, I am with you alway, even unto the end of the world."

The Episcopal Church in the United States had then sixteen bishops and seven hundred and sixty-one clergymen. Of the latter, eighty were in Connecticut, and this Diocese, next to New York, which was not yet divided, had the largest clerical list in the country. The world was the one field which the General Missionary Society, under its new organization, had in view, — the terms *domestic* and *foreign*, being only designations of the locality of its operations. While the missionary spirit of Connecticut would be confined within no narrower limits than those thus pointed out, the state of her parishes, and the religious aspect of many populous towns, seemed to plead for paramount sympathy and more generous contributions. Bishop Brownell, in his annual address to the Convention of 1835, referring to these things, and to the want of a proper interest in the operations of the Society for the Promotion of Christian Knowledge, called upon the clergy of the Diocese "to come up to the work with a spirit adequate to the urgency of the times."

"It is certain," said he, "that there is nothing in this department of missionary operations, which addresses itself strongly to the imagination. It is no region of romance. The results of our labor will not be magnified by distance, nor derive interest from associations with strange manners and a foreign language, yet they may not be less salutary to the souls of men, nor productive of less substantial benefit to the cause of Christ. It is not sufficiently considered, that in building up the Church in this Diocese, we are subserving the general cause of missions as effectually, though not directly, as though we were laboring among our scattered and destitute brethren of the West, or among the heathen of foreign lands. The whole Church of Connecticut has long been, in point of fact, *a Missionary Church.* Her lay emigrants, who have removed to adjacent States, and to the remoter West, have not failed to carry with them their love for the Church, and have ever been the first to rear up her institutions in the land of their adoption. She has, moreover, been a fruitful nursery of clergymen, and there is hardly a State in the Union where we may not find some of her sons ministering at the altar. Let it be borne in mind, then, that in extending the Church within our own borders, we are, at the same time, advancing the general interest of missions. Indeed, I may truly add, that with us every faithful parish minister is, in fact, a laborer in the missionary cause.

"But it is not through the medium of emigrations alone, that our building up the Church at home contributes to promote its advancement abroad. By multiplying the number of our congregations, and by increasing their strength, we not only augment the number of those who will spread abroad the institutions of the Church, but we increase our own direct ability to add to the amount of her missionary funds. This is another consideration that is not sufficiently borne in mind, because the effect is not so immediate, direct, and obvious; but it well deserves the attention of reflecting and judicious churchmen.

"It is true, the field of missions is the world. But we cannot reach the whole world at once. We must operate in the fields that are most accessible to us, and in places where our labors will, ultimately, turn to the best account. By extending the Church in our own State, and in our own country, we increase our ability to carry the light and the blessings of the gospel to the heathen nations. We may grieve at the slowness of our progress, and be impatient to leap from the means to the end. But both should be kept in view by the discreet Christian. Next to the salvation of our own souls, our great concern should certainly be to spread abroad the knowledge of the gospel, and to assist in building up the Christian Church, as it was originally founded upon the Apostles and prophets, Jesus Christ himself being the chief corner stone. Whenever we are conscientiously engaged in this work, in whatever field it may be, we may rest assured that we are in the performance of our duty, and we may confidently look to the great Head of the Church for His blessing on our labors."

The Diocesan Convention of 1835 was thoroughly missionary in its tone. Besides the Bishop's address, and the usual sermon in behalf of the Society for the Promotion of Christian Knowledge, the discourse before the Convention was on the subject of Missions, and each parochial clergyman, by a specific resolution of that body, was desired to take the earliest opportunity of carrying into "effectual operation," in such way as he might deem expedient, the principle publicly acknowledged and practically adopted by the General Council of the Church. The fruits of this new impulse to the cause of missions were visible, the next year, in every part of the Diocese.

CHAPTER XXII.

USE OF THE GENERAL CONFESSION; THIRD CHARGE OF THE BISHOP; ANOTHER VISIT TO NEW ORLEANS; AND MAINTENANCE OF THE CLERGY.

A. D. 1835 – 1840.

THE construction of the rubric admitted of a doubt, whether the General Confession in the Daily Morning and Evening Prayer was designed to be the joint act of minister and people. Hence a practice had arisen, borrowed from the usage of the English Church, whereby the minister pronounced each sentence of the Confession by himself, — the people not beginning until he had finished it, and then concluding the whole with the word "Amen," as their response, in which the minister did not unite. The attention of the House of Bishops was called to this practice, in 1835, by the other branch of the General Convention, and an opinion solicited with a view of promoting uniformity in the performance of all the offices of public worship.

The Bishops unanimously concurred in an opinion, which was thus expressed: "A regard to uniformity with what is practiced in other parts of the Liturgy, and also to the avoiding of a needless addition to the length of the service, and to its most decent performance, requires, that in repeating the General Confession in the Morning and Evening Prayer, the people should unite with the minister in saying it after him, in the same manner as is usually practiced in saying the Creeds, the Lord's Prayer, and the Confession in the Communion Service." A further opinion was given that, in those parts of the Liturgy in which the minister and people are to unite audibly, "as in the Confessions, the Creeds, the Lord's Prayer, the Gloria in Excelsis, the Trisagion, and the last prayer for Ash-Wednesday," the word "Amen" should be printed in the Roman letters, and the minister unite with the people in saying it, and wherever it is the response of the people to what the minister alone says, it should be printed in italics. A declaration that it is expedient to omit the Collect and Lord's Prayer, before the sermon, was annexed to the same opinion.

These proposed changes were carried into effect in most of the parishes of Connecticut on the afternoon of the third Sunday in October, 1835, and they were at once appreciated, both by the ministers and their congregations. Since that date, the Diocese has been marked by great uniformity in the performance of public services, and no serious departures from the rubrics have been noted.

The Annual Convention of 1836, composed of thirty-two clergymen and forty-six lay delegates, met in Christ Church, Hartford, and the Bishop delivered his "Third Charge." It was strongly imbued with the missionary spirit, and reiterated much that he had put forth on former occasions. The new vigor produced by the recent action of the General Convention, seemed to invite him to the consideration of this subject, and the kindred subject of an increase in the number of the clergy. He felt, with others, that our communion now, unfettered by any ties of human policy, and prospering with the prosperity of the country, was well situated to bear the tidings of Redemption into "waste and perishing borders."

"I find my Church," said the Rev. Dr. Jarvis, on his return to the United States, after an absence in Europe of nearly ten years, "once the feeble offspring of missionary labor, now, in her turn, extending the blessings of the Gospel to heathen lands, and repaying to another member of Christ's body, a portion of that aid which she herself formerly received. I find my country advanced in prosperity to a degree unimaginable and inconceivable by any who have not seen it with their own eyes. I find a life, and activity, and enterprise, a youthful ardor and vigor, arising from the freedom of our institutions, and our peculiar position, which, elsewhere, it would be in vain to look for. And from this united view of my Church and my country, I am constrained to ask, who are better situated than ourselves to become the heralds of the Cross? This life, and activity, and enterprise, and ardor, and vigor, which is the characteristic of our countrymen, needs only to be directed into right channels. In proportion as a lively sense of the unsearchable riches of Christ is diffused through our nation, in the same proportion will these energies be properly and successfully directed. In proportion as our Church is extended and strengthened in our own country, will the share be increased in which Christian America will act for the conversion of the world."[1]

[1] Sermon before the Church Scholarship Society, 1835, pp. 31, 32.

But the great want of the Church, in order to meet the exigencies of the times, was still the want of more ministers. The love of money, and the love of distinction, were absorbing passions that cast all the gentler occupations of life into obscurity and neglect, and it was natural that young men of affluence, education, and intelligence, should be tempted to other pursuits, and indisposed to undertake the toils and self-denials of the priestly office.

"Fortunately," said Bishop Brownell, "for the purity of the gospel ministry in our country, it holds out few pecuniary allurements to induce men to enter on its sacred functions. Though it requires an expensive education, and a long period of laborious preparatory study, the pecuniary compensation of a clergyman is barely adequate to his humble support. The mechanic, who learns his profession at little cost, is better paid, and has greater opportunity of laying up in store an adequate provision for his family. There is, therefore, no pecuniary inducement to call forth a supply proportioned to the demand. But, in this case, the maxim of political economy must be, in fact, reversed. We must procure a supply, in order to create a demand. It will not do to wait till the parish is organized, the church built, and the clergyman's salary provided. In the ordinary course of affairs, these things would never be done. The presence, the zeal, and the influence of the clergyman, are required to effect these arrangements. The first evangelists were not instructed to wait till the way should be thus prepared for them, and they called forth to enter on their ministry."

In this connection, he spoke of the necessity of

training and educating young men "for the altars of our Church by the liberality of her members," and in seminaries friendly to our religious principles. Then, too, there were other auxiliary means, which he would not have overlooked or neglected in seeking to promote the general prosperity of the Church.

"Christian parents," said he, "may do much towards directing the inclinations of their sons to the ministry of the sanctuary. They can dedicate them to God, in their infancy, and rear them up 'in the nurture and admonition of the Lord.' They can be instant in prayer for the renovation of their hearts, and they can lead their minds and direct their studies to this holy end. Were there more pious Hannahs in the Church, there would be more youthful Samuels consecrated to the service of the temple. The father of Hannibal was able to inspire an undying hatred to the Romans, when he was only nine years old. Cannot the Christian father be equally successful in filling the heart of his son with a prevailing love for the souls of men, and for the service of the altar.

"The ministers of Christ may do much towards filling up the thin and scattered ranks of their order. They can seek, through their Sunday-schools and their parishes, for youth of promising talents, to whom, in the morning of their days, the renewing influences of divine grace have been imparted. They can lay before them the destitutions of the Church, and the spiritual wants of the world; and, if they find any who feel themselves moved of God to labor in his vineyard, they can direct their studies, and facilitate their preparation for the work.

"But, above all, the prayers of the whole Church

should be put forth for the enlargement of her borders, for the increase of her zeal, and for the multiplication of her ministers."[1]

In November, 1836, Bishop Brownell consented to undertake a third journey to New Orleans. On the occasion of his visit to that city, two years before, he was instrumental in collecting together the scattered members of the Episcopal Church, and uniting them in an effort to erect a new house of worship. The edifice was now completed and ready for consecration, and, as there was not an Episcopal clergyman in the whole State of Louisiana, he was strongly urged by the vestry of the parish to make another visit, administer confirmation, and consecrate the new church, and officiate in the same so long as it might suit his convenience. He was absent from his Diocese five months, during which time he visited Mobile and confirmed several persons; and, before his departure for the North, the parish in New Orleans had extended an invitation to the Rev. Dr. Wheaton, President of the College at Hartford, to become its rector, and his acceptance had been received.

Dr. Wheaton left behind him many marks of his zeal and activity, and his exquisite taste was visible in an improvement of the grounds about the College. He was indefatigable in soliciting funds for its benefit, and, when he withdrew from its charge, he had laid the foundation of a system of judicious endowments, which his own private benefactions, subsequently yet unostentatiously bestowed, helped to foster.

Frequent changes in the presidency are always to be avoided, because always injurious to the prosperity

[1] Charge, 1836, pp. 22, 23.

of a college. Care should be taken to select for that office men who are well fitted to its responsibilities and duties by experience and attainment, and then none but the best reasons should be allowed to produce a dissolution of the connection. The Trustees resolved at length to fill the vacancy, occasioned by the resignation of Dr. Wheaton, with one who, though he had gained no celebrity in the Church, had yet proved himself eminently successful in one department of collegiate instruction. Thus they chose their own Professor of Mathematics and Natural Philosophy, the Rev. Silas Totten, D. D.

The constitution of the Episcopal Academy of Connecticut, at the instance of the Board of Trustees, was carefully revised by the Convention of 1836, and among the changes introduced, was one giving to the corporation the power of choosing the Principal, — a power hitherto held by the Convention of the Diocese. Other features, better suited to the object of a preparatory school of the highest order, were incorporated into the several articles, and as much of the old letter retained as comported with the design of the new organization. At a meeting of the Trustees in May, the Rev. Allen C. Morgan, Rector of St. John's Church, Waterbury, was appointed provisional Principal, but he did not accept the appointment until it had been renewed with great unanimity by the Convention of 1836, when he immediately prepared to enter upon its duties. Success attended his efforts to revive the Academy, and restore it to the measure of its ancient prosperity, but, at the end of two years, his sudden death, while on a journey to New York, again created a vacancy, which was filled by electing as Principal the author of this work, at that time the youthful Rector of St. Peter's Church in Cheshire.

The Convention of 1836 revised, also, the Constitution of the Church in the Diocese, in accordance with amendments proposed the previous year, and put back, to its old historic place in June, the time of the annual meeting.

St. James's Church, Westville, in the town of New Haven, St. Mark's Church, New Britain, and Christ Church, Westport, were new parishes, added, the first named in 1835, the other two in 1836, to the list of those in union with the Convention. Houses of worship were erected at once for each of these parishes, and, in several of the older ones, steps were taken which indicated the advancement of the Church. A chapel was built and consecrated in the autumn of 1835, at Bethel, in Danbury, out of which has since sprung a thrifty parochial organization. A spacious church of gray stone, not architecturally imposing or attractive, was built by St. John's parish, Bridgeport, and a smaller one, of like material and better design, by the parish in Guilford, and both were consecrated in 1838. Within the period embraced in this chapter, new churches were consecrated at North Haven, Bethlehem, Southport, Bristol, Oxford, Milton, Bridgewater, New Milford, Glastenbury, Brookfield, Trumbull, and Cheshire. Those at North Haven, Glastenbury, Bethlehem, and Cheshire, were constructed of brick, the rest of wood.

In his address to the Annual Convention of 1837, Bishop Brownell referred to the fact, that he had been able to visit all the parishes of the Diocese, with few exceptions, each year since his "withdrawal from the charge of Washington College." But, he went on to say, "it becomes a question of considerable moment, whether such frequent visitations are really useful to the parishes? I certainly deem it useful annually to become acquainted with the condition of each particular parish; and it affords me, personally, much gratification annually to meet each of my brethren of the clergy in his own domestic circle, to see the faces of my brethren of the laity, and to enjoy the hospitality and kindness which, on such occasions, I never fail to experience. Yet it may reasonably be questioned, whether such frequent visitations do not diminish the interest which would otherwise be attached to them? I would especially call the attention of the clergy and of the Convention to this question, in reference to the holy rite of Confirmation. When that rite is administered annually, there will be, of course, but a small number to receive it. Does not the smallness of the number sometimes detract from the interest which the clergyman and the congregation would otherwise attach to the administration of it? When it is felt, too, that the rite may be received the very next season, does not this consideration sometimes lead to a postponement of the preparation for it to another, and another, and another year? And do not such frequent visitations sometimes become rather opportunities for the gratification of private friendship, than the occasions for the performance of official duties? The question here presented is one on which my own mind is not yet definitely settled. I leave it with my brethren for their future consideration and ultimate counsel."

And his brethren, in taking up the subject the

next year, referred it to a committee, who suggested an alteration in the time and manner of making his visitations. "The number of congregations in the Diocese," said they, "is such, that if the Bishop visits them all every year, in those seasons which are favorable for an attendance on public worship, his stay in each parish must, necessarily, be very short. This circumstance, alone, may account for the occasional negligence which exists on the part of the clergy to accompany the Bishop in his visitations, and the consequent transient effects produced by them. Could the clergy be excited to take a deep interest in them, and accompany the Bishop in sufficient numbers to show the laity that they consider them important, and to enable the rector of the parish visited to have such additional services as the situation of his parish might require, this evil might be remedied."

Hence resolutions were adopted, to the effect, that it be not expected of the Bishop to visit each parish every year, — the canon then, as now, required an Episcopal visitation once in three years, — but that it be recommended to him, so to arrange his visitations as to allow more time to each parish, and that the clergy accompany him on such visitations as far as their respective duties would permit.

Great sensibility to the concerns of religion was evinced in Connecticut, soon after Bishop Brownell put forth his suggestions. A revival prevailed in some parts of the State, and symptoms of renewed vitality were seen in many parishes, that called for special visitations. As a consequence of this, he reported, in 1838, a larger number of persons confirmed than he had reported in any one year during the preceding five. The number of parishes visited was not much diminished in the next two years, and from 1829, when he summed up his confirmations, to 1840, he had added to the list four thousand eight hundred and seventy-two, making in all, to that date, since his consecration to the Episcopate, including those confirmed during his first two visits to the southwest, eight thousand two hundred and forty-six. The communicants, in 1840, as reported in fifty-eight parishes, were five thousand four hundred and sixty-eight, but as no returns were received from full a score of the smaller parishes, the whole number in the Diocese must have been, at least, six thousand. The aggregate of new communicants since 1819 exceeded this number.

The "Episcopal Watchman," a weekly paper devoted to the interests of the Church in Connecticut, was published in Hartford for seven years, and then, in the beginning of 1834, it was discontinued, and the list of subscribers was transferred to a New York publication. But the churchmen of the Diocese, who had been so long accustomed to a periodical of their own, were not content to be thus served, and a layman[1] was encouraged in a scheme of issuing another

[1] Alonzo B. Chapin, Esq., the son of a Congregational minister, and educated for the legal profession. He read himself into the Episcopal Church, and, becoming a candidate for Holy Orders, was ordained a deacon in 1838. He was a student of remarkable industry, and stored his mind with a fund of varied knowledge, some of which he put forth in the shape of pamphlets, reviews, and books, that gained for him a wide reputation among churchmen. He was too rapid a writer to be always accurate, and more care and scholarship would have added to the value of his historical publications. The work by which he is best known, is *A view of the Organization and Order of the Primitive Church.* He was honored with the degree of D. D. by the Norwich University, of Vermont, and died at Hartford, after much bodily suffering, in 1858, at the age of 50.

weekly paper, to be called the "Chronicle of the Church." It was an inauspicious time to begin an enterprise of this sort, for the embarrassments in the commercial world were great, and there was much derangement in the currency of the country. But, with liberal promises in the outset, and a partial indorsement of the object by the Convention of the Diocese, the paper, the first number of which was issued at New Haven, Epiphany, 1837, soon obtained a fair circulation, and was continued under the charge of its original editor for eight years, when it was removed to Hartford, and merged in "The Calendar."[1]

The number of candidates for Holy Orders continued to increase in Connecticut, without really adding many to the list of the parochial clergy. Age and infirmity gradually removed the names which had stood the longest on this list, and the Rev. Reuben Ives went to his rest in October, 1836, having several years before retired from the active duties of the ministry. But Ashbel Baldwin, Daniel Burhans, and Truman Marsh, each without any charge, still lingered, the only survivors of those belonging to Connecticut who were ordained by its first Bishop.

As fast as the new candidates were admitted to the priesthood, they seemed to be wanted in other Dioceses;

[1] This was a weekly paper published, under different editors, until 1866, when it took the name of the *Connecticut Churchman*, and the next year it assumed a broader title, *The Churchman*. No official sanction by the Convention, of what has become a strictly private enterprise, has been sought or given for nearly thirty years. It has long been the universal feeling that Church periodicals of all kinds, in this country, must depend for support upon their intrinsic merits.

and there were those among them who could not well decline the invitations to rectorships elsewhere, that promised a liberal support and a wide field of usefulness. In 1840, Bishop Brownell stated, in his address to the Annual Convention, that he had granted, during the previous year, letters dimissory to thirteen clergymen, — ten of them being natives of Connecticut. The parishes were constantly gaining strength, and the weaker ones were beginning to ask for more frequent services, and all for "clergymen who were supposed to possess higher qualifications of learning or talents." But there was an evil, in the power of the laity to remedy, which lay at the bottom of much of this uncertainty in the pastoral relations. While many of the necessaries of life had become more expensive, — some of them having doubled in value, — and while the wages of common laborers and of mechanics had been increased in the same proportion, there was not a corresponding improvement in the provision made for the maintenance of the clergy. Their salaries in Connecticut stood, substantially, where they had stood for twenty years, and, as taxing had ceased, and the support of religion was wholly voluntary, large parishes in the agricultural towns appeared to think they were doing liberally, if they each paid an annual salary of five hundred dollars. Even this, in some cases, was doled out in a way quite unsatisfactory and embarrassing to the receivers.

Bishop Brownell, therefore, very properly called the attention of the laity to the subject, in 1839, and urged them to inquire whether justice was extended to the labors of the clergy. He spoke of the constant demands for "higher qualifications in classical education," and then said: —

"The money now required to carry a young man through the Academy, the College, and the Theological Seminary, would purchase a considerable farm, or constitute a moderate capital for the young manufacturer, mechanic, or merchant. And yet how different are the worldly prospects of these classes? The industrious farmer may secure a competence for his family, or even rise to affluence. The mechanic, the manufacturer, and the merchant may become rich, through the many avenues of enterprise. But the clergyman, whose intelligence might find such scope in the pursuits of ambition, must be content with the mere necessaries of life. And if he leaves a family behind him, when he is called from his labors, they must be consigned to the charities of the world, or to the care of more fortunate relatives or friends.

"It is true that the clergyman has higher ends and aims than the acquisition of wealth. It is also true, that the cares of riches might tend to withdraw his thoughts from his more sacred duties. But it must be remembered that poverty has also its cares. And, though I would not wish to see a wealthy clergy, I would desire to see every clergyman's mind freed from corroding anxieties in regard to the immediate support of his family; and I think it not too much to desire, also, that he should be able to lay aside some little provision for the support of his old age, or to secure a bereaved family from absolute want.

"In this Diocese, I know of no clergyman with a family, who receives greater compensation for his services than is necessary for his immediate and moderate support. I know of many who are scarcely able to maintain their families, with the most rigid economy, and who have a hard struggle to keep free from the humiliation of unpaid demands for the common necessaries of life. The condition of the unmarried clergy is but little better, for, in most cases, any modicum they may be able to save from their necessary expenses must be expended in books, or applied to the payment of debts incurred during their preparation for the ministry.

"Brethren of the laity, these things ought not so to be. They are repugnant to justice, to humanity, and to Scripture. 'The laborer is worthy of his hire.' . . .

"I say not these things at the instance of the clergy, for they are as uncomplaining as they are self-denying. But, as Providence has placed me in a station to witness their privations, as well as their devoted labors, and knowing, as I do, the discouragements which those privations throw in the way of those who are looking forward to the sacred office, I should be unfaithful to my duty, and unjust to my feelings, if I failed to inculcate upon the several parishes of this Diocese the immediate necessity of a more adequate provision for the support of their clergy."

CHAPTER XXIII.

EDUCATION IN THE CHURCH; OXFORD TRACTS; FOURTH CHARGE OF BISHOP BROWNELL; AND NEW PARISHES.

A. D. 1840 – 1843.

The public schools of Connecticut offered so many advantages for a preliminary course of instruction, that churchmen committed their children to them, regardless of the evils by which they were attended. The munificent fund provided by the State for the purposes of primary education, continued to operate as a check upon the establishment of parochial schools or private seminaries. But the question was sometimes raised, whether efforts ought not to be encouraged for bringing a larger number of the children of Episcopalians under the constant influence of the teachings of the Church? It was felt to be unwise to subject to sectarian influences those youth, especially, who must be sent from home to finish their education, or who, having passed beyond the common schools, needed the higher instruction of the academy to prepare them for college, or for the counting-room. The Diocesan institution at Cheshire, though prosperous and doing its work well, could not provide for all of this class.

The fashion of family boarding-schools for each sex, separately, was now extending, and, from time to time, a few clergymen of the Diocese, with insufficient salaries from their parishes, or with a taste for teaching, were induced to advertise for scholars, and to make arrangements for their reception in the best manner they could. With limited accommodations, the number in each case was usually, at first, small, but out of these and similar efforts have grown private educational institutions, which, receiving pupils from different sections of the country, have had a long season of prosperity, and benefited the Church at the same time that they have rewarded, in a measure, the toil of their projectors. During the period from childhood to youth, external influences are the most potent in their operation, and for this reason, teachers who command the respect and affection of their pupils, will naturally impress upon them, even though they use none of the arts of proselytism, their own views of important questions concerning morals and religion. It is an inaccurate assumption, that if there be given to a child certain general principles, he will, of himself, erect upon them the proper superstructure. As the natural tendency of the human mind is not to right doctrines, so no Christian parent, living in the faith of our Church, can consent to leave it to the individual judgment of his son to fix what course he will pursue, and what creed he shall adopt.

The Convention of 1840, acting upon that part of Bishop Brownell's address which related to the subject of education, adopted the report of a committee, which contained these words: —

"Let churchmen patronize their own institutions. All similar institutions are now, by tacit and common consent, under the influence of particular denominations. If we send our children where their religious faith is in danger of being perverted, we have no one to blame for it but ourselves. Let the clergy exert themselves, by persuasion and remonstrance, to induce the laity, in their respective cures, not to sacrifice to convenience or to fancied intellectual advantages, the spiritual welfare of their children."

Appended to the whole report were several resolutions, and among them one : —

"That it is the duty of every member of the Church in this Diocese to unite in establishing, or improving, if already established, Episcopal academies or other schools for the higher instruction of youth, and not to expose the children of the Church to be perverted by sectarian influences."

All this was recommended in reference to institutions for males, and the College at Hartford, about which there was dissatisfaction in some quarters, because it did not attract a larger number of students, was presented to the Convention, not only as deserving a place in the hearts of Connecticut churchmen, but as entitled to the confidence and support of those who belonged to other dioceses. The education of females, quite as important in many of its aspects as that of males, was not touched directly in the report, and it has never been made a subject of legislation or public counsel by the Church in Connecticut. But seminaries for this purpose were established in some of the principal towns of the State by Christian women, upon their own responsibility, and under the patronage of leading clergymen and laymen ; and many parishes in remote parts of the land, as well as nearer home, have felt the influence of the good training of those who, from school-girls, have become mistresses of households, and zealous promoters of the interests of the Episcopal Church.

A theological movement in England, under the management of a few distinguished divines of Oxford, assumed a character which was beginning to create uneasiness and alarm. The growth of latitudinarian sentiments, and the ignorance which prevailed concerning the spiritual claims of the Church, were evils in the mother country, which the writers of the "Tracts for the Times" at first professed to be desirous of reaching and remedying. But, in their zeal to revive neglected usages and excite a veneration for Catholic antiquity, they seemed to be carried beyond their original purpose, as announced, and they were led to make statements in their writings which conflicted with the principles of the English Reformation, and rendered them liable to the charge of Romanizing tendencies. Feelings of strong partisanship were indulged in the controversy which followed the publication of the Tracts, and while the Oxford divines embraced every opportunity to clear themselves from the imputation of Popery, and denied that Church principles could ever become the path to superstition and idolatry, their opponents, on the other hand, persistently charged them with looking in the direction of Rome, and forsaking and condemning the spirit and doctrines of the English Reformers.

With the appearance of the Tracts in this country came much of the evil of the foreign controversy, and party spirit, for a time, ran high in the Church. As a consequence, the publications were both defended and denounced by those who had never read them; and the judgment of the clergy, and of intelligent laymen, interested in theological science, was, in a measure, forestalled by the discussions and statements about them in the popular periodicals of the day. Connecticut was not a good field in which to carry on a controversy of this kind, and, perhaps, no Diocese in the land manifested less concern in the progress of the whole movement. Bishop Brownell referred to the subject in his address to the Annual Convention of 1840, and he was so well convinced of the truth and propriety of the sentiments which he then expressed, that he repeated them in his address the next year without changing a word. After stating his repugnance to innovation, and his desire to see his brethren pursuing a course "equally free from the errors of the Romish superstition, on the one hand, and from the novelties and devices of sectarian dissent, on the other," he added some words about the controversies which had sprung from the Oxford Tracts, and said: —

"If the learned authors have sometimes manifested an undue veneration for the writings of the early Fathers of the Church, and an undue admiration for some ceremonies dropped at the Reformation, there can be little danger from their enthusiasm on these subjects, in a country of free discussion; and a nearer approximation to the truth will be the probable result in England of the present controversy. I cannot help thinking, however, that in that country much of the heat of this controversy, and much of the interest which it has excited, have been occasioned by its connection with those party politics, and sectarian prejudices, which prevail there. In our own country, the first of these causes can have no influence, and the latter must be much less strongly felt; and we should be unable to account for the sensation which the discussion has excited among us, were it not for the influence of those sympathies and antipathies which, in the present state of intercourse, are so easily propagated across the Atlantic.

"The circumstances under which our Church has grown up in this country, have led us to regard it in its true character, not as a State establishment, but as a divine institution. As a minor denomination of Christians, too, we have been constantly compelled to act on the defensive, and have been more generally accustomed, than our English brethren, to refer its constitution to the appropriate Scriptural authority, and its usages to those early Christian writings, by which they can be successfully defended.

"Though I do not imagine that the Tracts referred to, or the discussions which have grown out of them, will lead to any material change of sentiment in regard to the doctrines, discipline, or usages of the Church, as they are now received and practiced by us, yet the writers will not fail to command our respect for their learning, their talents, and their piety. And if the controversies which they have aroused, both in England and in this country, are attended with some violations of Christian charity, it is to be hoped that the evil will be counterbalanced, in the ultimate elucidation and establishment of truth.

"For ourselves, brethren, we are much less concerned about new discoveries in religion, than we are to preserve, in their integrity and purity, the faith and worship which now pertain to our Church; founded, as they are, in the Scriptures of truth, freed from the errors and incumbrances of superstition by the Reformation, and detached from all embarrassing alliance with the State, by the civil constitution of our country. We love the Church as it is; *Nolumus mutari*."

It will be seen in a future chapter, that the complacency with which the Bishop at first viewed this theological movement, was somewhat disturbed by its later developments and fruits, and he had reason to "deprecate the treachery of perverting the doctrines of the Church, or the teaching of dogmas alien to her faith, while ministering at her altars."

The Annual Convention of the Diocese, which met at Hartford in 1843, was composed of sixty-four clergymen and seventy-three lay delegates. On this occasion, he delivered his fourth and last charge to the clergy, entitled "Errors of the Times," — a suggestive subject, which admitted of a wide range of thought, and embraced a view of things that could not well be considered in his usual addresses. The tone and temper of the "dissenting press" were against the Church; and its various periodicals, taking advantage of the feeling excited by the discussions recently commenced at the University of Oxford, joined in a "general crusade against Popery, Puseyism, and Prelacy." The charge was the longest which the Bishop had delivered, and about one half of it was occupied with remarks on the abuses of the right of private judgment in matters of religion, and on some of the errors which have prevailed in modern times respecting the Church of God and its ministry. An extract from this part of it will show the tenor of his counsels upon one of the topics: —

"The general exercise of private judgment, and the freedom of the will, is, indeed, the natural and inalienable right of every man. But he is responsible to his God, and, in a minor degree, to his fellow men, for the manner in which he exercises those faculties. He may not rightly set them up in opposition to the word of God. He may not rightly exercise them in a spirit of vanity, of perversity, or of self-conceit. He may not rightly exercise them in a way injurious to the peace and order of society, nor without a due veneration for the judgment of the Church and its ministry, so far as that judgment is supported by primitive tradition and usage, and is in conformity to the divine word. We deem him self-sufficient and conceited, who pays no respect to public opinion, even though that opinion may, perhaps, be founded on the caprice of the day. Much less is he to be commended who sets at naught the opinions which have stood the scrutiny of ages, and which have, for centuries, received the sanction of the universal Church.

"It was under these views of the right of private judgment, that the Reformation of the Church of England was conducted through many vicissitudes, and brought to a successful issue. The result is fully embodied in our Book of Common Prayer, — a standard of faith and worship which seems to be almost the only permanent religious monument of the Reformation in Protestant Christendom. The communions planted by Calvin and Zuinglius, have become deeply imbued with Socinianism and infidelity. Those founded by Luther and Melancthon have been corrupted by Rationalism, and every species of vain philosophy. The stern Church of John Knox has shared, to a great degree, a similar fate, and is, moreover, rent by internal divisions. Has Puritanism enjoyed a happier destiny, either in Europe or in this country? Let the schisms, the heresies, the infidelity, the fanaticism, which have everywhere sprung up from its distractions, answer the question. The erroneous notions of the right of private judgment, under which all these communions were established, have been constantly growing to greater and greater lengths of extravagance, till the tone of public sentiment on this subject is utterly perverted. Under this state of things it seems to create but little horror, or even surprise, for a man to avow openly that *he is not a Christian.* The sentiment is still more common, that it is a matter of entire indifference with what particular sect a man connects himself; nor is it thought a matter of much importance that he should unite with any Christian denomination, provided that he be sincere in his religion. The same state of public sentiment has afforded a strong stimulant to the aspirings of religious ambition, and the arts of hypocrisy. Learned theologians have vied with ignorant fanatics and wicked impostors, in founding and extending new sects of religionists. No metaphysical quibble appears too slight to obtain partisans, no extravagance too absurd to gain disciples, and no imposture too gross to secure believers."[1]

[1] Charge, 1843, pp. 7, 8.

In the latter portion of the charge, the Sacrament of Baptism was considered, and some of those errors in regard to it noticed, which appeared to be the most deeply seated in the public mind, and the most injurious in their tendency. It was his belief that there was but little real difference of sentiment, among churchmen, as to the true interpretation of the baptismal office, and that the controversies which had been carried on concerning it were mainly disputes about words. The change of state effected in baptism is called in Scripture, and in the Prayer Book, regeneration, but the "New Light Theology," dating back to the times of Whitefield and Edwards, applied the term to the process of spiritual renovation, sometimes designated as the new birth or a change of heart.

"The use of the word," said the Bishop, "in a sense so different from its former acceptation, has led to a lamentable misunderstanding and misrepresentation of the doctrine of baptismal regeneration, as held by our Church. It is probable, too, that another error has concurred in producing this misapprehension. The idea of perseverance in grace is popularly connected with that of change of heart, and it is hence inferred, that if a person be regenerated in baptism, his salvation is secured. But the Church holds no such doctrine."

Profound deference was no longer paid to the authoritative teaching of the chief Protestant denominations on the subject. The Congregational ministers virtually rejected this teaching, by allowing so much latitude to the right of private judgment, and by yielding to the wide-spread influence of new views in religion. A few citations in the charge from the writings of the principal Continental Reformers, and from the standards of the Westminster and New England divines served to show that their doctrinal views in regard to baptism assimilated to those of the Church of England. But the great idea of the new heart absorbed all other considerations.

"Whatever vague generalities may be uttered concerning the duty of baptism, it is but too commonly regarded as a mere ceremonial observance, — a mere sign, unaccompanied by anything signified. Practically, there is an utter unbelief in its sacramental efficacy. And the pious nurture of children, whether baptized or not (so far, at least, as their religious state is concerned), is considered of no avail, until, some time during life, they shall become subjects of the 'new birth;' converted by a sudden 'change of heart,' of which they have a distinct consciousness, and in which they are entirely passive. Though, in reading the Scriptures, baptized persons are represented as members of the 'family' and 'household' of Christ; as 'fellow-citizens with the saints;' as 'members of Christ,' 'children of God,' and 'heirs of the kingdom of heaven;' as having 'put on Christ' by baptism; and as being 'buried with him in baptism,' — yet these are all regarded by those who are imbued with the new theology, as mere figurative modes of expression, from which they derive no distinct conception of the real efficacy of the sacrament."[1]

The charge provoked the hostility of all the ecclesiastical organizations which, following the lead of their ministers, inclined to lower the nature and obligation

[1] Page 30.

of baptism, and to exalt unduly the importance of experimental religion. Writers in some of the religious periodicals of Connecticut run their pens against it, and besides being subjected to long and searching reviews from the press, it was made the theme of discourse from more than one Congregational pulpit. The Bishop seemed to anticipate a reception of this kind, for, in the conclusion of the charge, he said: —

"I am aware that the plainness of speech which has characterized this discourse, will bring upon me the imputation of uncharitableness, by those who dissent from my opinions. I am not conscious of any such feeling, and it has been my desire to express myself with proper Christian courtesy. But charity consists not in the suppression of important truths, nor in overlooking important errors. It is sufficient that we entertain kindly feelings towards those whom we believe to be in error, and adhere to the great law of equity, by doing to others as we would have them do to us. The views which I have presented in relation to the right of private judgment in matters of religion, in regard to the nature and constitution of the Christian Church, its ministry, and sacraments, are widely different from the opinions held by many wise and good men around us. I question not their intelligence or their piety. I would judge no man, I would unchurch no man. I would decide nothing concerning the efficacy of a ministry which I may deem to be invalid, nor concerning the benefits which may be attendant on irregular or defective ministrations. It is the prerogative of God alone, who knows what allowance may be made for ignorance, pride, or prejudice, to determine what shall be the consequences to any man, of the errors he commits, — whether those errors be voluntary or involuntary. But, my brethren, it is the duty of all men to seek the truth, and to maintain it. And, for ourselves, it has been made our special care 'with all faithful diligence, to banish and drive away from the Church all erroneous and strange doctrines contrary to God's word.' Errors in religion, whether they relate to the theory or to the practice of it, are not only hazardous to those who embrace them, but they are injurious to the cause of religion itself. All the writings of infidels have, perhaps, done less to injure the cause of Christianity, than the heresies and schisms which have rent the Church, the multiplicity of sects which have arisen, and the hatred, the fanaticism, and the extravagances by which they have been attended."[1]

The errors of the day and the animating discussions which sprung from the Oxford Tracts did not prevent the erection of new churches and the formation of new parishes. The Diocese steadily advanced in prosperity, and larger edifices, built of wood to take the place of the old ones, were consecrated about this time for St. Paul's parish, Norwalk, St. John's, Stamford, and St. Stephen's, Ridgefield. A new church was also consecrated in the spring of 1842, for the parish at Poquetannock, in the town of Preston, — a parish representing the old Church in North Groton, which was among the earliest of those organized in the Colony before the Revolution.[2] During the same year a

1 Pages 32, 33.

2 The church originally stood about four miles south of the present edifice, but, before the Revolution, in order to accommodate the parishioners, the venerable Society for the Propagation of the Gospel, as appears from a "letter for that purpose," permitted it to be removed to any place in *the*

"spacious granite church" was built by St. James's parish, Derby, and small edifices of wood rose in the villages of Glenville[1] (Greenwich), and Zoar (Newtown). But there were better evidences than these of the increase of the Church. New parishes, which have since been blessed with prosperity, were formed in Hartford, West Hartford, Fair Haven, Wolcottville, and Windsor. St. John's parish, Hartford, sprung from the superabundant growth of Christ Church in that city, and immediately erected for itself, in a central position, what was called at the time, "a beautiful structure" of Portland stone. When it was consecrated in the spring of 1842, the Rev. Mr. Burgess, then Rector of Christ Church, preached the sermon, — a brief extract from which will show the need of a second parochial organization: —

"It is not yet thirteen years since the festival of

town of Groton. It was accordingly removed to the village of Poquetannock; and, to keep to the letter of the permission, was "placed so that the north side of the building coincided with the boundary line between Groton and Preston, the building wholly standing in Groton (now Ledyard), but touching Preston on its north side."

The Revolutionary War broke up the congregation, and the church went to decay. Occasional services were afterwards held in it, and it remained, as its successor still remains, the only house of public worship in Poquetannock. Ammi Rogers appeared among the people in 1815, and, being accepted as their minister, persuaded them to repair the church, but, in doing this, it passed from the control of the parish and became the property of individuals, other denominations having a right to use it when not needed by the Episcopalians. Subsequently different Episcopal clergymen officiated there, and, in 1839, the ministry of the Rev. Dexter Potter commenced. He succeeded in accomplishing the erection of a new church, which is located about a quarter of a mile east of the old one, and within the limits of the town of Preston.

[1] That at Glenville was due to the munificence of a single individual (Mr. Samuel G. Cornell), who conveyed it by deed to the Bishop of the Diocese, and his successors in office, in trust for the Protestant Episcopal Church.

Christmas was made more joyful by the consecration of that Church which now bears the name of Christ; and we are here met, in the season of His death and resurrection, to dedicate this by the name of that Apostle who, of all Christian men, was last at the cross, and earliest at the grave. The parish register of burials may, perhaps, better than any other record, display the actual increase in the number of persons who are to be furnished with the means of our worship. In 1811, the year at which this register commences, there were four burials; in 1841 there were forty-four. The regularity of increase may also be seen in the annual numbers of burials for a course of years; which were in their order, beginning with 1832, thirteen, sixteen, twenty-five, twenty-three, thirty-one, twenty-two, twenty-seven, thirty-five, thirty-four, forty-four; and in the present year, already fourteen, more than the whole number ten years ago.

"No signal event, then, has marked the history of our Church in this city, except such as has proceeded from its ripening vigor. No memorable struggle, no happy accident has filled its places of worship, till it demanded first a larger, and then another. It has but grown as bodies grow, which have a healthful life in their heart and their members. It has but received that place in the regard of men, which their impartial judgment and enlightened conscience must always, in the end, allow to truth, to unity, and to order. These are the principles on which it has sustained itself, and must sustain itself under the help of its Redeemer."[1]

[1] Pages 7, 8.

CHAPTER XXIV.

INCREASE IN THE NUMBER OF CLERGY; MOVEMENT FOR AN ASSISTANT BISHOP; DEATH OF REV. ASHBEL BALDWIN; AND IMPROVED STYLE OF ECCLESIASTICAL ARCHITECTURE.

A. D. 1843 – 1848.

FULL one hundred clergymen were now residing in the Diocese, but not more than seventy-five of them were engaged in active parochial work. Some of the remainder were prevented by age and infirmity from officiating, and others were employed as instructors in public and private seminaries of learning. The parishes also numbered nearly one hundred, and consequently, the smaller ones were obliged to continue united in cures or else have no stated ministrations. Though the list of candidates for Holy Orders rose from fourteen in 1843 to thirty-one in 1845, yet the growth of the Church in Connecticut was such as to require the services of all, and the parishes, which had been nursed with the bounty of the Christian Knowledge Society, were fast becoming self-supporting. All, however, did not remain in the Diocese, — many, as heretofore, being drawn to fields of usefulness outside of it, where the prospect of pecuniary support was better, and pastoral toils no more exacting.

An increase in the number of its clergy does not necessarily prove the prosperity of a Diocese. Internal troubles and theological controversies may check its advancement, and give to the enemies of Christianity occasion to triumph in their ungodliness. But Connecticut was happily free from evils of this sort, and furnished few incidents, at this period, to excite extraordinary interest. The condition of the Diocese was well described in the "Report on the State of the Church," made to the General Convention in 1844, and compiled from documents supplied by the different delegations which composed that body.

"The Church in Connecticut is now, as heretofore, at unity, and being strictly conservative in spirit, is in little danger of being seriously affected by unprofitable contentions. With reasonable and allowable differences of opinion on questions of policy and expediency, there is no diversity of sentiment with regard to the great principles of Christian doctrine and ecclesiastical polity. The mutual confidence subsisting between the clergy and laity and their Bishop, presents a beautiful exemplification of the tendency of our system, and the soundness of our principles. In no part of the Union has the Church been so rudely, unjustly, and unscrupulously assailed. But the hostile shafts have fallen harmless; and her steady progress affords satisfactory proof that she has nothing to fear from such an unsanctified warfare, and that, so long as these assaults shall stimulate men to examine her standards and her bulwarks, they will only tend to enlarge her borders and increase her prosperity."

The interest of the laity in the progress of the Diocese was shown, as in other ways, so, especially, by the more general attendance of their delegates upon the annual conventions. The new parishes were rarely unrepresented, and in the older organizations, where it had once been accounted somewhat of a burden, it was beginning to be esteemed a privilege to be chosen a delegate. Besides, it was a sign of deadness or indifference to be unrepresented, and hence, at the Easter meetings of the parishes, when vestries were elected, and all important business transacted, men were appointed to this office who would be pretty sure to attend. In 1844, the Annual Convention was held in New Haven, and the Rev. A. Cleveland Coxe, then Rector[1] of the new parish in Hartford (St. John's), preached the sermon. Seventy-two clergymen and eighty-six lay delegates were present, and on the same occasion, the next year, more than one hundred of the latter order were in attendance. This increase marked the growth of the Church in the Diocese, for, by the Constitution, each parish in union with the Convention was entitled to a representation by one lay delegate, and, if it contained "more than fifty families, by two," and parishes "composed of two or more congregations, having a corresponding number of church edifices," were entitled to a "representation from each of such congregations, as from so many distinct parishes."

Dr. Brownell had been in the office of the Episcopate for a quarter of a century, and, during that period, he had ordained one hundred and twenty-five deacons, one hundred and twenty priests, consecrated sixty-six churches, and confirmed, in Connecticut, eleven thousand three hundred and fifty-three persons. While such tokens of spiritual progress gladdened him, he could not but see that the generation which welcomed him to the Diocese was rapidly pass-

[1] Now Bishop of Western New York.

ing away. Four of the clergy only, who were present as members of the Convention of 1844, had participated in his election, and one of these was the venerable Burhans, ordained by the first Bishop of Connecticut.

The rest of the members, both clerical and lay, belonged to a new generation, and the Bishop already appeared among them as a patriarch among his descendants. Age and infirmity had produced their debilitating effect upon his constitution, and he was beginning to feel the need of some relief from the burden, which "the care of all the churches" in the Diocese brought upon him. He found it necessary to depend, for the most part, upon his clergy to preach for him, and frequently a presbyter was taken into his company for this purpose when he started on a visitation. Even with this assistance, the state of his health was not always equal to his duties. In his address to the Convention of 1844, he said:—

"Owing to an affection of my eyes, which continued through the past winter, and which threatened to terminate in blindness, I was advised to place myself under the charge of an eminent physician and oculist in the city of New York. His skilful treatment, aided by the divine blessing on the means, has produced a great mitigation of the disease, and I am encouraged to cherish sanguine hopes of the ultimate recovery of my sight. But the arrangements which I had proposed for Episcopal services through the spring have been almost entirely frustrated, and it is probable that several months must yet elapse before I shall be able to use my eyes for reading or writing."

Though he was afterwards restored, in a measure, to

his former health and able to resume his duties, the subject of permanent relief in the Episcopal office occupied much of his attention, and, while on his visitations the next year, he conversed freely with leading clergymen and laymen as to the expediency of applying for the election of an assistant bishop. Delegates, therefore, went to the Annual Convention which met at Hartford in 1845, fully persuaded that the matter would be introduced, and acted upon with due deliberation. But prior to the meeting, it had been discovered, that if an election was pressed, the candidate whom the Bishop might prefer, would not be the only one whose name would be brought forward, and there was danger that the choice of the clergy would fall upon some presbyter whose respectable support the Diocese would be indisposed to provide for, — at least, so long as it was still indebted to the Bishop, for arrearages of salary and interest, in the sum of nearly four thousand five hundred dollars. Under these circumstances, he would have been quite willing to relinquish the subject for the time; but he had gone too far in his consultations to do this, and therefore he closed his address with cautious words, and left the responsibility of further action, where it properly belonged, to the Convention: —

"In concluding this address, I have to bring before you a subject which cannot fail to be regarded with deep solicitude by yourselves and by me. It is known to many of you that, on account of permanent bodily infirmities, I have contemplated applying to the Convention for the election of an assistant bishop. Those of my brethren to whom I have mentioned this subject, have received the proposition in a way very grateful to my feelings, while they have generally expressed a wish that the measure might be deferred as long as practicable. The expression of this sentiment, in connection with the consideration that, for the last few weeks, my general health has been greatly improved, had almost determined me to defer the proposition for another year. But further consideration admonishes me that the bodily infirmities to which I have alluded are of a permanent character, and that I cannot count, with any confidence, on the continuance of the degree of health which I now enjoy.

"Under these considerations, I beg leave to refer the consideration of the election of an assistant bishop to the free discretion of the Convention. Whatever measure of health and strength may be vouchsafed to me by Divine Providence, I shall cheerfully devote to the service of the Church. But if my brethren of the clergy and of the laity shall be of opinion that the Diocese is likely to suffer for the want of a more efficient superintendence, it is my desire that the Convention should proceed to the election of an assistant bishop, either at the present session, or at such other time as their judgment may deem expedient."

This part of the address was referred to a special committee of seven, — four clergymen and three laymen,—with instructions to confer with the Bishop, and report to the Convention in the afternoon of the same day. The result was adverse to the agitation of the subject. In consideration of the improved health of Dr. Brownell, and of the want of means to sustain an assistant, the committee reported that it was inexpedient to proceed to an election; and the Convention, with entire unanimity, adopted a resolution to this effect, and even declined to authorize any measures to provide for the future support of an assistant bishop.

As early as 1821, a movement was made to establish in the Diocese a society to be called the "Society for the Relief of Decayed Clergymen and the Necessitous Widows and Orphans of Clergymen." It originated in a Convocation held at Waterbury on the day previous to the Annual Convention of that year, and a constitution for the Society was then presented and discussed, and definite action upon it postponed to a future meeting. Two years later a more voluminous plan, with accompanying forms for bequests, was substituted, which limited relief to "the widows and children of the clergy of the Protestant Episcopal Church in Connecticut;" but it was unacceptable to the Convocation, and the whole matter was finally dropped, and no earnest efforts again put forth in the direction of this charity until 1845. In that year both orders resumed it, and it was voted "as the sense of the Convention, that aged and infirm clergymen, who may be destitute of the means of support . . . have peculiar claims upon the sympathies and aid of the Church which they have served." Out of this resolution arose a canon which made it the duty of every parish to contribute annually towards a fund to be applied, under the direction of the Bishop and Standing Committee, for the relief of destitute and disabled clergymen, and of widows of clergymen belonging to the Diocese, who might need pecuniary assistance. The charity commended itself to the generous consideration of the parishes, and the fund, besides affording suitable relief in the cases which had arisen, soon accumulated to such an extent that it was deemed proper to provide a separate board under the authority of the Diocese, for its custody, management, and disbursement. Corporate powers and privileges were, therefore, solicited, and it was chartered by the General Assembly in 1855, by the name of "The Trustees of the Aged and Infirm Clergy and Widows' Fund."

But the organization was too late to render assistance to the needy among that class of clergymen who bore an important part in sustaining the principles and advancing the prosperity of the Church under the first and second Bishops of Connecticut. The number of these venerable presbyters was rapidly diminishing, and the last survivor — Rev. Ashbel Baldwin — of those admitted to Holy Orders by Bishop Seabury, at the first ordination held in the United States, died February, 1846, lacking one month to complete a pilgrimage of eighty-nine years. He was born in Litchfield, of Congregational parents, and graduated at Yale College in 1776, without changing the religious belief in which he had been reared. He held for some time, during the Revolutionary War, the appointment of a quartermaster in the Continental Army, and received a pension from the Government, which was his principal means of support in his latter days.

The story of his conversion to Episcopacy is worth telling. After leaving college, he engaged himself, temporarily, as a private tutor in the family of a gentleman on Long Island. The family belonged to the Church of England, and, at that date, where the Episcopal house of worship was, for any cause, closed on Sunday, it was customary for the stanchest churchmen to turn their parlors into chapels, and have the regular morning service. Mr. Baldwin, being the educated member of the household, was required to act as the family lay reader, and, ashamed to confess his ignorance of the Prayer Book, he sought the aid and friendship of the gardener, who instructed him in the use of the "Order for Morning Prayer;" and soon his love and admiration of the Liturgy and conversion to the Church followed. Frequent mentions have been made of him in the previous pages of this work; but it is proper to add that he was a man of more than ordinary talents, ready, cheerful, and the lover of a good joke, in which the clergy of his time often indulged. He was small in stature, and walked haltingly in consequence of one leg being shorter than the other, occasioned by an illness in boyhood; yet he was nimble in his movements and prompt in business. For a quarter of a century, he served the Diocese as Secretary of the Convention, as member of the Standing Committee and delegate to the General Convention, and he was chosen Secretary in the Lower House of the latter body for six triennial sessions, when he declined a reëlection. Though not the most careful keeper of records, he was familiar with the forms of ecclesiastical legislation, and understood the details of the organization of the Church and its institutions in Connecticut better, perhaps, than any of his contemporaries. He was, withal, an attractive reader of the Liturgy and a faithful preacher of the Gospel. His distinct enunciation added much to the force of his clear and instructive discourses, and the educated, as well as the uneducated, heard him with pleasure and profit. On the day of the Annual Convention of 1837, he was at Stratford, and addressed a letter to Bishop

Brownell, taking an affectionate leave of that body, and resigning to it the only office of trust in its gift which he had continued to hold. The reading of the letter produced a deep feeling in the Convention, and it is given here in full, because it is so characteristic of the man, so chaste, so exquisitely beautiful in its style, and so pathetic in its allusions.

"Rev. and Dear Sir: I was much pleased to learn that the Convention would be holden in New Haven this summer; as my present stay would be so near, that I might possibly be able once more to meet with my brethren. I had made arrangements to do so. But in that I am much disappointed, as the weather is such that I dare not venture abroad. The least cold affects my eyes immediately and produces much pain. In addition to an earnest desire once more to meet my clerical and lay brethren, I wished to be present at this annual meeting, for the purpose of resigning my office of Trustee of the Episcopal Academy. I was made one of the Trustees of that Institution at its first organization, and for many years I never failed to attend its meetings; but, for several years past, my health has been so bad, that it has not been in my power to attend to any of its concerns. Will you have the goodness, sir, to present me very affectionately to the members of the Convention, and request them to accept my resignation?

"My dear sir, when I first entered the Church, its condition was not very flattering. Surrounded by enemies on every side and opposed with much virulence, her safety and even her very existence were, at times, somewhat questionable; but by the united and zealous exertions of the clergy, attended by the blessings of her great Founder, she has been preserved in safety through every storm, and now presents herself with astonishment to every beholder, not as a grain of mustard seed, but as a beautiful tree, spreading its salubrious branches over our whole country. The Church, by a strict adherence to its ancient landmarks, its priesthood, its liturgy, and its government, has been preserved from those schisms which seem to threaten the peace of a very respectable body of Christians in our country. May the same unanimity and zeal which animated our fathers still be preserved in the Church. My days of pilgrimage, I know, are almost closed, and I can do no more than to be in readiness, by the grace of God, to leave the Church militant in peace. May I be permitted, sir, to ask the prayers of my Bishop and his clergy, that my last days may be happy.

"That your present meeting may eventuate in much good to the Church, is the sincere wish and fervent prayer of your friend and brother in Christ."[1]

Four new parishes were admitted into union with the Convention in 1845, but two of them were only developments into independency of the congregations which had worshipped in St. Paul's Chapel, New Haven, and St. Thomas's Chapel, Bethel. Dr. Croswell, the Rector of Trinity Parish, did not take the same view about permitting St. Paul's Chapel to separate from the mother church, which was entertained by the majority of his parishioners. He regarded the movement as a "suicidal measure," and would have preferred that those who advocated it the most strongly, should unite in a new organization and proceed to

[1] MS. Letter.

the erection of another house of worship. It was the natural feeling of an aged pastor. He desired to retain his cure unbroken to the last; and those who joined him in opposition to the proposed scheme, were governed more by a regard to his wishes than by a conviction that the time had not yet come for a separation. The new parish started at once upon a career of vigorous prosperity, — not being under the necessity of waiting to gather a congregation and to become consolidated and self-reliant. The church was remodelled, and extensive alterations made in it, at a cost of several thousand dollars, before the first Rector, Rev. Samuel Cooke, removed to New Haven to enter upon his duties.

A week after the adjournment of the Convention in 1845, St. James's Church, Fair Haven, built of brown stone, quarried in the vicinity, was consecrated; and also, at later dates, new churches of wood in the ancient parishes of Northford and Wallingford, — all of such appropriateness and ample dimensions, that the Bishop, in speaking of them in his annual address for the next year, was led to "congratulate the Diocese on the greatly improved style of church architecture which had been manifested within the last few years." Edifices of stone at Canaan, and in the new parish at Broad Brook, and another constructed of wood to take the place of the old church at Tashua, which had been standing for upwards of half a century, were added to the list of consecrated churches in the Diocese, not many months afterwards. Grace Church, Long Hill, — where a house of worship was begun in 1836, — continued, for ten years, a part of the parish at Tashua, when it was admitted into union with the Convention as a separate organization. At Nichols's Farms, another village in the town of Trumbull, a new parish was formed, and a new wooden church built in 1848. The era of a better order of ecclesiastical architecture had, indeed, now commenced. The improved taste of the day called for more beauty and fitness of expression in the house of God, and, instead of leaving it to builders to be guided by their own fancy, or to follow the model of the old structures, skilled and professional architects were employed to furnish designs for new churches, and to have a general oversight of their erection. A spacious and elaborate edifice, with a chapel annexed, built of granite from the neighboring hills, was begun by St. John's Parish, Waterbury, in the spring of 1846, and finished and consecrated in the second week of January, 1848. The growth of the town and of the congregation in numbers and wealth, called for this generous outlay, and it was cheerfully met by a people who have since been liberal in good deeds, and unceasing in their support of missions at home and abroad.

But two new churches of freestone, to be "more artistic and imposing than that at Waterbury," were already started, one in Norwich, and the other in New London. The plans were obtained from a New York architect,[1] and as these churches, when completed, were the most costly in the Diocese, so they were really the first into which the deep chancels and a high degree of decoration and adornment were introduced. The arrangements for conducting Divine service were made with an eye to the comfort and con-

[1] Mr. Richard Upjohn.

venience of the officiating clergy, and the position of the Lord's Table and the whole sacrarium were intended to impress Christian worshippers with greater reverence for the seat of the Eucharistical feast. Other parishes, with less wealth, could not but admire these noble specimens of a better style of architecture, but, in attempting to build anew, they shrunk from incurring such expense, and were content to sacrifice ornament and some of the accessories of divine worship in order to gain churches with an equal number of sittings.

The taste, however, for pointed windows, and the early English style, was extending everywhere, and building committees in the smallest parishes caught its influence and proceeded accordingly. A church of unhewn granite for the new parish at Stonington, was begun in the spring of 1848, and the corner-stone of another and a more spacious one, to be built of freestone, was laid in the ancient parish at Meriden on the 8th of June in the same year.[1] In this year also, the congregation at New Britain had prospered so much as to build a church, "capacious in its dimensions and distinguished for the good taste of its archi-

[1] "The church was consecrated by the Rt. Rev. Bishop Brownell on the 6th of February, 1850, and continued to be used for public worship until Trinity Sunday, 1866. The increase of the population in the western and northern parts of the town, and the necessity of providing additional accommodations for the parish, have rendered necessary the erection of another and a larger edifice. . . . The corner-stone of this third house of worship for the parish of St. Andrew's Church, is laid this 8th day of August, 1866, by the Rt. Rev'd Father in God, John Williams, D. D., Bishop of the Diocese." — *Extract from the Historical Sketch, MS.*, read by the Rector, Rev. G. H. Deshon, at the ceremony of laying the stone.

The second church was taken down, and the stone used in building the third, an edifice of much architectural beauty, from designs by Mr. Henry Dudley of New York. It was consecrated November 7th, 1867.

tectural arrangements;" and about the same time, mainly through the missionary exertions of the clergy in Litchfield County, a parish was organized at Winsted and a house of worship erected.

This outward growth of the Diocese was not unaccompanied by signs of the calm and pure ardor of increasing piety. The comfort and the power of Christianity were visible in the lives of those who had been "added to the Church," and the clergy and the "congregations committed to their charge" evinced, with every revolving year, a deeper interest in the spread of the knowledge which makes men "wise unto salvation." The evil, however, of clerical changes still continued, and the Bishop, in his address to the Annual Convention of 1848, said: "It is almost the only discouraging circumstance in the condition of the Diocese, that, during the past year, these changes have been more numerous than usual." Nine clergymen had removed from it with letters dimissory, and six had been received. Another prominent and accomplished presbyter had been fixed upon for a higher position in the Church, and his separation from his parish necessarily followed.

The Rev. George Burgess, D. D., was elected Bishop of Maine and consecrated in Christ Church, Hartford, of which he had been the Rector for thirteen years, on the 31st of October, 1847, the Rt. Rev. Philander Chase of Illinois, being the senior and Presiding Bishop in the United States, and acting as the consecrator on this occasion.

CHAPTER XXV.

MISSIONARY AND CHARITABLE CONTRIBUTIONS; CONVENTION AT NEW LONDON; ADDRESS OF THE BISHOP AND TENDENCIES TO ROMANISM.

A. D. 1848 – 1851.

THE progress of the Church in Connecticut was shown by the increasing contributions for missionary and charitable purposes. These, as reported from sixty parishes in 1848, amounted to upwards of ten thousand dollars, which was a great advance from the condition and feeling of the Diocese half a century before, when it was voted in convention "that the money formerly collected for the purpose of sending missionaries to the frontiers of the States be applied to the benefit of the Episcopal Academy." The impulse given to the missionary cause by the General Convention of 1835, and the new agencies then inaugurated, had helped to produce this improvement. But another reason is to be assigned for the change. Many of the parishes, from being weak and dependent, had now become strong, self-supporting, and able to contribute to outside objects; and with the enlargement of their prosperity came also an increase in the number and urgency of appeals from abroad for Christian sympathy and assistance. The duty of greater efforts for the support of Diocesan Missions, was pressed upon the attention of the Convention from year to year by the Bishop, and if there had not been extensive portions of the State where the services of our Church were yet to be established, the appeals of the "Domestic and Foreign Missionary Society" would have met with a more generous consideration.

In 1849, eighty-one towns and villages within the Diocese had no houses of Episcopal worship, and no stated ministrations from Episcopal clergymen, and one-half of these localities lay east of the Connecticut River, where the Church is still numerically weak. Something was done by the Convention of that year to awaken more interest in Diocesan Missions, and a large committee, previously appointed, of which the Bishop was chairman, in reporting on their state, and the means of their future support, said: —

"The strength of the Diocese is such, both in numbers and in pecuniary ability, that it must always be competent to take possession of every new point to which the way is opened for the introduction of the Church. In view of this truth, we cannot look at the unoccupied ground which is white with the waving harvest, without feeling that we have been, and still are sinfully slothful; that, as a people, we are in this, guilty of neglect before the God of the Church. It is certainly not to our credit that in a Diocese so old as this, and of such limited extent, the Church should be so partially known as it is."

The Annual Convention of 1850 met at New London on the festival of St. Barnabas, and seventy-nine clergymen and fifty-six lay delegates were present. There is no record that a similar meeting had ever been held in the same place, though New London was the residence of Bishop Seabury, and the scene of his latest parochial labors. The convenience of both clergy and laity had called for the selection of more central or more accessible towns in which to hold the annual conventions, and complaint was sometimes made, if the Bishop, who had the power of "determining" upon the place of meeting, chose an extreme part of the Diocese. But this was an extraordinary occasion, and the Diocesan Council was not its only attraction. The "holy and beautiful house" which had been erected by the ancient parish of St. James, and which contained, in one of the divisions of the chancel, the remains of the first Bishop of Connecticut, and a monument to his memory,[1] was now to be consecrated. The usual services before convention, and at the consecration, were blended together, and the sermon was preached by the Rev. John Williams, D. D., then President of Trinity College, having been elected to that position on the retirement of Dr. Totten in 1848. The sermon, which was upon the doctrine of the Holy Trinity, was published by order of the Convention and distributed with the Journal. It contained appropriate references to Bishop Seabury, and cited the memorable statement that, near the close of his ministry, he spoke often and earnestly to his clergy and people upon that mighty mystery of the faith which, he appeared to foresee, would one day be extensively corrupted and denied in New England.[2]

Trinity Church, Norwich, which had possessed itself of the edifice formerly occupied by the mother parish in that city, and Trinity Church, Ansonia, were new parochial organizations received into union with the

[1] Vide vol. i. pp. 440, 441. [2] Vol. i. p. 432.

Convention at this session. St. Thomas's Church, New Haven, had been admitted two years earlier, and, having erected a commodious chapel, the parish was beginning to exhibit signs of a vigorous prosperity. The Bishop, glancing in his annual address at the progress of the Diocese, said: —

"We have witnessed no sudden and remarkable changes; but a steady increase in numbers, strength, and vitality, has marked our course during the thirty years that I have been permitted to minister amongst you. I know of no serious difficulties in any of our parishes, and the unity of sentiment, and harmony of feeling, which have so long characterized the clergy of the Diocese, were never more happily exemplified than at the present time."

But he could not take the same cheering view of every part of our communion. Some unhappy fruits had sprung from the theological movement in England, and the fears of intelligent churchmen were not a little excited by the appearance of "Romish tendencies" among certain individuals who occupied positions of influence and importance in the Church. Towards the end of the year 1849, the Rev. Dr. Jarvis, with the approbation of his Diocesan, published a pamphlet of nearly fifty pages, which he entitled "A Voice from Connecticut, occasioned by the late Pastoral Letter of the Bishop of North Carolina," and in which he discussed very ably and learnedly "the power of priestly absolution, and the limits within which it must be exercised." It was addressed to Dr. Ives, whose "Pastoral Letter" had called it forth, and whose self-contradictions and doctrinal unsoundness, as manifested on several recent occasions, had given pain to his warmest friends, both in and out of his Diocese.

But prior to this, the alarm had been sounded, and editorial articles, evidently written with a full knowledge of facts, appeared in the Church periodical of Connecticut, stating that there existed a "Romanizing clique" in the city of New York, which was not only disloyal to the Anglican Church and its standard theology, but encouraged a practical reception of Popish standards of doctrine and discipline. The articles were sharp, and intended to attract attention and challenge replies. One of them closed with the warning — "Let churchmen be on their guard, and give the first symptom of this kind of Jesuitism its immediate and merited rebuke. We venture to promise it such a reception if it intrudes into the Diocese of Connecticut. We love our Prayer-books here with a loyal and virgin love." Attempts to justify or explain away the movements of the Romanizers were unsuccessful, and the progress of events showed that there was too much reason for the alarm which had been given. The principal part of the address of Bishop Brownell to the Convention of 1850, was occupied with the subject, and because his counsels are highly salutary and applicable to the times in which we live, as to all times, no apology need be offered for allowing them to fill up the remainder of this chapter. With the accompanying action of the Convention, they form an important passage in the history of the Diocese.

"In our parent country, excitements and dissensions prevail; and there have been some defections from the faith of the Church. A few such defections have also occurred in our country. But though these defections are much to be deplored, I see nothing in them to occasion serious alarm, in regard to the general soundness of the Church. The number of the apostates is small and insignificant, in comparison with the great body of churchmen who maintain their integrity. 'They went out from us, because they were not of us.' We may regret their secession, on their own account; but we may be well satisfied that they have placed themselves in a position where their real sentiments are known, and where they can no longer expect to corrupt and betray their brethren under false pretences. If their defection has been occasioned by conscientious conviction, however erroneous such conviction may be, we may respect and pray for them; but we cannot exercise the same charity towards those who would seek to Romanize the Church, while they remain within her pale. This is nothing less than treachery; and the clergyman who would persist in such a course, is false to his vows. Every clergyman, at his Ordination, solemnly engages to conform to the doctrine, as well as worship, of the Protestant Episcopal Church; and he promises, moreover, so to minister that doctrine, 'as *this* Church hath received the same.' He well knows what the Church expects from him, when she exacts these vows; and if he takes them, or acts under them, with a mental reservation, and resorts to the subterfuge of giving his own private interpretation to the doctrines of the Church, he is justly chargeable with treachery and falsehood. If he begins to doubt the catholicity of the Church in which he ministers, or the soundness of her faith, let him, as an honest man, suspend his ministrations till his doubts are solved. And if he believes the dictates of his conscience compel him publicly to withdraw from her communion, let him depart in peace, under his responsibility to his God. What we most deprecate is, the treachery of perverting the doctrines of the Church, or the teaching of dogmas alien to her faith, while ministering at her altars. And this treachery is equally to be censured, in whatever direction the false teaching may tend, — whether to the superstitions of Romanism, or to the coldness and baldness of Rationalism.

"Doubtless there may be allowed some latitude of construction, in the explanation of our doctrinal standards. But the discretion must be exercised with the most conscientious caution; and no individual caprice should go beyond the general understanding of the Church.

"Rationalism, or a leaning towards Rationalism, is, beyond all question, the prevailing error of our times and country. Its influence, indeed, is the most widely spread, and the most destructive, among the religious denominations by whom we are surrounded. But as our Church has been so rapidly increased by accessions from these denominations, it is not to be wondered at that traces of its influence should be discernible among some of the members of our own communion. This influence, however, is arrested in its proclivity to Infidelity, and is steadily fading away, under the more evangelical teachings and worship of the Church.

"It is now in the opposite direction, that the apprehensions of our Church seem to be more especially called forth. Several of her clergy, and some of her laity have recently seceded to the Romish faith; and yet this secession is not the principal occasion for the alarm. The number who have thus seceded is insignificant in comparison with those who yet remain behind, in a state of obvious sympathy with the feelings and doctrines of those who have departed. These sympathizers, and not the seceders, are the persons who are in a condition to make proselytes; and who, if they put forth their influence, either publicly or in private, as they will hardly fail to do, are the real traitors of the Church.

"Against the seductions of such, it behooves all the members of the Church to be constantly on their guard. This vigilance is more specially incumbent on those who are in a course of preparation for the exercise of the sacred ministry. These are yet in the position of inquirers. Their minds are open to instruction; and they have not yet acquired all that knowledge of the Scriptures, and of the history of the Church, which is necessary to enable them to distinguish between plain truth, and plausible error. In a few short years, too, these *learners* are to become teachers in the Church, and each one the centre of an important local influence. They are precisely in the situation that one would wish, who was ambitious of propagating favorite opinions, and of making proselytes. They may then expect to be addressed personally, or through the medium of the press, by those who wish to give a more Romish character to the Church. Under such circumstances, a watchful caution is the part of true wisdom. All novelties which are proposed should be received with distrust. There are too, certain doctrines and usages, much dwelt upon by the class of persons referred to, which, though true and proper under certain limitations, become erroneous when they are distorted or pushed to an extreme.

"One of these, which holds a prominent place, and is sometimes made to perplex the unwary, is the doctrine of *Catholic Unity*. Doubtless the Universal Church of Christ, holding one faith, — a belief in the way of salvation by the mediation and atonement of the Son of God; being baptized into one baptism, — a baptism administered in the name of the Father, and of the Son, and of the Holy Ghost; and all the members being joined together in one body, by being thus united to Christ their Head, forms 'One Holy Catholic Church.' But the Catholic Unity so much talked of, is something more vague and mysterious. Metaphysical subtilties are resorted to, in regard to the 'Notes of a true Church;' and many curious refinements are employed in reference to the precise line by which it is circumscribed. A visible centre of Unity, too, must be sought after; and the guide-posts are put up at such points as conduct the inquirer only to the Pope of Rome. In connection with the doctrine of Catholic Unity, the English Reformation becomes the subject of unfavorable comment and severe criticism. The licentiousness of Henry VIII., and the rapacity of his time-serving courtiers, are held up to just reprobation; while the corruptions and abuses of Romanism which were rejected, and the pure faith of primitive Christianity which was established, together with all the blessings which have flowed to mankind from that Reformation, seem to be studiously forgotten.

"The doctrines of *Auricular Confession*, and *Priestly Absolution*, are also favorite themes with the abettors of Romish error. The duty of confessing our sins to God in secret, as well as in the public services of the Church; and the agency of a divinely appointed ministry, in proclaiming God's pardon to the penitent, may be defended by 'most certain warrant of Holy Scripture.' The confession of particular sins to a spiritual guide, for counsel and instruction, is also commended in certain cases. But the private confession of *every particular sin* to a priest, and the procuring of his absolution as a necessary condition of God's pardon, is a 'fond conceit' of Rome. This latter view of the doctrine, taken in connection with its necessary adjuncts, — the doctrines of Popish penance, of Purgatory, and of Indulgences, has led to the most overbearing arrogation of priestly power, the grossest tyranny over the consciences of men, and the most degrading effects upon the intelligence and morals of society. Such doctrines could have gained footing in the world, only during the ignorance and superstition of the dark ages. They could receive no countenance in the present age, were it not for the tinge of superstition, and the love of ease, which are so congenial to the human mind. All men know that they are sinners before God, and that they are obnoxious to the penalties which he has made consequent on guilt. If, by simply confessing his sins to a priest, submitting to the mild penance he may enjoin, and receiving his plenary absolution, a man can believe that all the guilt of his past life is cancelled, to be remembered no more, and that he is entitled to the reversion of everlasting felicity, who would not purchase forgiveness and salvation at so easy a rate? And if, with a conscience thus at ease, he should again fall into a sinful course of life, with what alacrity would he again resort to the same efficacious sponge, to wipe away the traces of his guilt! And if, in worldly matters, the settlement of a man's accounts, and the extinguishment of his debts, afford him so much complacency, how much more so when his eternal interests are concerned. But God has chosen a different way for the exercise of His mercy towards mankind. He is, indeed, ever ready to pardon and save all who are sincerely penitent for their sins, who gladly embrace the way of salvation through His Son, who obediently keep His holy laws, and who walk in all the ordinances which He has appointed for His Church. But this is a way of salvation which demands a constant and anxious vigilance. The Christian must be ever solicitous that his repentance is sufficiently deep and sincere, that his faith is sufficiently strong and ardent, and that his obedience springs from the dictates of a heart influenced by the promptings of the Holy Spirit.

"The *performance of the Ritual* of our Church, is another medium through which tendencies towards Romanism may be encouraged. Among the multitude of ceremonial observances with which the Church was encumbered previous to the Reformation, some were significant of important truths, some were significant of pernicious errors, and some of mere unfounded superstitions. It was the object of our Reformers to free her from all such observances as did not conduce to the decency of public worship, and to the maintenance of sound doctrine. This object they happily accomplished. The Puritans and other Dissenters went to an extreme of plainness, in the order of their services and in their houses of worship, alike adverse to good taste and propriety. As one extreme begets another, there are those in our Church who would carry us back again to the showy ceremonial of the Romish ritual. They may be influenced partly by the promptings of a fanciful temperament, but are probably more strongly impelled by a love of certain Romish doctrines, of which these ceremonies are the exponents. Symbolic teaching was a mode of instruction adopted in the dark ages, to communicate, through the medium of the senses, that which could not be so readily apprehended by uneducated intellects.

"It may now be the policy of some to inculcate, by signs, doctrines from which the mind would revolt, if presented to it directly and plainly in words. The sacrifice of the mass, after the manner of the Romish priests, is pronounced, by Article XXXI. of our Church, to be a 'blasphemous fable,' and 'dangerous deceit.' And yet, when the sacrament of the Lord's Supper is administered at her altars, the priest may perform the service with such an appearance of overstrained veneration and awe, with such bowings, and crossings, and genuflections, as plainly to symbolize the doctrine of *Transubstantiation.* 'Let all things be done decently and in order,' is the precept of the Apostle. This precept should teach us to avoid all theatrical display, on the one hand, and all levity or carelessness on the other; and to follow a middle course, between the ostentatious ceremonies of Rome, and the baldness of Dissent.

"I may advert to one characteristic more, which

seems generally to mark the admirers of Romish doctrines and institutions; and I may, perhaps, best do it in their own favorite language — '*a yearning after greater holiness.*' I believe such professions are generally made in great sincerity. But there is much difference between a mawkish desire and an earnest endeavor; between romance and reality. Young persons, and others of imaginative temper, who have felt the hindrances to piety and devotion which are created by the amusements and business of life, often envy the seclusion of the monastery or the nunnery; as if religious affections could be cultivated only in solitude. And as such seclusion is generally unattainable, the feeling often seeks relief in the performance of a round of ceremonial observances.

"The indolence and corruption which was brought to light at the breaking up of the monastic institutions of England, has demonstrated that such institutions may be the nurseries of vice, as well as of piety. And it is probable that the like institutions now existing in Europe, would hardly be found in a better moral condition.

"Pure religion is founded in an unfeigned love to God and to mankind. As such, it must be an *active* principle. It exhausts not itself in solitary meditations, nor in elaborate ceremonial observances. It is best demonstrated by sincere devotion in the public and private worship of God, and by an unfeigned obedience to all the Divine commands, while pursuing the active duties of life. He who is earnestly engaged in the performance of these duties, will find abundant scope for the exercise of his religious affections, without the '*strenuous inertia*' of counting beads, or a yearning after — he knows not what.

"Brethren: In the remarks which I have now addressed to you, you must be aware that I have had in my mind a class of persons who are desirous of assimilating the character of our Church more nearly to that of Rome. Their numbers I do not pretend to estimate, though I am well convinced of the existence of such a class, comprising laymen as well as clergymen. They may not, and probably do not, all entertain the same views in regard to the changes they would effect. Some may be satisfied with holding all Romish doctrine, as matter of opinion, and yet remaining quietly in the exercise of their ministry. Others have been determined to *revolutionize the Church*, or to quit her communion. Some have already abandoned it; more may follow.[1] It is quite time, then, that the Church should be on her guard.

. . . .

"I think you will bear me witness that I am no dis-

[1] The Rt. Rev. Levi S. Ives, D. D., Bishop of North Carolina, accompanied his wife to Europe in 1852, and writing from Rome, under date of Dec. 22d of that year, to the Convention of his Diocese, he resigned into its hands his office of Bishop, and further stated his determination to submit to the Roman "Catholic Church." The "doubts" which had "goaded him at times to the very borders of derangement," have "grown," he said, "into clear and settled convictions; so clear and settled that, without a violation of conscience and honor, and every obligation of duty to God and His Church, I can no longer remain in my position."

His defection was not unexpected. In consequence of his strange course, his own Diocese had lost all confidence in him before he took this step, and had learned to distrust his recantations and the sincerity of his promises. Not one of the clergy or laity of North Carolina is known to have followed him in his abandonment of the Church. The House of Bishops, at the meeting of the General Convention in 1853, solemnly pronounced him, according to the terms of the Canon, "*ipso facto*, deposed to all intents and purposes from the office of a bishop in the Church of God, and from all the rights, privileges, powers, and dignities thereunto pertaining."

Dr. Ives died October 13, 1867, near Fordham, N. Y., where he had acted for many years as a professor in St. John's (Romish) College.

turber of the peace of the Church, and that I am not addicted to unnecessary controversy. But when errors are abroad in the Church, those whom Providence has placed as watchmen upon her walls should not hesitate to give the necessary warning. It may, perhaps, be apprehended by some, that, in the present case, the sound of alarm may create too general a distrust, and that it may bring suspicion upon those who do not justly deserve it. But in regard to Romish errors, the position of no churchman, and especially of no clergyman of the Church, should be in the least equivocal.

"It is true, indeed, that religious controversy is very liable to be carried on with uncharitable feelings. This consideration should lead us to guard our own hearts with care. But the good Providence of God, which brings light out of darkness, often illustrates important truths by the exposure of error. Let us devoutly pray that the same good Providence may so direct the discussions which are now going on in the Church, that prejudice and uncharitableness may be restrained, that the cause of truth and righteousness may prevail, and that the Church itself may be built up, enlarged, and established in the most holy faith."

The foregoing extracts from the address of the Bishop were referred by the Convention to a special committee of three clergymen and two laymen. On the morning of the second day of the session, the committee reported a series of resolutions, which, if they did not rise to the tone and dignity of the address, fully responded to "the opinions, counsels, and warnings" of the Bishop, and bore witness that he had shown no disposition to provoke "unnecessary controversy," or to disturb the peace of the Church. A brief and spirited debate followed, and a few members, who expressed concurrence with the purport of the address, evinced an unwillingness to sustain the resolutions on technical grounds. For this reason it was decided to take the question upon their adoption by yeas and nays, and a stranger, dropping into the assembly at that moment, would have judged by the course of half a dozen clergymen, that they were in actual sympathy with the Romanizers, and yet as much afraid to follow the dictates of their consciences as to indorse the views of their Diocesan. Some retired from the church before their names were called; two or three asked to be excused from voting, but their request was denied, and thereupon they either refused to vote, or voted nay.

The final result was the adoption of the resolutions with almost entire unanimity — five only of the clergy, and two of the laity, appearing in the negative. This action was a fresh proof of the conservative spirit of the oldest Diocese in our country, as well as a solemn protest against every Romanizing movement. The fears of those who doubted the wisdom of the Bishop in bringing the subject before the Convention, and manifested some solicitude at the peculiar turn which it took, never were realized. Dr. Croswell, who voted to sustain him, said, "An evil has been done which an age will not cure," — but he lived long enough to change his opinion, and to see good reasons for the counsel "that the Church should be on her guard."

CHAPTER XXVI.

DEATHS AMONG THE CLERGY; ELECTION OF AN ASSISTANT BISHOP; AND THEOLOGICAL EDUCATION IN THE DIOCESE.

A. D. 1851 – 1853.

As the draft upon Connecticut by other dioceses still continued, the real working force of the clergy in parishes was diminished rather than increased. Death, which is ever finding its way among all bodies of men, fell upon a few of the older presbyters, and now and then upon those who had just begun to prove their Christian armor. Isaac Jones and Truman Marsh, both far advanced in years, died at Litchfield — one in the spring of 1850, and the other a year later. They had been formerly united in the charge of the "associated churches in Litchfield," and Mr. Marsh was Rector of the mother parish there (St. Michael's) for thirty years before he resigned and went into retirement.

But the name of a more distinguished presbyter disappeared from the list of the clergy at this time. A few weeks before the death of Mr. Marsh, the Rev. Dr. Jarvis, son of the second Bishop of Connecticut, died at his residence in Middletown, leaving unfinished those literary labors for which he had long been qualifying himself. Since his return to this country from Europe in 1835, he had resided in Connecticut, and acted first as a professor in the College at Hartford, and then as Rector of the parish in Middletown. He resigned his parochial charge in 1842, and devoted himself to the completion of a work, the importance of which the General Convention had recognized by appointing him "Historiographer of the Church, with a view to his preparing, from the most original sources now extant, a faithful Ecclesiastical History reaching from the Apostles' times to the formation of the Protestant Episcopal Church in the United States." The first volume was a mere "Chronological Introduction" to this history, and the second had scarcely been issued from the press, when aggravated disease came upon him and closed his labors. He occupied positions of honor and influence in the Diocese which were due to his profound scholarship and great theological attainments; and the Church at large was benefited by his wisdom and experience in her general councils, and by numerous publications setting forth her doctrine, discipline, and worship. Bishop Brownell, speaking of his decease in his annual address, said, he "has been called away in the midst of his usefulness, and while the Church was looking anxiously forward to the fruits of his future labors. For the extent of his knowledge in Biblical literature and sacred history, he has left few equals behind him, in this or any other country."

Two weeks after the meeting of the Annual Convention in 1851, the Rev. Seth B. Paddock, who was twenty-two years Rector of Christ Church, Norwich, and who had been Principal of the Episcopal Academy, since the autumn of 1844, died at Cheshire, after a protracted and painful illness, leaving two sons[1] to inherit his good name and succeed him in the ministry of the Church. His departure was soon followed by that of another. The oldest presbyter of the Diocese, born and serving in it, and the last survivor of those ordained by Bishop Seabury, Daniel Burhans, D. D., died on the 30th of December, 1853, having passed nearly six months beyond his ninetieth birthday. For thirty years he labored faithfully and successfully as Rector of Trinity Church, Newtown, and, after relinquishing this charge, he continued to officiate in other parishes of the Diocese, until age and infirmity compelled him to retire from the exercise of ministerial duties. His fine personal appearance, good elocution, and sound practical judgment supplied, in some degree, the defects of early education, and gave him, in his better days, great influence in his parish, and in the councils of the Diocesan and General Conventions.

The venerable "Society for the Propagation of the Gospel in Foreign Parts," having "been permitted to complete a century and a half of missionary labor," resolved to commemorate with thanksgiving and prayer the close of its third Jubilee. The commemoration commenced in England on the 16th of June, 1851, — being the anniversary of the signing of the royal charter, — with full services in Westminster Abbey; and on the following Sunday, sermons appropriate to the occasion were preached in the principal churches of the metropolis, and collections made for the promotion of missionary objects. The Archbishop of Canterbury, President of the Society, addressed a

[1] Rev. John A. Paddock, Brooklyn, N. Y.; Rev. Benjamin H. Paddock, D. D., Detroit, Mich.

letter to the several bishops of our Church in this country, apprising them of the proposed celebration, and inviting their Christian sympathy and coöperation.

"The Society," said he, "has good reason to expect, that what may be called its Solemn Jubilee, will be observed in all the colonial churches, but the occasion seems to justify the hope of a still more comprehensive union of prayer and praise.

"Bearing in mind the relation of our two countries, and the intimate connection which subsisted between the Society and many of the States during the greater part of the last century, I feel some confidence in proposing to you the joint celebration of a Jubilee, in which all the members of our Church must feel a common interest. I venture, also, respectfully to submit, whether, in a time of controversy and division, the close communion which binds the churches of America and England in one, would not be strikingly manifested to the world, if every one of their dioceses were to take part in commemorating the foundation of the oldest Missionary Society of the Reformed Church, — a Society which, from its first small beginnings in New England, has extended its operations into all parts of the world, from the Ganges to Lake Huron, and from New Zealand to Labrador. Such a joint commemoration, besides manifesting the rapid growth and wide extension of our Church, would serve to keep alive and diffuse a missionary spirit, and so be the means, under the Divine blessing, of enlarging the borders of the Redeemer's kingdom."

The Church in Connecticut had many reasons to be specially grateful to the Society for aid in her establishment. Its fostering care and protection had been bestowed upon her for a period of more than fifty years in colonial times, and God had brought the seed, then planted and watered, to a marvellous increase. Hence the Annual Convention, which met at Waterbury, in 1851, sent a cordial response to the letter of the Archbishop, and having designated a Sunday to be devoted to a participation in the Jubilee, requested the Bishop to set forth a proper form of prayer to be used in all the churches of the Diocese on that day, and the clergy to preach appropriate sermons, and make collections for missions within the borders of Connecticut. The contributions thus received amounted to about eighteen hundred dollars; but one of the happiest results of the service was the interest which it awakened in the memories of the past, and the information which was thereby diffused throughout the Diocese concerning the early charities and operations of the venerable Society in New England.

The celebration was observed by other dioceses of our country; and towards the end of the year of Jubilee, a second letter came from his Grace, the Archbishop of Canterbury, accompanied by resolutions of the Society, acknowledging the cordiality with which the original invitation had been received and acted on by the bishops and clergy of the American Church, and asking the House of Bishops to depute two or more of their number to join in the concluding services. These were to be held on the 15th of June, in the same glorious temple where, a year before, the celebration had been commenced, and two American prelates,[1] designated by their brethren

[1] Bishop De Lancey, of Western New York, and Bishop McCoskry, of Michigan.

for this purpose, and several American clergymen were present to share in the interest and joy of the occasion. The whole movement was one which served, not only to manifest the essential unity of the churches of England and America, but to "promote a spirit of Christian good-will and harmony among the members of our Communion, in all parts of the world."

Connecticut was benefited by the missionary spirit thus excited among her clergy and laity, and England felt the influence of the special efforts made to increase the funds, and extend the operations of "the oldest purely missionary institution" in the realm. Dr. Wilberforce, the Bishop of Oxford, in his eloquent sermon at the closing services in Westminister Abbey, said: —

"The earth, which is girdled by our colonies, is beginning to be gemmed by our colonial sees. This year of Jubilee has brought its own blessing; our work has been more supported, and aided largely by parishes as parishes. For this, too, let us this day bless God, and that not so much for the £1000 a week of added resources, which He has poured into our coffers, as that, by means of this increase, we have, we trust, already been enabled to add three new sees to our colonial Episcopate, and to aid in founding various colleges from whence may issue forth through all lands that only true means of converting nations, a native clergy to minister amongst their brethren." [1]

Thirty years had elapsed since the Annual Convention met in Waterbury. It was then a village of few inhabitants and little enterprise, but now it had

[1] Sermon, p. 12.

become a place of extensive business, large wealth, and increasing population. The Convention which assembled in it, and took action upon the Jubilee celebration, was composed of ninety clergymen, and upwards of one hundred lay delegates, — about three times as many of each order as formed the body which convened in the same place in 1821, and heard the primary charge of Bishop Brownell. The attendance was, no doubt, larger from the fact that an important movement was expected to be made in this Convention. Every year it was becoming more manifest that the infirmities of the Bishop were lessening his ability to perform his Episcopal duties, and that the best interests of the Diocese would suffer if some relief was not soon provided. For a long time he had not attempted to preach, and it was rare that he even addressed the candidates presented to him for confirmation. He was, himself, conscious of his weakness and decline, and a few weeks before the assembling of the Convention in Waterbury, he "addressed a circular letter to all his brethren of the clergy, in regard to the election of an assistant bishop," and requested them to communicate the same to their lay delegates. The substance of this letter was recapitulated at the close of his annual address as follows: —

"It will be remembered that, owing to bodily infirmities, which disabled me from preaching, and which were a hindrance in the performance of other Episcopal duties, I brought this subject to the consideration of the Convention six years ago. Difficulties were felt at that time in regard to the selection of a candidate for the office, as well as in regard to his support; and, after due deliberation, it was decided to *defer* the further consideration of the matter. Believing that the difficulties which then existed may now, in some good degree, be obviated; feeling that the weight of six additional years has been accumulated upon the infirmities which then beset me, and being now in the seventy-second year of my age, I feel myself justified in bringing this subject once more to the consideration of the Convention of the Diocese. Before coming to this conclusion, I have thought it right to consult extensively the views of my brethren with whom I have had the opportunity of conferring; and the great unanimity of sentiment which I have found to prevail, encourages me to believe that the proposition will be received with general favor by the Convention. To this brief statement, I feel impelled to add the expression of my humble gratitude to the great Head of the Church, for his unmerited blessing on my poor labors in his service. Nor may I withhold my grateful acknowledgments from my brethren of the clergy, for the indulgence they have shown to my infirmities, and for the uniform kindness which they have bestowed on me. From not one of them have I ever received an unkind word, or been conscious of an unfriendly act. May the blessing of Almighty God rest upon them, and upon the people of their charge."

The subject of choosing an assistant bishop was referred to a judicious committee, with instructions to confer with the venerable Diocesan, and report to the Convention at nine o'clock the next morning. Their unanimous report in favor of the proposed measure was readily acquiesced in, and the two orders having separated for the purpose of an election according to the terms of the Constitution, the clergy proceeded with due solemnity to cast their ballots. The number in the Diocese entitled to vote for a bishop, was ninety-seven, of whom nine were absent. Upon counting the votes after the first balloting, seventy-three were found to be in favor of the Rev. John Williams, D. D., President of Trinity College, and a graduate from it in the class of 1835, and fifteen were scattered among half a dozen candidates. This happy result was communicated to the House of Lay Delegates, who immediately confirmed the nomination of the clergy by a vote of eighty-seven yeas, and fourteen nays. Those in the negative did not raise any objection to the candidate himself, but their opposition lay rather to the uncertain or indefinite provision for his support, and to the combined relations which he was expected to sustain to the College and to the Diocese. The unanimity of both orders was very remarkable, and Dr. Williams, in signifying his acceptance of the office which had been conferred upon him, said: —

"To be associated with the clergy of Connecticut, and with her laity, is an honor which I feel most deeply. I am most willing, too, to devote my life to the service of a Diocese in which I was confirmed, and received both my orders; in whose principles I was educated; to which I am warmly attached; and whose spotless history I reverence and love. The unanimity and good-will which, you assure me, marked the proceedings of the Convention, afford other and strong encouragements. May it be a pledge for the future, that by no fault of mine the harmony and peace which have ever made this Diocese 'a city at unity in itself,' shall be disturbed."

The requisite testimonial in behalf of the Assistant Bishop elect, was signed by eighty-seven clerical members of the Convention, and ninety-three lay delegates. Of the lay delegates, twenty-nine were from New Haven County, twenty-five from Fairfield County, twenty from Litchfield County, eight from Hartford County, five from each of the Counties of Middlesex and New London, and one from Tolland County.

The consecration of Dr. Williams took place in St. John's Church, Hartford, on Wednesday, the 29th day of October, 1851. It was upon the same day of the week, thirty-two years before, that Bishop Brownell had been consecrated in Trinity Church, New Haven. Now he presided at the consecration of one chosen to be his own assistant, and he was aided in the impressive services by the bishops from all the New England States, and by Dr. De Lancey, the Bishop of Western New York. The sermon was preached by Dr. Burgess, the Bishop of Maine, in which he drew an admirable portraiture of the character of a man, filling the highest office in the ministry of our Church. Of the eighty-six clergymen, most of them in surplices,[1] gathered within the nave and around the chancel, and of the vast crowd which thronged the edifice, not one could have gone away without a feeling of thankfulness for being permitted to witness and share in the solemnities of so great an occasion.

[1] The vestment in general use by the clergy of the Diocese at the time of the consecration of Bishop Brownell, was a gown. This was worn on funeral and other public occasions, and a surplice was rarely, if ever, seen in any service outside of a church. In 1825, the Annual Convention by a formal resolution, recommended to the wardens and vestrymen of the several parishes in the Diocese, "to provide a suitable gown for the use of the officiating clergyman."

The Assistant Bishop and the Diocesan set out immediately on a visitation, beginning the next Sunday at Seymour, and passing into Fairfield County, and spending a week in some of its oldest parishes. On this visitation, the senior Bishop confirmed the candidates, and his Assistant addressed them and preached the sermons. They were everywhere warmly welcomed, and the ability of the junior prelate, and the favorable impression made by him upon churchmen with whom he was brought in contact, were cheering indications of his success under God in the future administration of the Diocese.

Gratuitous instruction had been given for some time at Trinity College, to a few candidates for Holy Orders, without attracting much notice beyond the precincts of Hartford. "The work was begun in no narrow spirit of localism, but simply under a strong feeling of the growing necessities of the Church in reference to the sacred ministry, and an earnest wish to do something towards meeting those necessities." It increased upon the hands of those who commenced it, and in the autumn of 1851 a full course of theological studies was regularly organized, and afterwards "adopted by the Trustees as an integral department in the College." The appointment of a professor in Ecclesiastical History was, in part, the origin of this scheme, and the subsequent action of the trustees gave shape to it, and warranted the presumption that it was to be more than a mere experiment.

Bishop Brownell, in his annual address to the Convention of 1852, called attention to the establishment of the theological department in the College; and the Convention approved of it, and adopted a sentiment that the training of our candidates for Orders in this way, so that the Bishop might have them under his immediate direction and superintendence, was "in accordance with the early practice of the Diocese, and the universal practice of the primitive Church." As the cares of the Episcopate multiplied with every revolving year, and demanded more of the time and attention of the Assistant, Dr. Williams resigned the Presidency of Trinity College at the Commencement in 1853, and soon after this, propositions were made to place the theological department on a new basis, and with a liberal endowment, provided it was removed to Middletown, and established in that city. One generous layman,[1] and one presbyter[2] of the Diocese offered such inducements, that subscriptions to fill up the endowment were readily obtained, and the removal having been effected, Bishop Williams transferred his residence to Middletown, and assumed the oversight of students in their theological course. The institution was incorporated by the Legislature in 1854, under the name of the "Berkeley Divinity School," and with a provision in the charter, which gave to the Convention of the Diocese the future election of the trustees. The Convention readily accepted the charter and the trust, and thus it became a Diocesan institution.

A commodious building for the use of the students — the contribution of five friends of the School — was added, in 1860, to the large edifice originally purchased; and three resident professors besides the

[1] Edward S. Hall, Esq., of Millville, Mass., subscribed twenty thousand dollars.

[2] Rev. Wm. Jarvis, ten thousand dollars.

Bishop, occupied themselves, as from the first, in dispensing a thorough course of theological instruction. About the same time, a memorial chapel (St. Luke's) built of stone, was presented to the institution, — "the munificent benefaction of a single individual,"[1] whose husband, from its foundation, had been interested in its success, and in other undertakings for the glory of God and the advancement of the Church.

It is not easy to estimate the good results to our communion from the establishment of Trinity College, and the Berkeley Divinity School. How much more, or whether any more would have been accomplished by keeping them together under one corporate name, and giving to the College somewhat of the character of a University, is not a question for the historian to decide or examine. They have both been highly useful, and the College has done a work far beyond that of educating young men with a view to the Christian ministry. Among its graduates scattered over our land, are those who adorn the professions of law and medicine, and the higher walks of learning and science. Bishop Brownell said, in 1852, "Nearly one third of the clergy in our Diocese, and nearly one tenth of all the clergy of our Church have been educated at this institution, while a much larger number of its graduates occupy important stations in other learned professions, or in the various occupations of society. Its influence would be greatly extended by more ample endowments; and by a fuller appreciation of its advantages by such members of our Church as would seek a safe and healthful collegiate education for their sons."

[1] Widow of the late Thomas Dent Mütter, M. D.

The "more ample endowments" were afterwards received, — a special effort being made to add to its funds one hundred thousand dollars. One fourth of this amount was immediately subscribed by four laymen[1] of Waterbury, who thus founded a new professorship, and contributed a handsome sum for the use of the library. The effort was not completed before a general financial embarrassment led to its suspension. When it was renewed, the original sum, exclusive of the contributions from Waterbury, was sought, and ultimately obtained. It was a timely replenishment of the treasury of the College, and, with the exception of a few thousand dollars, the whole amount was subscribed by churchmen in the Diocese of Connecticut.

[1] J. L. M. Scovill gave ten thousand dollars, and his brother Wm. H. Scovill, both since deceased, seven thousand, and Scovill M. Buckingham, three thousand to endow the "Scovill Professorship of Chemistry and Natural Science." The late John P. Elton gave five thousand dollars for the Library.

CHAPTER XXVII.

NEW PARISHES AND NEW CHURCHES; GENERAL CONVENTION; FUND FOR THE SUPPORT OF THE EPISCOPATE; AND SALARIES OF THE CLERGY.

A. D. 1853 – 1857.

NOTHING appeared now to stand in the way of the more rapid advancement of the Church in Connecticut. With institutions to educate candidates for Holy Orders, and with a youthful and vigorous element introduced into the Episcopate, the spiritual life of the Diocese was quickened, and parishes put forth efforts which, with the divine blessing, were greatly conducive to their prosperity. The total number of communicants already exceeded ten thousand, the candidates for the ministry reported in 1853 were twenty-one, and the contributions for missionary and charitable objects nearly twenty-two thousand dollars — an amount more than twice as large as had been contributed for like purposes five years before.

Besides an increase in the strength and liberality of the existing parishes, the organization of new ones was effected not so much on the principle of aggression as to meet the calls for the services of the Episcopal Church in populous places, where they had been only occasionally performed, or where more room was needed to supply the wants of our growing communion. A week previous to the meeting of the Annual Convention in 1851, a new church was consecrated for the new parish at Pine Meadow, in the town of New Hartford. The inhabitants of that village, none of whom were then Episcopalians, erected it with the aid of a few friends in the Diocese, and contributed liberally in the outset to provide for the support of a resident clergyman. A month later, "a very perfect edifice, built of Portland stone" in the early English style, but with too much chancel for the size of the structure, was consecrated at Milford, to take the place of the old church begun there before the Revolutionary War. The ancient parishes at Litchfield and Branford found it necessary to enlarge the accommodations for their people, and hence a new church of wood was completed and consecrated in each of them, during the ensuing winter. From that time to 1857 only three new edifices — two of wood, and one of stone — were erected for parishes with a colonial origin. The two of wood, were for Christ Church, Watertown, and Trinity Church, Southport, a borough in Fairfield, where the church consecrated in 1835 had been accidentally burned; and the other, of "rubble stone, with Caen trimmings," was for the parish at Greenwich.

But much was accomplished during the same period, in the way of improving and enlarging the old edifices — the alterations, in some instances, being almost equivalent to rebuilding. Chancels and towers were added to them, organs were introduced, and parsonages provided for the comfort and convenience of the rectors and their families. In the first six years succeeding the consecration of Bishop Williams, the churches at Salisbury, Naugatuck, Fair Haven, Stamford (St. John's), Woodbury, Middletown,

Bethel, Norwich (Trinity), Warehouse Point, Marbledale, and Middle Haddam, all underwent alteration and enlargement, and were reopened with dedicatory services.

Within the same period, the ground was broken for seven churches in as many new parishes — three of these being in the city of New Haven. The temporary chapel erected by St. Thomas's parish in 1849 was insufficient for the wants of the increased congregation, and a complete edifice in the early English style of architecture, with the walls and tower of Portland stone, and capable of seating nine hundred persons, was built to take its place, and consecrated by Bishop Brownell, amid the joys of the Easter season in 1855. This was his last official act in New Haven, and, though he lived on for nearly ten years, yet he performed only once again the same service elsewhere.[1] Two mission churches, both of wood, and small at first, arose in New Haven, not long before the date of this consecration, — one under the auspices and patronage of St. Paul's Church, and the other under those of Trinity. They soon developed into independent parishes, and took the names, respectively, of St. John's Church, and Christ Church. The evidence of their prosperity appeared in the immediate rebuilding and enlargement of their edifices. Through the renewed efforts of St. Paul's Church, another mission chapel of wood was erected in an outskirt of the city, and consecrated early in December, 1857. It was established upon the free principle, like the other two, and the poor and men of low estate in the neigh-

[1] About three months afterwards, he consecrated St. Paul's Church, Hartford.

borhood were invited to enter it, and learn the way of salvation. It has not yet acquired complete independency; for though recently organized as a parish, it still derives aid in the support of its minister from the mother church.

On the eve of the Advent season in 1850, Bishop Brownell called together, at his residence in Hartford, the clergy of the city and several influential laymen, for the purpose of consulting about the establishment of a free Episcopal Church, and City Mission. Out of this movement grew what is now St. Paul's Church, Hartford, a substantial stone edifice, provided for those who had no settled place of worship, as well as for those who might find inconvenience or embarrassment in the workings of the pew system.

The rectors in Hartford and some of the clergy attached to the College, with a few zealous churchmen from that city, commenced services at earlier dates in Windsor,[1] Manchester, and West Hartford, which subsequently led to the formation of parishes, and the building of churches in all those places. The church in West Hartford, constructed of brick, was completed in the spring of 1855.

In midsummer, 1856, a new church, built of wood, was opened at Central Village, in the town of Plainfield, the fruit chiefly of missionary efforts by the

1 The first Episcopal Church in Windsor — a small wooden edifice — was consecrated January, 1845.

A larger and more attractive church, built of stone in the early English style, and on a different site, was consecrated by Bishop Williams, September, 1865. Its cost was over twenty-five thousand dollars — a portion of which was contributed by friends outside of the parish. The land on which it stands was the gift of Mr. H. Sidney Hayden, who, in addition to this and his original subscription, paid a debt of some five thousand dollars, to free the church from all incumbrance and allow it to be consecrated.

clergy in Eastern Connecticut. A movement was made, about the same time, to establish the services of our Church in Yantic, a manufacturing village within the limits of Norwich, and the movement was attended with success.

Steps towards the organization of a second parish in the city of Bridgeport, by the name of Christ Church, were taken in the latter part of the year 1850. A building was procured and fitted up, in which to hold religious services, but in less than ten months it was destroyed by fire, and the loss occasioned thereby was supplied by the erection of a costly and substantial edifice of brown stone, with sittings for about eight hundred persons. This was consecrated in April, 1853. A new parish formed in the adjoining town of Fairfield, was admitted into union with the Convention in 1856, and its projectors purchased an unfurnished brick building in a central location, which, with some changes and additions, was made, architecturally, one of the most beautiful and church-like structures in the Diocese.

All the parishes in the shore towns, from New Haven towards New York, were beginning to feel the impulse of an increase in the number of their inhabitants, and more room and better edifices were needed to meet the wants and suit the wishes of wealthy residents. The work of Church extension was visible, too, in every part of the Diocese, and the Society for the Promotion of Christian Knowledge made the most earnest appeals for larger contributions to enable it to extend its operations. The Assistant Bishop preached a sermon in its behalf during the Annual Convention of 1853, and showed by what he emphatically styled "the rhetoric of facts, and the logic of statistics," how important it was to be more zealous in the cause of Diocesan Missions. The Convention indorsed his sentiments, and recommended to the several parishes to contribute, on an average, to the funds of the Society, not less than fifty cents for each communicant, and the amount received into the treasury during the ensuing year, rose from one thousand to more than three thousand dollars. The interest thus excited in Diocesan Missions continued, and no backward steps have since been taken.

The General Convention held its triennial session in October, 1853, in the city of New York. The House of Clerical and Lay Deputies was composed of exactly two hundred persons, and the whole number of the clergy of our church in the United States was then sixteen hundred and sixty-three, including thirty-one bishops. By the death of Bishop Philander Chase, of Illinois, in September of the preceding year, Dr. Brownell had become the senior and presiding prelate, and he was present at the opening services of the Convention, and took an active part in its proceedings. The session was marked by the visit of a deputation[1] from the venerable Society for the Propagation of the Gospel in Foreign Parts to the Board of Missions of the Protestant Episcopal Church in the United States. This was a suitable return of kind sympathy for the interest shown by the American bishops, in sending two of their number to represent them, and to participate in the concluding exercises

[1] The Rt. Rev. Geo. T. Spencer, D. D., late Lord Bishop of Madras, the venerable John Sinclair, the Rev. Ernest Hawkins, and the Rev. Henry Caswall.

of the Jubilee of the venerable Society referred to in a previous chapter. Those who composed the deputation must have looked with pride and joy upon the council of the daughter Church, gathered now in so much strength from every section of the land to legislate for her best interests, and to provide for any new emergencies that had arisen in her history. One painful circumstance, — the complete abandonment of our Communion by Dr. Ives, late Bishop of North Carolina, and his submission to the Roman hierarchy, — might have been noted by them; but the solemn and canonical deposition of him from the Apostolic office was almost immediately followed by the elevation to the Episcopal bench of two presbyters, — one (Dr. Atkinson), to take his place, and the other (Dr. Davis), to fill the vacant see of South Carolina. On the occasion of their consecration, all the Bishops of the American Church were present, together with Bishop Spencer, and Dr. Medley, the Bishop of Fredericton, New Brunswick, who both joined in the imposition of hands. The latter preached the sermon, and the House of Bishops thanked him "with fraternal greetings," and solicited a copy of it for publication.

A bold step towards the extension of the Church was taken by the same Convention in the choice of two presbyters,[1] to be consecrated Missionary Bishops for the Pacific coast, — one for California, and the other for "Oregon, having jurisdiction in Washington Territory." The rapidity with which that region, especially California, was filling up with an active

[1] Rev. Wm. I. Kip, D. D., of Albany, N. Y., and Rev. Thomas F. Scott, of Columbus, Ga.

population, forbade the policy of waiting for the perfect organization of dioceses before sending out the chief shepherds to oversee the scattered flocks.

The pastoral letter of the House of Bishops at this time was from the pen of the presiding prelate, and it breathed with the spirit of peace, moderation, and wisdom. A single extract from it will be of interest in the present connection: —

"The world around us is pervaded by forms of error, against which nothing but active controversy can be successful. It should be a controversy, however, dictated and modified by love. On the one hand, we behold an all-grasping Romanism, which gives no quarter, allows no truce, but demands an unconditional submission. On the other hand are various forms of error, still pervaded, more or less, by the true spirit of Christianity, but constantly breaking into fragments, and steadily tending to latitudinarianism and infidelity. Amid these erratic tendencies, the best hopes of Christianity are centred in the Church of England, and in the Protestant Episcopal Church in the United States.

"The spread of Romanism in this country is inevitable — not much, indeed, by proselytism, but by immigration. A few romantic and sentimental minds may be captivated by its imposing ceremonial, and its specious claim to holy living, but the hollowness of its pretensions, and the imposing parade of its impostures cannot stand the scrutiny of an enlightened public opinion. In most Roman Catholic countries, there is, probably, a wide-spread infidelity among the more intelligent classes of the community. They regard with contempt the impostures which the ignorant eagerly receive. The Roman Catholic religion, too, wears a very different aspect in Italy, Spain, and Portugal, from that which it exhibits in this country. Superstitions and mummeries there pass unquestioned, which, in this country, would not impose upon the credulity of its most ignorant devotee. The remission of several hundred years of the pains of purgatory, by the dropping of a few shillings, and repeating a few *aves* and *paters* at the shrine of some supposed saint, which is so frequently advertised in the countries referred to, would hardly impose upon the most ignorant Romanist in this land of free opinions.

"The wonderful immigration of Roman Catholics to this country is often looked upon with alarm by the friends of other religious institutions. Who knows but it is the way designed by Infinite Wisdom for their reformation? We would hope that Romanism cannot withstand even the popular influences of our country. Besotted ignorance cannot long prevail in a land of free schools. Servile superstition must gradually decline in a land of free inquiry. Priestcraft and imposture cannot long flourish in a land of newspapers. It should seem to be our wisdom, therefore, as well as our duty, to treat our less favored brethren with kind consideration, to improve their temporal condition, to enlighten their minds, and to afford them the full benefit of all our free institutions. Under their own organization, they can hardly fail gradually to emancipate themselves from the thraldom which has been imposed upon them in times of ignorance and imposture. There can be little doubt that, from the very circumstances of their position, they will be making rapid advances towards a more intelligent and a purer faith; and it is hardly possible that more than a century or two can elapse before, by a gradual progress, they will relieve themselves from those superstitions and corruptions of the Dark Ages, which, in our parent Church, were thrown off by a more sudden revolution. We may be too sanguine in these anticipations, but it is certainly a consummation most devoutly to be wished."

No positive provision was made for the support of the Assistant Bishop at the time of his election. It was understood that he would not immediately retire from the presidency of the College, and that the matter of salary, at least during his continuance in that office, would be a private arrangement between him and the venerable Diocesan. The Episcopal Fund had been nursed with the greatest care, but the income from it, together with the annual assessments upon the parishes in the proportion of two and one half per cent on the salaries of their respective rectors, scarcely amounted to three thousand dollars. The amount should have been larger, but many of the parishes neglected to pay these assessments; and at the Convention of 1853, a committee of laymen, in a voluminous report not free from mistakes, reviewed the history of the Fund, and urged upon the Convention the necessity of taking effectual measures to increase its permanent and productive capital. By this time, the whole of the considerable balance, principal and interest, due to the senior Bishop ten years before, had been paid, together with his regular salary of eighteen hundred dollars per annum, to April 1, 1853.

When the subject came up for discussion in the

Convention of that year, the two Bishops withdrew, and afterwards sent in a joint communication, in which they stated that they would be "entirely satisfied" with receiving the present income of the fund, and the assessments on the parishes; and concluding with the expression of their earnest hope, "that the available resources of the Diocese may be applied, as far as is practicable, to the *Extension of the Church;* by aiding the weaker parishes, and by the establishment of missions, and the organization of new congregations in those populous portions of the State where the Church is yet unknown." This was certainly generous to the Diocese, if it was not strictly just to themselves.

The original charter, under which the Trustees of the Bishop's Fund acted, gave them no power to hold property at any time, "the annual product of which exceeded the sum of one thousand dollars," and upon their petition, the General Assembly, at its May session in 1853, authorized and empowered them to receive and hold for the purposes for which they were incorporated, funds "the annual income of which, at the rate of six per cent per annum, shall not exceed five thousand dollars." In opening the charter, the Legislature took away the rights of a close corporation, and required of the Trustees an annual report to the Diocesan Convention of the condition of the fund, its investment and proceeds; and also empowered that body to fill all vacancies in the Board, and in case of the neglect or refusal of the Trustees to render an acceptable report, to remove any one or more of them from office, and appoint others in their place. The result of these changes in the charter was beneficial. The Diocese now gained, as a matter of right, the information which formerly it had acquired only as a matter of courtesy. The effort to collect from the delinquent parishes what was due on the old assessment of 1813 was finally abandoned, and reliance for the full support of the Episcopate placed with more wisdom on the annual assessment, which had been renewed by a special vote of the Convention, and directed to be continued during the life of Bishop Brownell.

The Trustees had managed the fund well, and notwithstanding one heavy loss, — the loss by the failure of the Eagle Bank, — it had grown upon their hands, and in the language of Mr. Sigourney, when, on account of age and infirmities, he resigned the office of Treasurer in 1854, after having held it for upwards of forty years, "the little brook had become a river." The Diocese was grateful to him for his long-continued services, and he retired from his trust with a vote of deserved thanks.

When the Assistant Bishop resigned the presidency of Trinity College, it was with the understanding that he was to receive from the Trustees of the Episcopal Fund the surplus revenue of that Fund, as increased by the amount paid in by the parishes, after the salary of the Bishop had been paid. This arrangement was to take effect from the 1st of January, 1853, antedating so far the time of his actual separation from the College. But the revenue thus received was insufficient to afford him a competent income, and in 1856, the Convention voted to give him twenty-five hundred dollars per annum, and to double the assessment upon the parishes, — "the extra sum so raised, to be appropriated to meet the increase of the Assistant Bishop's salary." The resolution in regard to doubling the assessment was not carried into effect. Bishop Brownell, on learning what had been done, directed the Treasurer of the Episcopal Fund to pay to his assistant twenty-five hundred dollars annually, and accepted for himself whatever balance there might be, without the additional tax. He had become too infirm to make any visitations, or to be depended upon for the discharge of any official duties. His last communication to the Convention of the Diocese, and his last appearance in that body, were at its assembling in Christ Church, Hartford, in 1859. Providence had thrown into his hands a sufficiency of this world's goods to make him comfortably independent in his declining years, and he freely relinquished, for the benefit of his assistant and successor, what he might have equitably claimed on the score of past services. The salary of Bishop Williams was increased, in 1864, to three thousand dollars,[1] and the resolution assessing the parishes two and one half per cent, was reaffirmed and ordered to be in force until the annual income of the Fund should, at least, be equal to that amount.

The special attention of the laity was directed, in 1853, to a more liberal support of the parochial clergy. Nowhere in the Diocese, unless in a few city parishes, were their salaries more than sufficient for the absolute necessities of their position. "An intelligent mechanic," said Bishop Brownell, in his

[1] In 1866, it was increased to four thousand dollars, and in 1868, the Convention, upon the suggestion of the Trustees of the Bishop's Fund, added five hundred dollars more, — making it four thousand five hundred dollars per annum.

address to the Annual Convention of that year, "receives better compensation for labor than many a clergyman who has devoted years to hard study, and spent much money in acquiring the necessary literary and theological preparation for the duties of his profession." The age had become extravagant, and the cost of living was greatly advanced. Individuals devoted to other pursuits demanded an increased remuneration for the fruits of their toil on the ground that it was necessary to enable them to maintain their families, and provide them with suitable comforts, and the demand thus made was irresistible. But the salaries of the clergy, though a matter of contract between them and their people, could not be regulated simply on the principles of a hireling. This was a low view of the question, and the parishes that entertained it were unmindful of their best interests.

The whole subject was referred by the Convention to a committee of laymen, who, in their report, recognized the fact that the salaries of the clergy, especially in the rural districts, were not what they ought to be, and they appealed to the laity to awake to a proper sense of duty and justice in this matter. "No greater blessing," said they, "can exist in any village, than the influence of an educated, an intellectual, cheerful, and happy clergyman, and his family. This influence is felt in all our social or domestic relations, softening the asperities, refining and elevating the propensities of our nature. In sickness and in health, in our joys and in our sorrows, he is with us to alleviate and to heighten; and gratitude should unite with interest in the laity to strengthen that influence. Much, very much, depends in this respect upon a comfortable support, cheerfully and promptly given."

Whether the suggestions, emanating from the Convention in this way, were the cause or not, the parishes soon began to make better provision for the support of their rectors. The salaries were generally increased, and with the development of more life, as shown in the erection of new churches, or the enlargement of old ones, several parishes proceeded to supply themselves with rectories, which were to be free of rent for their respective pastors. This was a movement in the right direction, and tended to prevent the evil of frequent clerical changes. Besides the direct advantage to the clergyman, there are pleasant memories for the people lingering about the rural rectory. They often come to it for the relief of their burdened souls, and for guidance in the day of trouble and adversity. They watch with delight the hand of improvement, as applied by some tasteful occupant, and a priest of God in the next generation may thus have reason to cherish feelings of gratitude towards his predecessor, and to be excited thereby to good works. When the celebrated George Herbert had rebuilt, at his own charge, the greatest part of the parsonage at Bemerton, he caused to be engraved upon the mantel of the chimney in the hall, for the benefit of his successor, these significant lines: —

"If thou chance for to find
A new house to thy mind,
And built without thy cost,
Be good to the poor,
As God gives thee store,
And then my labor 's not lost." [1]

[1] *Temple and Country Parson*, p. 43.

CHAPTER XXVIII.

PROGRESS OF THE DIOCESE; DEATH OF DR. CROSWELL; NEW CHURCH AT STRATFORD; AND EFFORTS TO INCREASE THE RANKS OF THE MINISTRY.

A. D. 1857-1860.

MANY proofs of steady and continuous growth were now visible in every part of the Diocese. Its clerical force, — besides the two Bishops, — consisted of one hundred and thirteen presbyters, and eleven deacons. The names of twenty-three persons appeared on the list of candidates for Holy Orders in 1857, and the number was the same two years later. At the Annual Convention of 1858, which was held in Waterbury, ninety-five of the clergy of the Diocese were present, and one hundred and six lay delegates. Bishop Williams, in his address on that occasion, noted a large list of clerical changes — too large for the good of the Church; but he expressed his belief that the action of the Convention five years before, in regard to the increase of the salaries of the clergy, had served to lessen this evil, and that the laity had it in their power, if they pleased, to render the pastoral relation more permanent in the future. "The mere perfunctory performance," said he, "of the duties of preaching, administering the sacraments, and going through with services and offices, can be as well done by an itinerant ministry, or occasional supplies, as in any other way. But to secure the real work of a pastor, to insure that it shall be any thing more than an ephemeral and spasmodic effort, the pastoral relation must be made an enduring one."

A remarkable religious interest pervaded Connecticut in the beginning of 1858. Unlike revivals in previous years, it was attended with no special excitement, and the influence of noted preachers in originating and carrying it on was scarcely perceptible. The financial embarrassments of the country led men to pause in their career of worldliness, and daily prayer-meetings, and the ordinary instructions of the pulpit on Sundays, and occasionally on other days, were followed by the conversion of many sinners, and their pursuit of a new and better life.

The clergy of the Church, particularly in those places where the revival prevailed, were more diligent in their ministrations, and probably the Lenten services in no former season had been so numerously attended. The number confirmed in sixty-three parishes of the Diocese, as reported to the next Annual Convention, reached eleven hundred and twenty-five, and of these confirmations, nearly one fourth were for the parishes in New Haven. The religious interest manifested itself very largely in that city, and the opportunity was improved by the several rectors, to draw together their flocks more frequently for the purposes of Christian instruction, and, by stirring appeals, to warm the hearts of established believers, encourage the timid and the wavering, and awaken the careless from the sleep of insensibility, to the duty of a living faith in the Son of God, and of practical obedience to His laws.

There was no reaction to the Episcopal Church in the movements and results of this revival. During the next Conventional year, the Assistant Bishop visited all the parishes and missionary stations in the Diocese except four; and administered the rite of confirmation to one thousand and twenty-nine persons. This was the most extended visitation which he had ever made in any one year, and he was as much gratified as surprised to find so soon again large classes of candidates presented for the Apostolic rite. The quiet and earnest work of the pastors seemed to be producing the blessed fruits for which some of them had patiently waited. The aggregate of communicants in the whole Diocese went up, in 1859, to eleven thousand and five hundred, though the loss by death and removal, as reported at the same time, was fully equal to one third of the yearly increase by new admissions. These admissions, from year to year, coincided for the most part with the number of persons confirmed, — it having, for a long period, been the practice of the clergy to teach that "what is required of those who come to the Lord's Supper," is substantially no more than what should be required of those who present themselves for the rite of Confirmation. The number of families, too, fell but little short of nine thousand, and the Sunday-schools and the missionary and charitable contributions steadily increased.

One by one, the venerable presbyters, who, since the death of Bishop Jarvis, had been conspicuous actors in the affairs of the Diocese, disappeared, and left their places to be filled by younger men. On the last day of December, 1854, the Rev. Dr. Croswell,

Rector of Trinity Church, New Haven, preached a sermon, which was afterwards published, commemorative of the fortieth anniversary of his connection with the parish. If any of his parishioners were disappointed that the occasion was not more largely improved by one who had been "forty years in the mount," his brief reminiscences must have, at least, touched their hearts, and made them grateful to God, for the vast amount of parochial duty which He had enabled His servant to perform in the several offices of the Church.

"Forty years," said he, "constitute a large portion, even of the longest life; and when considered with reference to the relationship between pastor and people, it seems, indeed, like a very long period. Such instances of unbroken pastoral connection are extremely rare, and especially in this age of fluctuation and change, where hearers sometimes become fastidious, critical, and fond of novelty, and preachers exhibit at least a corresponding degree of sensitiveness, restlessness, and instability. But to one who has been permitted to enjoy such a protracted relationship, the passage of so many years would appear but a mere span, were it not for the considerations that present themselves to the mind on an occasion like the present.

"I stop at this point in my journey, for recollection and review; and who can tell what memories crowd upon the thoughts? Surrounded by the same parish, into whose service I entered forty years ago, what can I behold to show its identity? What has become of the familiar faces of my immediate contemporaries? Where are those who stood with me, side by side, at that period? Alas! how many of their number have passed away! How few continue to accompany me on the short remainder of my journey! Here and there, indeed, a senior's voice may be heard in the congregation; and they verily seem like the last 'shaking of the olive tree, or like gleaning grapes, when the vintage is done.' But as for the residue,—they have risen up to occupy the places of those who have gone before; and the generations by whom I am now surrounded, are pressing forward to fill the ranks vacated by their predecessors. But still an identity may be traced. It is the same parish. Those who have grown up under my pastoral care, or have been gathered from the fields, constitute but one and the same household. All maintain the same relationship; and, amid perpetual changes, the parish remains the same."[1]

Dr. Croswell, at this time, had an associate[2] in the rectorship, and for many years he had not been without aid in his ministrations. He dwelt among his own people, and was rarely absent from his post, but his strong and robust constitution was beginning to feel the effects of an insidious and complicated disease, and he finally fell before it, on the 13th of March, 1858, when he was approaching his eightieth birth-day. Bishop Williams preached the sermon at his funeral, which was attended by a great concourse of people, and by forty-seven of his brethren in the ministry,—a larger number than was present at the special Convention of the Diocese in 1819, when Bishop Brownell was consecrated.

[1] Sermon, pp. 5, 6.

[2] Rev. Thomas C. Pitkin, D. D., now Rector of St. Paul's Church, Detroit Mich.

It is the privilege of few clergymen to pass through a life of such varied experience and momentous events as that of Dr. Croswell. He was brought up to the occupation of a printer, and in early manhood became the editor and proprietor of a political newspaper, published first in Hudson, and then in Albany, N. Y. He showed much talent and tact in that capacity, and gained for himself the confidence and friendship of a circle of distinguished men. Some of his severe and pungent editorials brought him into collision with his political foes, and being prosecuted for libel, he was defended by Alexander Hamilton in a speech, remarkable as the greatest forensic effort of one of the greatest minds of his age.

The arena of politics proved unsatisfactory to Mr. Croswell, and "turning his thoughts to the solemn subject of religion, and the Christian duties that rest on our race," he conformed to the Episcopal Church in 1812, and immediately applied his vigorous intellect to the study of theology. From the time of his ordination in the spring of 1814, until his removal to New Haven, a period of eight months, he officiated in Christ Church, Hudson. It has been seen, in previous chapters, how much he was identified with the interests of the Church in his native state, and how resolutely he stood up to defend her doctrines, discipline, and worship, when he found them misrepresented and maligned. He was widely known in our communion, and filled the most important posts of honor and usefulness in her councils. From 1816 till the day of his death, he was chosen uninterruptedly by the Diocese, one of its clerical delegates to the General Convention, and from 1822 to 1852, when he declined a reëlection, he was a member of the Standing Committee.

His native shrewdness and sagacity, and his self-control, gave him great influence in public bodies, and as a manager he seemed to have been made wiser by the experience which he acquired in the struggles of political life. He had a way of saying sharp things without intending to give offence, and he sometimes spoke disparagingly or sarcastically of those who failed to come up to his own standard of ritual and churchmanship. Though not a scholar himself, and, therefore, incapable of fully appreciating scholarship in others, he was better read than most busy pastors in polite literature, and what he knew of the works of the old English divines, he knew well.

But his chief excellences of character were exhibited in his own parish. He went to it without the advantages and supports of a liberal education, and though surrounded by the culture and learning of "the Standing Order," he so bore himself in his pastoral duties, so went in and out among his people, so preached, and so prayed, that "the word of God grew and multiplied," and men of all shades of opinion and religious belief, became reverent admirers of his fidelity to the Church, and of his kind attentions and ceaseless charities to the sick and the needy. He was an eminently practical and instructive preacher, and his style of writing was pure, perspicuous, and free from redundancy. His majestic figure, and massive head, crowned, in the latter years of his life, with silvery hair, invited the attention of a congregation when he arose before it; and a stranger, meeting him in the streets, would have been struck with his form as that of a Christian gentleman of the old school. It was in reference to this that his gifted son[1] wrote the lines which are just as true as if they were not prompted by filial affection: —

> " My father, proud am I to bear
> Thy face, thy form, thy stature ;
> But happier far, might I but share
> More of thy better nature."

A fitting and tasteful monument, erected in the chancel of Trinity Church, marks the remembrance and gratitude of the parish for his long continued and faithful services.

The death of Dr. Croswell was followed a month later by that of the Rev. Zebediah H. Mansfield, a graduate of Trinity College, and still in the prime of his usefulness. He returned in 1854, from a warmer climate to Norwich Town, and the home of his childhood, and though a sufferer from disease and occupied to some extent in teaching, he rendered important missionary services to Yantic, and bequeathed to the parish there valuable legacies, which will cause him to be held in grateful and lasting remembrance. In

[1] Rev. William Croswell, D. D., " Poet, Pastor, Priest." The hand of death fell upon him while closing the services in the Church of the Advent, Boston, of which he was Rector, on Sunday afternoon, November 9th, 1851. He knelt down at the chancel rail, and repeated from memory — his book having fallen noiselessly by his side — an appropriate collect. Unable to rise, from the exhaustion of his strength, he remained on his knees, and pronounced with faltering voice the Apostolic benediction. A general alarm immediately pervaded the congregation, and he was borne by his friends through the church to the vestry-room, and from thence in a carriage to his residence, where he soon ceased to be mortal. His bereaved and sorrowing father prepared and published, in an octavo volume, a tender " Memoir " of him, containing not only a somewhat minute history of his life, but many of his charming poetical productions, and extracts from his voluminous correspondence.

his first report to the Bishop, after his return to the Diocese, he mentioned his ministrations in this place, and said: "It is within my recollection that there was but one church in Norwich, and the congregation not larger than the new parish" of Grace Church, Yantic.

As the venerable presbyters of a preceding generation passed away, so did the wooden churches, associated with the memories of colonial times, and with the labors and prayers of self-sacrificing and godly men. Only two or three of these were now left standing. That which belonged to the oldest parish in the Diocese, Christ Church, Stratford, was the most remarkable of them, and the richest in historical associations. Around it clustered the memories of more than a century — memories connected with the first foundation and early trials of Episcopacy in Connecticut. Its walls had echoed with the voice of Dr. Johnson, and as an interesting link, uniting them with the past, the people cherished it, and were reluctant to take the necessary steps to replace it by another of larger dimensions, and more in accordance with the prevailing style of ecclesiastical architecture. But the prosperity of the parish and the march of improvement demanded a new edifice, and friends from abroad, — "they of the city," — mindful of the fragrant blessings of the Church in their native village, made generous contributions to aid in its erection. It was constructed of wood, in the Gothic style, with sittings for about seven hundred and fifty persons, and is the third house of worship built by the parish. It was consecrated by Bishop Williams, on the 29th of July, 1858, one hundred and fourteen years after its immediate predecessor had been opened with suitable services by Dr. Johnson. He described that second temple in one of his letters to the Society for the Propagation of the Gospel, as "almost finished in a very neat and elegant manner, the architecture being allowed in some things to exceed anything done before in New England."

At the time of the consecration of the new church, a scene was presented in Stratford very different from the one witnessed there a century and a half before, when Heathcote and Muirson rode into the village, and were met with vehement opposition because they came to initiate the services of the Church of England. They came upon the invitation of a few families, who were attached to the faith of their forefathers, and desirous of worshipping God in the forms of the Liturgy. But how changed now! Instead of the lone presbyter appearing with his lone attendant, and seeking in some private dwelling to "sign with the sign of the cross," a child in baptism, or to minister to a little despised flock, forty-nine clergymen approached the village in various groups, and from different places, and uniting in a surpliced band with a bishop at their head, entered the newly erected edifice, and were welcomed by a waiting multitude, who joined them in the glad response, "This is the generation of them that seek him; even of them that seek thy face, O Jacob." The sermon at the consecration was preached by the writer of these pages, and published at the request of the vestry of the parish, and whatever merit it possessed was due to "an occasion fraught with holy memories, and suggesting the most solemn and weighty duties."

Additions to the sacred edifices of the Diocese, and

improvements in the old ones, still continued. A new parish was formed in an outlying district of Bridgeport, by the name of the Church of the Nativity, and a neat though small structure of stone was consecrated for it in the middle of January, 1859. Three weeks later, the corner-stone of a church for the new parish of St. James, Glastenbury, was laid, and not long after, a similar ceremony was performed for St. Mark's Church, Bridgewater. "Up to the second Sunday in August, 1859, no service of the Book of Common Prayer had ever been celebrated in that part of the town of Farmington" called Plainville. Lay reading was then commenced by a candidate for Holy Orders, who, shortly before, was a licentiate among the Congregationalists, and supplied their church in that place. An Episcopal parish was duly organized, and a convenient brick church erected, and consecrated Tuesday, in Easter week, 1860. On the following Tuesday, another "beautiful structure" of brick was consecrated for St. Andrew's Church, Thompsonville, — a manufacturing village in the town of Enfield. This was a new parish admitted into union with the Convention in 1855. Internal troubles in the ancient parish at Simsbury, the scene of the labors of the unfortunate Gibbs, and the faithful Viets, led to the formation in 1849, of Trinity Church, Tariffville, at that time a prosperous village of the town, where carpets were extensively manufactured. The church of the Presbyterian Society was ultimately purchased and fitted up for our services, and a clergyman sustained there by the people, with the aid of appropriations from the Missionary fund. During the next month, the ground was broken for a chapel at South Norwalk, and for another at Stamford. They were respectively projected by the mother parishes in those places, and a conviction that they were needed to meet the spiritual wants of the people, was not too soon put into practice. They were built of stone, capacious enough to hold several hundred persons, and the worshippers in them have since organized into independent parishes, each one of which is now supplied with a rector, to whom a liberal salary is paid. A neat stone church was commenced in the summer of 1856, for the new parish in Darien — a town about midway between Norwalk and Stamford; and though finished, and an object of interest to its little band of devoted supporters, it was not consecrated, owing to the encumbrance of a debt, until early in the spring of 1863.

Connecticut was now better supplied with clergymen than at any former period. She had twenty-three candidates for Holy Orders, nearly all of whom were pursuing their studies at the Berkeley Divinity School, and scarcely a parish within her borders was destitute of a minister. But a like favorable statement could not be made of other Dioceses in our land. The new ones were rapidly filling up with an active and intelligent population, and their bishops were constantly calling for more men of the right stamp to do "the work of the ministry" — men of holy and unselfish character, who were willing to take the risk of a support anywhere, or rather to depend mainly on opening the fountains of charity and grace in the hearts of the people for aid and sympathy in carrying out the design and offices of the Church. None of the old and favored Dioceses were overstocked with working clergy, and vacant parishes in any of them were generally filled by turning to quarters where there was the greatest supply. This was the natural course of things, and Connecticut continued to be the bed from which many flowers were transplanted to grace other gardens.

The ranks of her ministry would have been thinner, but for the agency of the "Church Scholarship Society" — a strictly Diocesan institution. As this failed to reach the great want of the whole Church, a scheme of wider influence was projected and carried into operation. Bishop Williams, in his address to the Convention of 1859, speaking of the number of candidates for Holy Orders, said: —

"In this connection, I would call attention to the 'Society for the Increase of the Ministry,'[1] organized about a year ago, but lately incorporated by the Legislature of this State, and commencing its labors under flattering auspices, and with every prospect of eminent success. The favor with which it has already been received by the clergy and laity of the Diocese, may, I trust, be regarded as only the beginning of an ever increasing interest in the important duty which it has undertaken. Let the heart of the Church be

1 The "Society for the Increase of the Ministry" originated in Connecticut, and the first public meeting after its organization was held in Hartford, on the last day of June, 1858. The officers chosen were chiefly from New England, and this gave an impression abroad that it was to be an institution of a local character. But the Society, which from necessity appeared to be local in its earliest movements, soon became general in its work, and furnished practical evidence that it was not to operate in favor of one particular section of the country. "The object of this corporation," as defined by the charter, "shall be to furnish means for the education of candidates for Holy Orders in the Protestant Episcopal Church of the United States."

fully roused to the real grandeur of the work which is here opening before her, for the increase of a well-trained and educated ministry, and it will afford the best of all possible endowments; an endowment the income from which will be made living in prayer and love, and bless alike givers and receivers to the glory of their God and Saviour."

The General Convention, held at Richmond, in the autumn of the same year, appointed a large committee of laymen for the recess, with instructions "to devise and carry out such means and measures as they might deem advisable," for the welfare of the Church; and especially to impress upon their lay brethren the great necessity for more ministers. The same Convention, in view of the impossibility of supplying regular clerical services in parishes and congregations already in existence, "earnestly requested the parochial clergy to bring the Church's pressing need of additional laborers before their respective congregations," and also to solicit from them contributions to aid in the education of indigent and deserving young men seeking admission into the sacred ministry. The next year, 1860, the number of candidates for Holy Orders in Connecticut rose to twenty-eight, and it may have increased in a similar ratio in several of the older Dioceses; but upon the breaking out of civil war, and the general prostration and derangement of business during its frightful desolations, the call to arms was made a paramount duty, and the country demanded for services in the field the freshness and flower of her youth. Under these circumstances, the candidates for the ministry were slightly diminished, and the yearly number in Connecticut has not been so high since that date.

The necessity for them, however, in this Diocese and throughout the country has not ceased. For never did the Church require a larger supply of educated, intellectual, and judicious ministers. The spread of knowledge, the propagation of infidel opinions, and the secret growth of loose views in religion and morality, all render it more than ever important that candidates for the ministry should not only be multiplied, but be well trained and taught, and fitted for their godly work. There is much for Christian men to do in the way of checking the progress of moral evil. The lapse of years has not changed the truth of what Bishop Williams said in his sermon before the Diocesan Convention of 1857: —

"Surely, in an age and land like ours, where wealth, and the worldliness and luxury that wait on wealth, are pouring in upon us; when that simple state of society, which was at once our pride and safeguard, is giving way to an artificial civilization, which ever bears in its bosom the elements of the most fearful barbarism; when, before this tide of worldliness, public morality is falling to a lower standard, the private life is sinking to a lower level, the 'old domestic morals of the land,' are becoming matters of history; when all this is so, then, I say, it does become us, clergy and people alike, to see to it, each for ourselves, each in our place and station, that something shall be done to stay the plague." [1]

[1] Sermon, pp. 18, 19.

CHAPTER XXIX.

CONVENTION AT NEW LONDON; DIOCESAN MISSIONS; EPISCOPAL DUTIES; CIVIL WAR; AND DEATHS AMONG THE CLERGY.

A. D. 1860 – 1862.

THE opening of a railway, through the towns along the shore from New Haven to New London, made the latter place more convenient of access by residents in the interior and western parts of the State. The power of steam tends to annihilate distances, and the Annual Convention which met at New London, in 1860, was as numerously attended as the same Convention which assembled in Waterbury two years before. The interest of the laity in the legislation of the Church carried their delegates to these yearly gatherings, and by a canon of the Diocese, it is declared to be "the duty of every clergyman, having a seat in the Convention, to attend every meeting of the same, or send a reasonable excuse to the Bishop for his absence."

The Convention at New London was marked by an effort to introduce greater efficiency into the work of Diocesan Missions. Discontent with the operations of the Society for the Promotion of Christian Knowledge, and also with its cherished title, prevailed to some extent, and nine clergymen from different sections of the Diocese were appointed a committee to "inquire into the character and condition of the missionary work," with instructions to present to the next Annual Convention any further measures that might be deemed necessary to excite in its behalf more zeal and sympathy among churchmen. Time was thus given for considering the subject, in order that the several members of the committee might have an opportunity to produce such statistical and other information as would lead to satisfactory results and conclusions. The year went round, and they had embodied their researches and views in an elaborate report, which covers nearly six closely printed pages of the Journal. Testimony was borne in it to the immense good accomplished by the Society in former days; and while "the Church in Connecticut seemed called to a bolder and more enlarged line of effort," the debt of gratitude for its humble charities to feeble and destitute parishes, was not to be forgotten.

"There are two forms of Church work and Church growth," said the committee, "which may be respectively called the spontaneous and the aggressive. Hitherto the Church in this Diocese has confined herself almost exclusively to the former. But she will never fulfill her mission till she enters upon and prosecutes the latter energetically. Hitherto she has grown as the plant grows that sends out its leaders, and multiplies by their clinging to the neighboring soil, and repeating itself in the spot to which they adhere. When from any cause an interest in favor of the Church has sprung up in any locality, and measures have already been taken in her favor, she has recognized the movement, and extended to it her fostering care. But she has followed, not led. Rarely has she gone into any place, and set up her Master's banner, and called men to enroll themselves under her standard, and stood among them, and proclaimed the truth, and patiently waited to see the effect. Yet this is true missionary work, and without it she will never diffuse herself through the land, and do her Master's work as it ought to be done. There is a multitude of places where the Church is scarcely known and greatly needed, and where, by suitable efforts, she could be firmly established and permanently maintained, if her services were sent to them, and steadily and perseveringly sustained. It will not do to wait till we are invited to come. It will not do to expect the people to pay for the services to any considerable extent. This supposes the previous existence of the very interest which it is the object of true missionary work to awaken. There are places where a prejudice exists against a paid clergy, who are stigmatized as hirelings — the fruit of fanatical excitements that began more than a century ago. What is needed is that suitable men should be sent upon the ground, sufficiently paid, and kept there long enough to give the experiment a fair trial."

The Convention, in accepting the report, adopted a series of resolutions, the object of which was to create a greater interest throughout the Diocese in the work of its missionary organization. As no economy would enable the Society to do its appropriate work without a greatly enlarged income, the Board of Directors was required to hold four public services, during the year, at such times and places as the Convention might designate, and by addresses and statements of facts to stimulate churchmen to be more liberal in their contributions to Diocesan Missions. In view of the necessity of special attention to the spiritual wants of many neglected places, it was further recommended to the Board to appoint at least one itinerant Missionary "to explore, and as far as may be, occupy the vacant fields of the Diocese."

The result of these new movements was not as beneficial as had been hoped for and anticipated. The quarterly missionary meetings were held on week days, and therefore, large congregations were not generally drawn out to hear the appeals and statements of the Directors. Some progress, however, was made, and the annual amount afterwards received from collections in all the parishes compared favorably with those reported in preceding years. But the stream of sympathy, and of alms, did not rise high enough for the necessities of the Church. An itinerant Missionary was sent into the destitute localities lying east of the Connecticut River; but his solitary work was, for the most part, confined to a survey of the whole field — essential, indeed, to intelligent action in selecting the best places for building up parishes; but not reaching to the extent of occupying them, or even of supplying them with stated ministrations.

The western and southern portions of the State, especially the Counties of New Haven, Fairfield, and Litchfield, afforded, at this time, the least room for missionary effort. Scarcely in any of them might a call for the services of our Church be made without finding a response from some parochial clergyman. Only three or four towns, and those thinly inhabited, either in New Haven, or Fairfield County, were destitute of houses of Episcopal worship. A few of the towns had several, and the Church in these sections was full of vigor and steadily progressing. But this could not be said of the eastern and northeastern parts of the Diocese. The counties of Windham and Tolland, as a whole, were the most spiritually destitute, and presented some of the best openings for the introduction of faithful missionary labor. More attention has since been given to them, and liberal and special contributions made to sustain the services of the Church in places where there seemed to be rapidly rising a flood of "that evil which is worse even than original heathenism — the evil of a lost Christianity."

Bishop Williams opened his annual address in 1861, with these words: —

"Ten years have elapsed since I was elected by the Convention of this Diocese to the office of its Assistant Bishop, and it may not be amiss, that, before I present the customary statistics, I should lay before you a summary view of the period, which this day closes. Ten years form a large part of an average Episcopate, and one who has gone through them cannot but feel that he has reached a point, the like to which he very probably will never reach again. In some sort, then, a summing up of such a period is like the summing up of all one's stewardship; and though the briefly stated results cover but little space, and occupy but little time in the statement, yet they are surrounded with thoughts and memories, with hopes and fears, with consciousness of shortcomings and failures, with joys and sorrows, that give to the otherwise dry statistics, at least for him who makes them, a very real and a very solemn life.

"Seven thousand six hundred and forty-four persons have received the laying on of hands.

"Eighty-five candidates for Holy Orders have been ordained to the Diaconate.

"Sixty-five Deacons have been ordained to the Priesthood.

"Twenty-eight churches and chapels have been consecrated, and two, which have been erected, and are in use, are awaiting consecration — making thirty new churches and chapels in all.

"Twenty-four churches have been reopened after enlargements and improvements in various ways. So that fifty-four churches and chapels have been built, or re-edified and enlarged.

"During the period under review, I have preached on one thousand four hundred and seventy-three occasions, delivered six hundred and two confirmation and other addresses, and administered the Holy Communion two hundred and twenty times. It ought also to be recorded, with feelings of devout gratitude for God's protecting mercy, that in travelling more than fifty-nine thousand miles, I have met with no serious accident, and very rarely with even a detention, though illness has sometimes prevented me from fulfilling my appointments.

"From among the clergy we have lost thirteen by death. One hundred and sixteen have taken letters dimissory, and left the Diocese. Eighty-one have been received from other Dioceses. This makes our loss by death and removal exceed, by forty-eight, the number received from other quarters, and yet through our accessions by ordination the roll of clergy has increased from one hundred and ten to one hundred and forty-five. I mention this more especially because it demonstrates the necessity of Trinity College and the Divinity School to the efficient working of the Diocese, and shows that by their agency we can not only supply our own wants, but also furnish pastors for other portions of the Church."

In closing this retrospect, grateful mention was made of the "paternal kindness and confidence," received from the senior Bishop. For several years, his advanced age and bodily infirmities had disqualified him for the performance of any of the active duties of the Episcopate; but he was still a judicious counsellor, who "had understanding of the times," and "knew what Israel ought to do."

New and startling events now occurred in the civil and political history of the country. All the better blessings of "unity, peace, and concord," were forgotten amid the rage of envenomed feelings, and ungoverned passions, and the excitement of mustering hosts for the battle was followed by actual warfare. The foot of civil strife was treading wildly, and the land was overspread with oppressive gloom. The dismemberment of the national Union, under which all sections had been signally prospered and blessed, was attempted, and a fearful expense of life and treasure, of suffering and sorrow, was before the country. In such an alarming crisis, the Church could not remain unaffected, and her clergy and laity had momentous duties to perform. While no political revulsions can furnish any excuse for overlooking the infinitely great interests of the soul, a godly submission to the laws and constitutional rulers of the land is ever a matter of religious obligation,— and nowhere is this submission more faithfully taught than in the Protestant Episcopal Church.

Bishop Williams, in his address for 1861, referred to the national troubles, and uttered sentiments and suggestions in unison with the feelings of the Convention. It would be doing injustice to him, to withhold from the reader the following extended extract: —

"Brethren, this seventy-seventh Convention of our Diocese meets in a crisis of our country's history, which few of us, probably, had ever anticipated. Until within the last few months, we had been fain to believe that the forces which bound together the different portions of this great Republic were so much stronger than those which tended to separation, that under all misunderstandings and jealousies there was such a substantial basis of mutual good-will and common interest; that, in a word, there was such a national life and unity among us, that we were as safe as any human government could make us. And it certainly appeared, in contrasting our condition for fifteen years past, with that of almost all other civilized countries, as if we had grounds for this belief. 'Our country,' to use the eloquent words of a late English statesman, 'was as a land of Goshen. Everywhere else were the thunder and the fire running along the ground, a very grievous storm, such as there was none like it since man was on the earth, and yet everything tranquil here; and then, again, thick night, darkness that might be felt, and yet light in all our dwellings.' But the storm and the darkness are upon us now, and the season of fierce trial has overtaken us.

"At such a time, it could hardly be expected that an Episcopal Address should contain no allusion to our special duties as Christian ministers and people, no words of counsel or suggestion. My words will be few; but uttered, let me say, with a deep sense of the responsibility which they involve, and a constant remembrance that they are spoken in a Council of that Kingdom, which is not of this world. I am authorized to say that they are spoken for the Bishop of the Diocese as well as for myself.

"It is a great comfort that our chief duty in this exigency is so plain before us, that we need not be perplexed or at any loss about it. It is a great comfort, too, that in bringing it home to ourselves, or, if such be our office, urging it upon others, we have only to follow on in that line of teaching which our Church has always commended to us, and placed before us. We have no new lessons on this point to learn, no old lessons to unlearn.

"Our American Prayer Book, as doubtless we all remember, was adopted in 1789, two years after the framing of the Federal Constitution. Since then, every child in our communion has been taught as a part of his Christian vocation, 'to honor and obey the civil authority.' On all ordinary occasions of our public worship, when that book has been used in its integrity, we have prayed for the 'President of the United States, and all others in authority;' and regularly besought the good Lord to deliver us from 'sedition, privy conspiracy, and rebellion.' Our articles were adopted in 1801; and the XXXVIIth of these declares, 'The power of the Civil Magistrate extendeth to all men, as well clergy as laity, in all things temporal; but hath no authority in things purely spiritual. And we hold it to be the duty of all men who are professors of the Gospel, to pay respectful obedience to the civil authority, regularly and legitimately constituted.'

"Such is the clear, outspoken, unmistakable teaching of our Church; and it does but echo the teaching and injunction of God's Holy Word. Whenever and wherever her ministers have taught anything else, they have done it in plain dereliction of their duty, and in contravention of their ordination vows. So far as we in this Diocese are concerned, I have never known or heard of any other teaching. 'Through evil report and good report, applauded or condemned,' we have always taught that 'every soul' is 'to be subject to the higher powers; for there is no power but of God, the powers that be are ordained of God;' and that this subjection is 'not only for wrath, but also for conscience sake.'

"And what else need we teach now, in regard to the great question that stirs the depths of this nation's heart? Surely, there is no room for the least doubt as to what and where that civil authority is, to which, as 'regularly and legitimately constituted,' we are bound 'to pay respectful obedience.' Surely, if this teaching had been everywhere received, and acted on as a part of a Christian's personal religion, things would never have come to the pass which they have reached now.

"Here, then, I am content to leave this matter. Patriotism, loyalty, every sentiment and every emotion, which man can know in his relations to the State, find their living utterance and only true life in loyal obedience to the lawful government under which we live. Apart from that obedience, they are utterly valueless, and become empty words. When then, Christ's ministers teach that, they teach all the rest; they teach what God's own Word declares; they teach what their vows of ordination bind them to inculcate."

As the battle-fields of the civil war were remote from New England, the clergy in Connecticut were not disturbed in their pastoral relations, except that a few of them fell under the operation of drafts for troops by the General Government. They were relieved, however, by the provision of substitutes, and devoting themselves to their ministerial duties, the Church continued quietly to gain in numbers and in strength. With some minds under divine grace, the tendency of national anxieties and excitements is to lead them nearer to God, while with others, — and this is the more general effect, — it is to carry them away from Him, to make His Word less precious, His holy day less sacredly regarded, and the ordinances of religion less faithfully observed. The present peril is ever more absorbing than the future, and in such a crisis the contributions and sympathies of Christians naturally follow their thoughts, and go largely to the relief and consolation of those who have enlisted in the service of their country, and become disabled by wounds or sickness.

But much was now done also for the advancement of the Church and her institutions. In the changes of private fortune, which war commonly produces, the ability of many to multiply their gifts to Christian charities was suddenly increased, and different sections of the Diocese reaped advantages from special efforts of benevolence made easier by an expanded currency. In some cases, parish debts of long standing were liquidated, and churches relieved from embarrassment, showed new life and vigor, and responded liberally to appeals for external objects. According to the summary of parochial reports in 1862, the contributions to these objects for the previous Conventional year amounted to upwards of forty thousand dollars, and were nearly equal to those, "not including ordinary expenses," furnished for purposes within the parishes.

Death again fell among the elder clergy of the Diocese; and the list no longer contained the familiar names of David Baldwin, Stephen Jewett, Ambrose S. Todd, and Nathaniel S. Wheaton.

Mr. Baldwin, who was the senior presbyter of Connecticut, died in August, 1862, and Mr. Jewett in the same month of the preceding year. They were both ordained by Bishop Jarvis, and one for a quarter of a century was rector of the parish at Guilford, where he continued to reside after relinquishing it; and the balance of his ministerial life was devoted to the service of feeble churches in that vicinity. Mr. Jewett for thirteen years held the cure made vacant by the death of the patriarchal Mansfield; and for some time before he resigned it and removed to New Haven, he showed his unselfish heart by surrendering his salary, Providence having given into his possession the means of support without calling upon his people. But this was a step which he afterwards regarded as wholly unwise. The laborer in the vineyard of the Lord is worthy of his hire, and it is no excuse for the people to withhold it from him, on the ground that he is not actually in a state of penury. There never was a clergyman who had so large an income that he could not find ways to dispense it all in charity. In consequence of bodily infirmities, Mr. Jewett was compelled to withdraw from the active duties of the ministry many years before his death, but he left behind him the memory of faithful services to the Church, and of generous benefactions wisely bestowed in his lifetime to promote objects of learning and religion.

Dr. Todd was a son of the Rev. Mr. Todd, of Huntington, and like Mr. Jewett, acquired his classical and theological education at the Episcopal Academy in Cheshire. He was ordained to the Diaconate by Bishop Hobart, in the spring of 1818, and the whole period of his ministry, with the exception of the first five years, was spent in the service of St. John's Church, Stamford. From 1823 to the day of his death in 1861, he fulfilled the office of a priest of God among the same people, and was "permitted to see five parishes with seven churches and chapels grow up out of a single cure."

The Diocese must ever bear in grateful remembrance the name of Dr. Wheaton.[1] After graduating from Yale College in 1814, he proceeded to Maryland with the design of occupying himself as a teacher, and while there, pursued the study of theology, and was admitted first to the Diaconate, and then to the Priesthood by Bishop Kemp. He returned to his native State in 1819, having been appointed to fill the vacancy in the rectorship of Christ Church, Hartford.

It has been seen in other chapters of this work, how his skill and taste in ecclesiastical architecture were applied to the erection of the stately edifice belonging to that parish, as well as what fidelity and power

[1] He received the degree of *Doctor of Divinity* from his Alma Mater in 1833.

he evinced as a Christian minister, and the head of a collegiate institution, which he befriended from its very foundation. He never ceased to love the people to whom he had given the vigor of his best days. After resigning his church in New Orleans, in 1844, and spending a year in Europe, he returned to Connecticut with broken health, and resided for a time at Hartford among the cherished friends of earlier years, officiating for his former parish during a vacancy in the rectorship, and rendering as they were needed services in other places. But disease increased upon him, and being a bachelor with ample means, he retired to Marbledale, his native village, and the humble home of his boyhood was as great an enjoyment to him in the decline of life, as had been the dwelling of his wealthiest parishioner. He was a benefactor to the parish in Marbledale — for besides assisting in the enlargement and remodelling of its house of worship, and supplying it with services on alternate Sundays when his health permitted, he endowed it with a parsonage and suitable grounds.

He died in March, 1862, showing to the last his interest in Trinity College, by leaving to its Trustees the sum of ten thousand dollars, to be applied in the erection of a chapel, and a residuary legacy, for the general fund of the institution, amounting to as much more. The pamphlets, which came from his pen, and the writings and occasional discourses that he published, are among the best and purest productions of the Connecticut clergy. "For myself," said Bishop Williams, mentioning his death to the Convention, "I desire always to remember him as I first knew him, when he occupied the Presidency of the College, as the clear and able expounder of the Word of God, the patient and accurate instructor, the well-balanced Christian man, carrying under a reserved and sometimes cold exterior, an unselfish, warm, and generous heart."

CHAPTER XXX.

MORE NEW CHURCHES AND PARISHES; PROVISION FOR THE CLERGY; DONATIONS AND BEQUESTS FOR CHURCH PURPOSES; PROLONGED RECTORSHIPS; AND DEATH OF BISHOP BROWNELL.

A. D. 1862–1865.

EARLY in December, 1862, Bishop Williams consecrated Trinity Church, Southport, a spacious edifice reconstructed of wood, after having been completely ruined on New Year's night by a frightful tornado. The parish had just finished the payment of a debt, incurred in the erection of a church, which was a successor to the one destroyed by fire, when this unexpected calamity arose, and produced scarcely less devastation. Had the edifice been originally built of stone, and without a tall wooden spire, it would have been proof against the fury of the gale, that carried sorrow to the hearts of a band of zealous churchmen. It was located in the borough, where the shore of the sea trends to the southwest, and about a mile distant from the old Fairfield Church, which filled up for Dr. Dwight the vision of the "finished landscape," when he penned the lines in his "Greenfield Hill"[1]—

> "Beside yon Church that beams a modest ray
> With tidy neatness reputably gay."

If suitable stone can be dug out of the hills and quarries in the vicinity, or conveniently obtained else-

[1] A Poem in seven parts with notes, 1794, p. 41.

where, it is the best material for use in the construction of churches; and the practice is becoming more common for parishes in the rural districts of Connecticut, to adopt it on the score of economy in the end.

Notwithstanding the pressure of the times, several enterprises were projected at this period, which put to the test the faith of clergymen and the benevolence and zeal of their people. The corner-stone of a new church for St. Matthew's parish, Wilton, was laid a week after the Annual Convention of 1862, and towards the end of August in the same year, a like ceremony was performed for Trinity Church, Bristol. The edifice at Wilton, in the cruciform style, was built of stone, with brick quoins and arches; the other was constructed of wood. St. John's Church, Pine Meadow, was burnt in 1860, while the people were preparing it for the celebration of the Christmas festival, and another of wood to supply its place was consecrated in June, 1863.

An effort was begun in 1864, to provide a new stone church of attractive architecture for the ancient parish at Brooklyn. The venerable sanctuary built before the Revolution, chiefly at the expense of Godfrey Malbone, though beautiful for situation, and dear to the hearts of many from the associations of a lifetime, and the memories of the dead who sleep around it, was too far from the village, and every way unsuited to the wants and growth of the congregation. The work of building on a choice site in the centre of the population, progressed slowly, but with the aid of contributions from other parishes it was finally completed, and the toil of the faithful rector, who for nearly thirty years had stood at this lone outpost of the

Diocese, was rewarded. The old church remains as a relic of former times, "overshadowed by huge oaks in the quiet churchyard," one of the very few buildings in New England which show the ancient style of ecclesiastical architecture. It is to be preserved from decay, and kept in repair for occasional use, by the interest of a legacy left for that purpose.

But important steps were now taken in the direction of new parochial organizations. As the result of the labors of some of the students of the Berkeley Divinity School, working under the supervision of Bishop Williams, parishes were formed, and churches of wood built in Durham and Middlefield, towns adjoining the city of Middletown. On Good Friday, 1863, a parish was organized at Hazardville, in the town of Enfield, and a brick church erected mainly through the liberality of a wealthy gentleman[1] whose name the village bears. About two years earlier, Trinity Church, Hartford, was consecrated. This was a handsome edifice of Portland stone, originally built for a Unitarian Society, and located in a central and busy street. That Society was unsuccessful, and finally disposed of its property for secular uses, and it was a fitting thing in the new parish of Trinity Church to purchase the building, take it down, and reërect it in another and rapidly growing part of the city. The last public act of Bishop Brownell was to lay its corner-stone, and at the time of its consecration to the worship of the Triune God, the Rev. Dr. Huntington, of Boston, formerly a distinguished Unitarian minister, and now a presbyter in the Episcopal

[1] A. G. Hazard. He died in 1868, remembering among his bequests the parish which he had founded.

Church, was present to preach the sermon,—"an exceedingly well-written and impressively delivered discourse on the doctrine of the Trinity."

A stone church, finished with great taste, was consecrated on the 30th of June, 1863, for the new parish of the Holy Trinity in Westport. It was due to the design of a single individual who died before the walls were raised, but his widow,[1] without regard to cost, more than completed the plans, and then dedicated the beautiful structure as a memorial to her late husband, and executed a deed conveying it to the "Trustees of Donations and Bequests for Church purposes," to hold the same in perpetuity for the benefit of the parish of the Holy Trinity. It was the first memorial church erected in Connecticut, and the whole cost of it, with the land and appendages, was about fifty-five thousand dollars.

A movement, stimulated by a peculiar state of feeling among the supporters of St. John's Church, led to the formation of a third parish within the compact limits of the city of Bridgeport. The swarm does not always leave with the utmost good will of the old hive. Unpleasant things often occur in the establishment of new parochial organizations, and jealousies and contentions, from which Christian men are not free, sometimes spring up and produce estrangements that last for a generation, and conflict with the best interests of the Church. The movement in Bridgeport was attended with a little trouble in its earlier stages. Sixty-three heads of families, most of whom had been connected with St. John's parish, went through the legal and canonical form of organizing

[1] Mrs. Mary Fitch Winslow.

themselves into a society by the name of Trinity Church, and then, 1863, applied for admission into union with the Convention of the Diocese. The committee, to whom the documents were referred, reported unanimously in favor of the application; but when it came up for consideration, it was warmly opposed, on the ground that no such parish should be received, especially if it was permitted to build its church on a site which had been selected almost under the very droppings of the old sanctuary. The Convention refused to be guided by any partial view of the case, and admitted the parish to the usual privileges upon the broad principle that the necessary legal and canonical steps having been taken, and the sanction of the ecclesiastical authority obtained, the right of admission could not be denied. The responsibility of choosing a lot on which to build, so near the mother church as to be in the judgment of many a perpetual reminder of strife and division, was for those to bear who were immediately concerned in the enterprise.

Measures were at once adopted to erect a stone church in early English style, without spire or tower, and affording sittings for six hundred persons. The expense of its erection, furniture, and lot — about twenty thousand dollars — was promptly provided for, and the edifice consecrated on the 2d of November, 1864. The parish entered upon a life of zealous activity, — which served to attest the claim of its founders, that "it was formed to do the work of our Master and only Saviour Jesus Christ, and to advance His Kingdom, a kingdom of truth, righteousness, mercy, candor, and honor."

The two older parishes in the same city relieved

themselves of the inconvenient debts which they had carried for many years, and as something which belongs to that period, it may be mentioned that the Mission established by St. John's, in East Bridgeport, now (1868) promises, under a resident minister, who devotes his whole energies to its welfare, soon to become a strong and vigorous parish with a substantial stone edifice, — the erection of which has already been commenced.

The clouds of civil war hung heavily over the country when most of these enterprises were initiated. Money was easily earned, and circulated freely, and judicious schemes for the advancement of the parish, or the institutions of the Church at large, were sure to meet with favorable attention. Some charities, however, conceived before the war, now took shape. Two homes for aged and destitute women, one under the auspices of Trinity Church, New Haven, and the other under the direction of the Church of the Holy Trinity (formerly Christ Church), Middletown, arose at this season, and were the beginning of a new form of parish work in the Diocese. Wealthy laymen whose "liberal things," were suspended by the outbreak of national troubles, returned to them, and what was not given or laid out immediately, has since been bestowed with generous and unostentatious benevolence.[1]

[1] Mr. Joseph E. Sheffield, of New Haven, has recently commenced on the same grounds in that city suitable buildings, including a chapel, which will cost when completed, about seventy thousand dollars, intending the whole as a free gift for the use and benefit of the "Parish School of Trinity Church," and "The Trinity Church Home." This, with his previous donations to the cause of education, and to the Church in the Diocese, will perpetuate his name as a liberal benefactor.

All commodities are enhanced in price as money cheapens, and clergymen with salaries barely sufficient to support their households at former rates had before them a gloomy and disheartening prospect, as the year 1863 was drawing to its close. The two bishops, therefore, shortly before Christmas, addressed a pastoral letter to the vestries, and to the members of the parishes of the Episcopal Church in Connecticut, calling their attention to the condition of many of the clergy, and asking them to make further provision for their wants in a "period of the advanced and advancing prices of all the necessaries of life." Unless relief in some shape was afforded, it was evident that there were parishes then faithfully served by their ministers, which must either be abandoned, or else "indebtedness, suffering, and untold trials" would ensue. The circular of the Bishops reached the laity in a season of thankful joy for the mercies of redemption, and met with such a general and cordial response that Bishop Williams, in his address to the Convention the next year, referred to it with gratitude, and said: —

"The cases, so far as I have been able to ascertain, where, with the ability to do, nothing was done, were altogether exceptional, and exceedingly few. The subject is one which we trust will not be lost sight of. It involves not more a Christian duty than it does the well-being of our parishes and our Diocese. A provision, which was sufficient a few years since, is very far from being so to-day. I rejoice, however, in the belief, that this whole subject of clerical support may be safely left to the generosity and justice of the laity."

Hitherto there had been no incorporation in the Diocese to receive and manage such donations and bequests as devoted friends of the Church might design for its benefit. Charities are sometimes perverted or misused when those who bestowed them are out of the way, and this operates as a discouragement to benevolence. For Christians with liberal dispositions may well hesitate to provide endowments for specific church purposes, where there is no security from the influence of individual or parochial selfishness. The subject was brought before the Diocesan Convention in 1863, and the preliminary steps taken to apply to the General Assembly for an act incorporating a Board of "Trustees of Donations and Bequests for Church Purposes." The charter granted, enabled them to receive, hold, and manage all funds entrusted to them "for the support of the institutions, parishes, and missionary work of the Protestant Episcopal Church in the Diocese of Connecticut, and for the promotion of any of its general interests according to the doctrines, discipline, rites, and usages of said Church." The net income of productive property was to be disbursed by them upon the conditions of the respective trusts as stated in the original gifts, bequests, or transfers. Thus benevolent churchmen, who apprehend the alienation of charities, may have through the incorporation of this Board a feeling of security that the donations which they would make for a specific purpose, will be sacredly applied according to their intention and desire.

The prosperity of the Diocese was visible in spiritual as well as temporal things. It is true of some men that they are often liberal in contributing to the erection of churches,[1] while they appear to forget the real object of public worship, and the claims of God upon us to "walk before Him in holiness and righteousness all our days." But of the nine hundred and twenty-two persons confirmed during the preceding year, Bishop Williams said in his address to the Convention of 1864: "A very gratifying feature of the confirmations has been the large number of males who have come forward to receive that Apostolic rite. In several instances, they have composed the entire class; and in most cases, their numbers have increased from those of previous years."

The preface to the order of Confirmation provides that those who are to receive it shall have been duly instructed in the principles of the Christian religion as taught by the Church, and the custom is not common in Connecticut to present any for the rite whose age disqualifies them for a proper understanding of its nature and solemnity. Most rectors now prepare their candidates with special reference to the Holy Communion, and it is worthy of note that a great change in this respect has taken place during the lapse of half a century. In the same address above alluded to, Bishop Williams, glancing back over a period of ten years, mentioned that seven thousand six hundred and sixty-eight persons had been confirmed in that time, and seven thousand two hundred and fifty-two persons admitted as new communicants. The figures for the last four of these years, as well as

1 "Though stone and brick and wood, are not salvation, they may become subsidiary to it in various ways. They not only furnish the opportunity to recommend and urge it, but by a suitable employment and disposition, they do themselves instruct and educate and refine." — Rev. Dr. Hallam's *Anniversary Sermon*, 1860, p. 11.

for the year then closing, showed a more favorable comparison. "And this, my brethren," the Bishop went on to say, "it seems to me, is as it should be. For while it cannot be laid down, as an unalterable rule, that no one shall be received to confirmation, unless on the condition of immediately coming to the Lord's Table, yet, surely, all who are presented for that holy rite should be affectionately admonished that they ought to come, with the honest purpose of 'going on' from 'baptism, and the laying on of hands,' to those 'holy mysteries,' by which we are 'assured of God's favor and goodness towards us, and that we are very members incorporate in the mystical body of His Son.'"

Hence, though not a season of tranquillity in national affairs, it was a season of growth for the Church in Connecticut, and good impressions, through the sanctifying agency of the Holy Spirit, were produced upon the souls and characters, the life and conversation, of her members. The list of the clergy, numbering upwards of one hundred and forty, was chiefly composed of those in youth and middle age, and there were no rectorships in the Diocese at that time which began at so early a date as the consecration of Bishop Brownell. Death, and the changes incident to the fluctuations of human society, had often sundered the pastoral ties, so that seven only among the clergy could be found who had been connected with their parishes for a period of twenty-five years.[1]

[1] The Rev. Dr. Bennett, Rector of Christ Church, Guilford, in his twenty-fifth anniversary sermon, preached July, 1865, says, p. 13: —

"At the present day, when the pastoral tie is so frail and so frequently severed, the rectorship of a quarter of a century's continuance is eminently noticeable. Of above one hundred and forty clergymen in this Diocese, only five besides your Rector have remained for that period in the same

Prolonged rectorships generally leave behind them lasting fruits and blessed memories. They serve to increase the sacredness attached to the pastoral office. Members of a parish who were born and educated under the ministrations of the same clergyman come to regard him as their spiritual father, and to confide in his instructions even when they cease to be attractive to other minds. But it is a privilege which very few are permitted to enjoy, to consecrate faithful labor through youth and through age, to the spiritual benefit of one people. John Beach, of Newtown, was the only Episcopal clergyman in Connecticut before the Independence of the Colonies was acknowledged, whose ministrations in the same cure were continued without interruption for half a century. Since the Revolution to this day, only three rectors in the Diocese — Dibblee, of Stamford, Mansfield, of Derby, and Tyler, of Norwich — have had a like experience, and these all, with Beach, were missionaries of the venerable Society, and went beyond the limit of his ministry in the Episcopal Church. Hubbard, of New Haven, nearly reached it; and Croswell his successor, Fogg, of Brooklyn, and Shelton, of Bridgeport, were each forty years or more in unbroken charge of the same parish.

What is true of a protracted rectorship, is much more true of a protracted Episcopate. Though Bishop

field of labor: the Rev. Dr. Hallam, of St. James's Church, New London; the Rev. Dr. Mead, of St. Paul's Church, Norwalk; the Rev. Dr. Clark, of St. John's Church, Waterbury; the Rev. Dr. Emery, of Trinity Church, Portland; and the Rev. Dr. Camp, of Trinity Church, Brooklyn."

To this list should have been added the name of the Rev. B. M. Yarrington, Rector of Christ Church, Greenwich. His charge of that parish commenced in April, 1839.

Brownell had long been languishing under the infirmities of age, and unable to discharge the full duties of his office, yet he still lived fresh in the affections of his clergy, and of all who knew him, and was revered and esteemed for his good example, his simple virtues, and unostentatious piety, not less than for his official character, his uniform prudence, and accurate knowledge of human nature. The lustre which Christian learning throws over talents and over station, beautified the evening of his days, and the dignity and grace of his manners, which had always commanded respect and excited affection in the circles of rank and affluence, lingered to the last. Among the lowly and the poor also he was deeply beloved for his generous kindness and ready sympathy.

But the worn thread is easily broken. Just before Christmas he became seriously ill and died, after much physical suffering, on the morning of the 13th of January, 1865, surrounded by his family, and his assistant and successor, for whom as for others "he spoke words of farewell and of blessing never to be forgotten." Not only was the Diocese, by this event, bereaved of its venerable head, but the Church throughout our land was deprived of its senior and presiding Bishop. It was a bitter cold day, on the 17th of the month, when he was carried forth to his burial. Thousands of persons thronged Christ Church to see the remains, which, clothed in the episcopal habit, had been "placed on a *catafalque* in front of the chancel."

When the hour appointed for the public service arrived, the Bishop of New York, and all the bishops of the New England Dioceses, except the Bishop of New Hampshire, together with the clergy of Connecticut and representatives from its parishes, and clergymen from other States were present, and participated in the solemn and imposing ceremonies. Dr. Burgess, the Bishop of Maine, delivered the address — a finished and graceful portraiture of the deceased prelate. No one could speak with a better understanding of his private and official character, for he had learned to love and esteem him when he was fulfilling under his immediate supervision the duties of a rector in Hartford.

At the close of the services in the church a procession was formed, and moved towards the cemetery on the northern edge of the city. The body was borne upon a bier, and all who followed it, except the immediate family and friends, were on foot, the bishops in their official robes, and the clergy in their black gowns. "As the long procession passed on to the cemetery, the snow fell thickly on the pall, changing its blackness to the purest white." Thus were buried the mortal remains of the third Bishop of Connecticut.

He was the fifteenth in the line of succession consecrated in these United States, and of all our prelates, with the exception of the patriarchal and saintly White, whose episcopate reached into the fiftieth year, he held the staff of his office the longest, and there was not a bishop in the Church of England at the time of his decease, whose consecration, like his, dated back to 1819. "The image of a pure and a long episcopate, left on the most sacred recollections in so many parish churches, in so many Christian families, in so many chambers of prayer, and in so many secret hearts, is something which an angel might almost emulate. What care or toil, what sacrifice or burden, would it not recompense?" But how great are the changes produced by death in the silent lapse of forty-five years. Three only of the clergy who welcomed him to the Diocese survived, and of the more than fifteen thousand persons upon whom he had laid his hands in the apostolic rite of confirmation, a vast number had preceded him to the world of spirits, as had also full one third of those to whom he had given authority to execute the office of deacons and priests in the Church of God.

If it is the sad feeling of such a lengthened age to find itself alone among new generations, it is yet a privilege that it has witnessed the progress of human events, and the advance of the Church from weakness to strength and great prosperity. At the time when Bishop Brownell was invested with the oversight of the Diocese, there were but *seven* parishes in it capable of supporting full services; the rest were united in cures, and imperfectly sustained. Forty clergymen, scattered along the shore towns, and back in the interior of the State, led their thin flocks, and ministered to them in the rude wooden edifices, erected for the most part before the storms of the Revolution.

But what a change in these respects did he live to witness, the whole of which was accomplished under the blessing of his own Episcopate! Like a vine running over and mantling the wall, the Church had covered the land where she was once so weak and dependent, once most bitterly and persistently opposed. The pages of this work have traced the successive steps of her growth, and the events which contributed to the establishment of her principles. From the summary of parochial reports in the Journal of the

Convention for 1865, it appears that the parishes of the Diocese then numbered one hundred and twenty-nine, the clergy one hundred and fifty, and the communicants twelve thousand five hundred. The amount of missionary and charitable contributions, for the same year, not including ordinary expenses and canonical assessments, was upwards of two hundred thousand dollars.

It would be wrong to say that this growth, in the order of Divine Providence, was due to Bishop Brownell. It was what he lived to see, and it was attained under his wise and paternal administration. Zealous laymen who confided in the wisdom of their spiritual overseers, a body of faithful and earnest clergy, and an energetic, self-sacrificing, and scholarly Assistant Bishop were the largest contributors, humanly speaking, to the later and more abundant prosperity of the Diocese. The senior prelate exercised a silent influence, and did his work without knowing that the work had been done.

"He was endued with those natural attributes, physical and mental, which form the completeness of manhood, and come only from Him who made us, not from ourselves. The endurance and vitality of his frame he shared with a very numerous family of brothers and sisters, not one of whom died till an advanced period of maturity. In him it resisted, through fourscore and five years, the encroachments of decay, bending, at all times, rather than breaking, under every assault of disease. A manly stature, an attractive person, a noble aspect and voice, were easily united with a dignified bearing, a kindly manner, and a graceful elocution. The mind, corresponding with the outward frame, uttered itself in calm and lucid thought, in harmonious sentences, and in perspicuous arguments. These qualities were due to the direct gift of the Creator, in his very nature, or to the blessing which attended such a nature under the usual process of educational culture. . . . .

"His equability, his sagacity, the impartiality of his determinations, the largeness of his views, the avoidance of needless collisions, the decision of his conduct, when decision became needful, had their result in this strong and united and confiding Diocese. He sought no constrained uniformity. He entertained no fanciful ideal. He leaned towards no extreme tendency. He was steadfast, because his mind was clear. He brushed away all that was not essential to any question or purpose, or smiled, and suffered it to pass by. He recognized the rights of all. No one had cause to suppose himself wronged with him by any prejudice; and when 'swift to hear, slow to speak, and very slow to wrath,' he spoke at length, the Church listened and was satisfied."[1]

This extract gives a just though brief outline of his "qualities" and character. What it lacks may be well supplied by applying to him in his connection with the Church and its institutions in the Diocese of Connecticut, that passage of the Psalmist, which Bishop Williams, in his commemorative sermon,[2] said he never could read without the involuntary application: "So he fed them with a faithful and true heart, and ruled them prudently with all his power."

[1] *Address of Bishop Burgess*, pp. 8, 9. [2] Page 14.

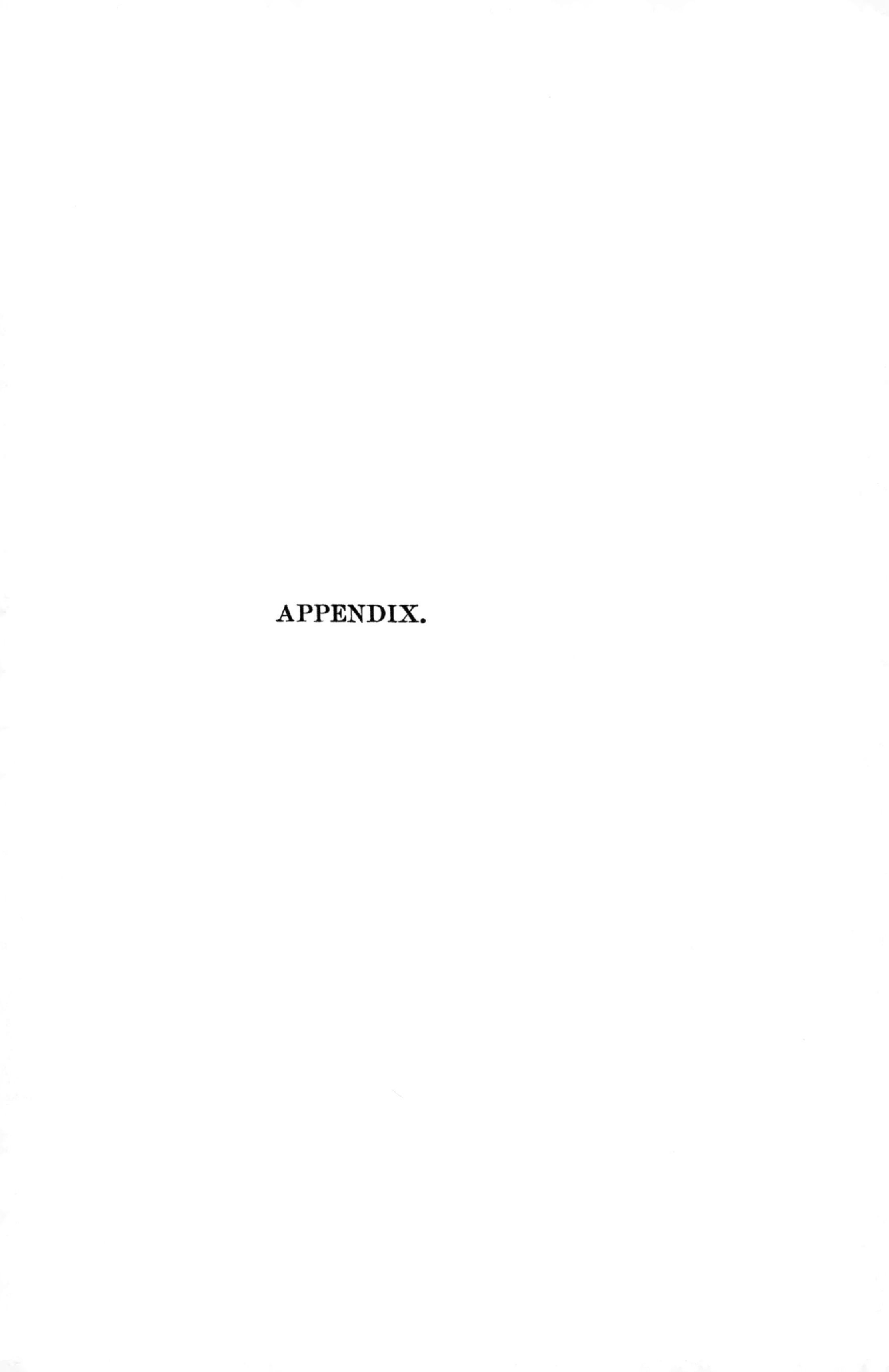

APPENDIX.

APPENDIX A.

The following letter was addressed to the Rev. Ashbel Baldwin, Stratford, Ct.: —

"Croom, 12*th January*, 1807.

"Rev. and Dear Sir, — I had the honor to receive a letter from the Reverend Convocation of the Diocese of Connecticut, together with a resolve of that body, requesting you as their Secretary, to forward a similar one to all the bishops who sat in the last General Convention of our Church. This letter I received about three months ago, and for reasons which will appear below, I have hitherto declined answering it. In their letter the Convocation inform me of the step the Convocation of the Church of Connecticut had in the year 1804 thought themselves authorized to take in Mr. Rogers's unhappy affair, in consequence of its being referred to them by the House of Bishops, of their reasons for taking that step, and the consequent misunderstanding that had arisen between them and two of the House of Bishops on the subject, by which a great danger of a schism in the flourishing Church of Connecticut had arisen. They go on to profess the purity of their intentions in that transaction, and in the true spirit of the Gospel, their hearty desire to do everything in their power for the peace and prosperity of the Church, and conclude their letter by requesting that I, in *conjunction* with the other bishops, concerned in that business, would as soon as convenient transmit a statement of our view of the whole subject, together with our advice to Connecticut, how it would be prudent in the present state of things to proceed, and particularly, whether it would be advisable to give Mr. Rogers a new trial on the ground of nullity in the Act of Degradation.

"For reasons which will presently appear, however desirous I may be, it is impossible that I should at present, with my stock of information on the subject, comply with this request. However, I think it my duty to state to you the view I myself had of the cause, and the part I took in it. You will recollect, my dear sir, the very ill state of health I was in during the whole session of that Convention. Notwithstanding which, as I conceived Mr. Rogers's appeal to be amongst the most important affairs which the House of Bishops had to transact, I attended closely to it, and endeavored to view it in all its bearings. On the last day of the session of Convention, just before its adjournment, the deputies from the Church of Connecticut, and Mr. Rogers, were desired to retire out of the House of Bishops, when, according to the best of my recollection, every bishop present, except Bishop Jarvis (who I presume, thought himself too much implicated to give any opinion), expressed a decided conviction of his guilt, and I then thought nothing remained to be done but to award the sentence denounced by our Canon law against such criminals. But in this particular I was mistaken; for I was invited to dine in the evening of that day in which Convention adjourned, together with the rest of my Rt. Rev. Brethren, with the Rt. Rev. Bishop Moore, and told that Mr. Rogers's business would be then and there finished. In the course of the morning, I was informed by some clergyman (I have forgotten whom), that it was the wish of some of the bishops to have the cause referred back to some of the State Conventions. This gave me some uneasiness, for my illness having increased, I had determined to return by the first opportunity, and before the meeting at Dr. Moore's. Thus circumstanced, I sent for my Rt. Rev. Brother Dr. Parker, to my friend Dr. Beach's, where I lodged, took him into a private room, and informed him of my situation, and of my intention to leave town immediately, and also of what I had heard concerning the wish of some of the bishops, respecting Rogers's cause. I told him that I was pointedly against the adoption of such a measure for the following reasons. Because, as I understood the matter, Mr. Rogers did not hold himself amenable to the Church, either of Connecticut or New York, and had on that ground appealed from the prosecution commenced against him by the Church of Connecticut, to our House, so that the cause appeared to me to come very properly before us, and that it did appear to me also after what had passed in our House in it, that we could not possibly refer it to any earthly tribunal whatever, without derogating from that authority given by the great Head of His Church to His Apostles *collectively*, and through them to their successors in office to the end of the world, when He delivered to St. Peter the keys of the Church, which authority I conceive was by his appointment paramount to that of any *single* Bishop or *Church* in our

Union, and therefore, in cases of this sort, especially, not transferable by them to any earthly tribunal. I added, that if it should appear that a majority of the House of Bishops was determined to refer this cause to some State Convention, I hoped they would not refer it to the Church of Connecticut, as I was persuaded that such a measure would have a direct tendency to make the confusion already occasioned by it in that flourishing Church still more confused, and endanger a schism.

" In these sentiments Bishop Parker appeared at the time to coincide with me, and I concluded the conversation by requesting him to set my name to the act, if the bishops should determine to do the only thing in my opinion remaining to be done, namely, to award the sentence against Mr. Rogers, required by our Canon law ; but if a reference to any Convention, or any other half-way measure was adopted, not to put my name to the deed, as I was *exanimo* against them all. The good Bishop promised to conform to the premises, and I have not had any information since on the subject, excepting what has been afforded me by the journals of the last General Convention, and the letter of your Convocation. I did think it possible, that in consequence of the resolution of your Convocation lately sent me, some of my Right Reverend friends might have stated to me by letter their motives for referring this cause, as also their intentions with respect to the powers to be vested in your Convention by the act of Reference, and this circumstance delayed my answer to the Convocation.

" All expectations of information on the subject sufficient to enable me, *conjointly* with the other bishops concerned, to give any further statement of that unhappy business, being now at an end, I have thought it my duty, by way of apology to your Convocation, to make this candid communication of the subject to you, and through you to them.

" The conversation with Bishop Parker above cited, contains the substance of my sentiments on the subject at the time, and with great deference to the opinion of the three learned prelates, who finally determined the matter in the House of Bishops, I have seen nothing as yet to induce me to alter them. There is a wide difference to be sure between us ; but this difference may be accounted for by supposing, what their *determination*, as they call it, would lead us to suppose, that a Canon of the General Convention was necessary to clothe them with authority in this case, which I did and do suppose Christ himself gave them independently of any lay or clerical authority whatever.

"As for advice, my dear sir, insulated as I am from all intercourse with my Rt. Rev. Brethren, placed in a corner of the country where I can seldom, except at church meetings and visitations, see my own presbyters, and at the same time, in an ill state of health, I should consider it a high degree of presumption to offer it *individually* to the good Bishop of your Church, aided as he is by his truly pious and learned presbyters. However, my solicitude for the preservation of the ancient principles of the Church, impels me to hint a wish that your Bishop and learned presbyters would make a solemn pause, and well weigh the consequences to the Church of Christ before they suffer themselves to be induced to pronounce their own degradation a nullity, for I think it may well be questioned, whether they or any other power upon earth, in cases of this sort, are competent to such an act. Mr. Rogers, indeed, upon his true repentance, might be loosed from those sins which occasioned his degradation, but nothing but reordination can, in my judgment, restore him to his former standing in the Christian ministry. In this sentiment, I think I am supported, not only by the nature of the commission given to the Church by Christ, to bind and loose, but also by the practice of the Primitive Church. Sure I am, that such a step, was it to be taken by your Convention at this time, and in this country, when and where the minds of men on the subject of Church discipline are so very unsettled, and tremblingly alive to what they call Liberty, would militate strongly against all ecclesiastical authority whatever, so necessary to the well-being of the Church of Christ upon earth.

"If this unhappy business cannot be amicably settled before in some other way, rather than thus endanger so important a pillar in our venerable spiritual edifice founded upon the Apostles and Prophets, Jesus Christ himself being the chief corner-stone, I should think that your Convention had much better abide by the consequences, until the meeting of our next General Convention, when they may avail themselves of far better advice than that of

"Dear and reverend Sir, your sincere friend and affectionate brother in Christ,

"THOMAS JOHN CLAGGETT,

"*Bishop of the Protestant Episcopal Church of Maryland.*

"P. S. — If you can make it convenient to send me a dozen numbers of the "Churchman's Magazine," beginning with this month, I shall forward the money to any person you may appoint. Direct to me near Upper Marlborough, Prince George's County, Md."

APPENDIX B.

"THERE was presented to this House a letter signed William H. Winder, enclosing two documents, signed Ammi Rogers. Mr. Winder informs this House, that he is counsel for the said Ammi Rogers, who, in the documents referred to, appeals to the General Convention, from a sentence of degradation said to have been passed on him without trial or hearing, by the Right Rev. Bishop Jarvis, of Connecticut.

"This House having considered the contents of the aforesaid papers, are of opinion that, agreeably to the Constitution of this Church, they have no authority to act on an appeal in regard to the matter stated; and that there is no existing mode by which any bishop or bishops of this Church can take cognizance of the conduct of any other bishop, unless at the desire of the Convention of the Diocese to which such a bishop should belong, and conformably to rules of process by them established.

"And whereas this House acted on the concerns of the said Ammi Rogers, in the session of 1804, as appears by the minutes; they now wish it to be known that their proceedings at that time originated in his own petition, relative to the following points: —

"1. Whether he belonged to the Diocese of Connecticut, or to that of New York.

"2. The recalling which he proposed, of a circular letter written by Bishop Jarvis, forbidding the petitioner to perform divine service in the Diocese, and the clergy and laity of the same to countenance him as a minister.

"3. A candid and impartial inquiry into his conduct and character.

"On the first of the said points, the House then assembled, being assured that both the parties were disposed to submit to their determination, declared it to be, that Ammi Rogers was a clergyman not of New York, but of Connecticut.

"The second point being a matter of internal concern of the Church in Connecticut, was not acted on judicially by this House; although as their opinion was expected on both sides, they expressed it as it was, approbatory of the measure.

"On the third point, they were of opinion that Ammi Rogers, far from having been treated with injustice, had not received a sentence sufficiently severe.

"To the opinions thus given, no addition or alteration is intended by this House; and they finally dismiss the subject from their consideration.

"This House, wishing the House of Clerical and Lay Deputies to be informed of their proceedings on the application now before them, direct, that the Secretary deliver to them a copy of the minute now made, with the papers on which it is grounded. They also direct the Secretary to deliver a copy of the minute to William H. Winder, esquire, and for the further information of that gentleman, to deliver with it a copy of the Constitution of this Church.

"The above was accordingly communicated to the House of Clerical and Lay Deputies, and a message was received from them containing the following unanimous resolution: 'That it is the opinion of this House, that, agreeably to the sixth article of the Constitution, the General Convention have no cognizance of the case of Ammi Rogers, and that he therefore have leave to withdraw his petition.'" — *Journal of House of Bishops*, 1808.

"There was no doubt on the minds of the two bishops present, that there had been an oversight in not granting to this man a trial in the Church in that State. But the oversight, if they were correct in supposing one, was not theirs, nor was it in their power to correct it. Nothing could have been easier than the convicting of him of faults which deserve degradation. But it did not become the Bishops to advise the recalling of the act, and the giving of him a trial." — *Bishop White's Memoirs*, etc., p. 199.

APPENDIX C.

THE following is a copy of the letter of Mr. Rayner, to Bishop Brownell, upon the terms of which his sentence of suspension from the ministry was grounded: —

"MONROE, *October* 9, 1827.

"RIGHT REV. AND DEAR SIR, — Although I am not conscious of having violated any Canon or Rubric of the Episcopal Church, in which, for many years, I have had the honor and happiness to officiate as a minister and public teacher; and although I have endeavored with great care and diligence to read and study the Holy Scriptures, and to teach and disseminate only such doctrines as, according to my best judgment, 'may be proved by most certain warrants of the same;' yet forasmuch as it has appeared that my views of Scripture doctrine, in some points, which are thought important, are in the view of my clerical brethren and others considered inconsistent (if not expressly with the Articles, Creeds, and Liturgy) with the commonly received opinions of the ministers and members of the Episcopal Church; and whereas, under these circumstances, there is little hope that I can be useful as a clergyman of said Church; I hereby beg leave to resign to the Bishop, as well my official standing as an Episcopal clergyman in this Diocese, as my rectorship of the parish in which I at present officiate; and though the terms of this communication are not the same as those used in the second Canon of the General Convention of 1817 [Canon vii. 1820], yet by a liberal construction of that Canon, I believe my case may come within its provisions. I trust, therefore, the Bishop will consider himself at liberty to record this 'declaration' of my views, and also to take such other measures as in his judgment the Canon may require.

"I am aware that my present resignation must probably deprive me of the Bishop's pastoral superintendence, which I sincerely regret. That it should also forfeit me his private and personal friendship would be a misfortune to which I truly hope I shall not be subjected. I shall still humbly claim to be considered as a member of the Church, entitled to all its common privileges.

"With great respect, I am, Right Reverend and Dear Sir,

"Your obedient servant,

"MENZIES RAYNER."

The Bishop in his annual address for 1828, alluding to this matter, said: —

"It is known to the Convention that the Rev. Menzies Rayner has relinquished his ministry in this Church, and connected himself with another religious communion. Having communicated to me in writing, the relinquishment of his 'official standing as an Episcopal clergyman in the Diocese,' that I might 'record' the same, according to the provisions of the Canon, in that case made and provided, 'and also take such other measures, as in my judgment the case might require,' I have, therefore, recorded his said declaration so made; and also, in the presence of the Rev. George W. Doane and the Rev. Norman Pinney, have pronounced the said Menzies Rayner to be suspended from the exercise of the ministry of the Protestant Episcopal Church, and have recorded his suspension, pursuant to the provisions of the Canon above referred to. The Rev. Mr. Rayner, by making his suspension the result of his own voluntary act, has greatly relieved me from the pain which such an act of discipline is otherwise calculated to create. And however we may regret the cause which has led to it, we are not to be judges of other men's consciences, — 'to his own Master he standeth or falleth.'"

INDEX TO VOL. II.

C.

D.

M.

N.

U.

V.

W.

www.ingramcontent.com/pod-product-compliance
Lightning Source LLC
LaVergne TN
LVHW020916110826
845150LV00004B/689